# CIVILISING
# BARBARIANS

# CIVILISING

# BARBARIANS

Missionary Narrative and African Textual Response
in Nineteenth-Century South Africa

LEON DE KOCK

WITWATERSRAND
UNIVERSITY PRESS

LOVEDALE PRESS

Witwatersrand University Press
1 Jan Smuts Avenue
2001 Johannesburg
South Africa

ISBN 1 86814 298 1

First published 1996

The cover illustration shows Major W.L. Geddes at the head of the Lovedale boarders in drill
formation in the grounds of the famous institution. Geddes was boarding master at Lovedale *circa*
1940 when this picture was included in R.H.W. Shepherd's *Lovedale South Africa: The Story of a
Century*. Picture by courtesy of the Cory Library, Rhodes University.

Typeset by Photoprint, Cape Town
Cover design by Photoprint and Celéste Burger
Printed and bound by Kohler Carton and Print, Pinetown

This book is dedicated to Margaret, Luke, and Charis,
without whom it would have appeared
too soon or not at all

# ACKNOWLEDGEMENTS

I wish to acknowledge the support and encouragement of Ivan Rabinowitz, a fine listener and a highly discerning reader, who has given generously of his time, sympathy, and imagination. Greg Cuthbertson has been an unfailing friend and supporter, always willing to offer moral support and material help.

Others whose discussions with me made an impact on this study include Stan Ridge, David Attwell, Tim Couzens, Richard Elphick, Keith Dietrich, Annamaria Carusi, Mike Hyman and Johannes du Bruyn. Among librarians, Dawie Malan, Monique Smith and Mary-Lynn Suttie have been friends and assistants of the highest calibre.

Acknowledgements are due to the following journals, in which earlier versions of material in this book have appeared: *The English Academy Review*, *Journal of Literary Studies*, *Missionalia*, *Journal of Theology for Southern Africa*, *English in Africa* and *Alternation*.

# CONTENTS

# INTRODUCTION

Nations, writes Benedict Anderson in *Imagined Communities*, share with individuals the predicament of having to construct identity out of simultaneous acts of memory and forgetting. Awareness of being embedded in what Anderson calls secular, serial time, with all its implications of continuity, yet of *forgetting* the experience of continuity, engenders the need for a narrative of identity (1991:205). In the wake of South Africa's supposed rebirth as a nation in 1994, it is perhaps apposite to consider what has been remembered, and what forgotten, in the country's popularly imagined regeneration.

We know, from innumerable items of news and talk, as well as the *news-talk* characteristic of that more recent form of public communion, the radio talk show, that apartheid died for South Africa to be reborn. Less frequently, but no less volubly, we have also heard calls for the death of colonialism. The history of colonialism, however, has all too often found its enunciation in the coarser tones of militant anti-colonial rhetoric. The word 'colonialism' is then used as a thunderblow, to denote a self-evident evil, not an object of analytical enquiry. Even in university essays, perhaps on J.M. Coetzee's *Waiting for the Barbarians* in a second-year literature course, 'colonialism' is likely to be brought into service as a conceptual bludgeon: the colonisers were the real barbarians; 'they' did bad things.

For the most part, however, the popular imagination seizes upon apartheid and its supposed birth in 1948 – only a year after India unshackled itself from British imperialism – as an all-encompassing evil of the last resort in the modern world, the apotheosis of colonial domination, transformed into the legislative fiat of a modern, if perverse, nation-state. In the remembered genealogy of the 'new' South Africa, apartheid often figures as an incorporative, originary point of emergence, while the finer distinctions of continuity and discontinuity between the nineteenth and twentieth centuries, between colonialism in a past as strange as another country, and apartheid in the second half of this century, seem to have become so blurred as to be almost invisible. Even the more recent memory of apartheid itself is becoming difficult for the very newest, emerging generation to recall. The history of

1

formal apartheid is slowly but surely passing beyond phenomenal, lived experience and, for many young people, now resides only in books, pictures, documentaries – sources which must themselves compete with thousands upon thousands of visual information items in a time of acute information overload.

Yet in a very real sense the meaning of the imperial past, and its consequent colonial conditions, cultures, and polities, have, as Edward W. Said observes in *Culture and Imperialism*, 'entered the reality of hundreds of millions of people' and still exercise tremendous force as a 'highly conflictual texture of culture, ideology, and policy' (1993:11). I do not profess in this book to explain the persistence, in contemporary reality, of the imperial or colonial past in the form of Said's categories. That would be a vast undertaking indeed. My more modest aim is to recall more fully the memory of that particularly pervasive strand in the making of a South African nation, and of African nationalism, the nineteenth-century 'civilising mission'. In view of the contemporary belief that nations and their constitutive identities are brought into being partly, but significantly, by acts of imagining and of narration (Anderson 1991; Bhabha 1990; Said 1993), this book seeks to explore some of the ways in which a relentlessly book and print-driven civilising colonialism sought to *inscribe* in 'barbarous' Africans the precepts of a largely Protestant, Western modernity (contemporaneous, in southern Africa, with the telegraph and the press) and to implant in their minds dreams of a 'rational', Christian community of peasant individualists drawn away from what was conceived as heathen abjection in degrading tribal conditions.

Whether this was right or wrong is not really the issue, although the recalling of it is likely to stir up many emotions. The more general interest in the project is to understand the negotiations of identity in the many *narrative* forms by which African subjectivity was brought into question and reformulated under conditions of tremendous upheaval in the nineteenth century. The term 'narrative' in this sense refers to all those enunciative acts, whether verbal (the sermon, classroom lesson, informal talk, public lecture) or in print (the bible, newspaper, book, periodical, letter) which derived from a master narrative of Protestant conformity, and found their form in the lofty medium of English. These narratives sought to retell the story of proper human subjectivity in a context of coercive military and cultural warfare. My particular interest in the nineteenth century, therefore, lies in the dramatic contests over the moral destiny of South Africans, and over the very nature of identity. It has become common cause in recent interdisciplinary scholarship to point out that both Africans *and* Europeans were transformed by these processes (Comaroff 1991, Elphick 1992, Hofmeyr 1993), even though the ostensible thrust of the civilising mission was to remake Africans in the European image. As Jean and John Comaroff have argued so forcefully in their influential, if controversial book, *Of Revelation and Revolution* (1991), the signifying dimensions of cultural exchange (in contrast to earlier emphases on capital, class, and official politics) can be seen as central to such 'contests of conscience'. In particular, scholarship has begun to regard what has come to be known as 'identity politics' (cf. Greenstein 1994) as a revealing source of insight into both micro- and macro-contexts of colonial contestation.

The negotiations of identity, and the struggles involved in sustaining, modifying, or revolutionising the self in the nineteenth century found their form in narratives, in story, projection, and response. To be sure, these narratives and counter-narratives were implicated in the larger play of power and conflict, unity and dislocation. They were the stories people told each other in diverse contexts and they include the more philosophical 'narratives of legitimation' employed to underpin ideological positions. They involved, in addition, the complex, back and forth interpenetrations of orality and literacy, the establishment of literate orthographies for 'vernacular' languages, as well as the growing ascendancy of English as a master code, the ultimate fount of civilised life from which lowly 'Kafirs' were benignly invited to drink.

It will be clear that, broadly conceived, this is a very large subject. My aim in this book is to keep this broad sense in mind while concentrating selectively on various written sources in which one can detect traces of the larger process. Not surprisingly, then, missionary interactions are examined as one of the prime sites of the civilising mission and its generating narratives, although the subject of this book is not missionary discourse *per se*. In addition, some key responses of Africans who were themselves missionary subjects are examined, as are other sources in which the confines of textually imposed identity can be seen to undergo intriguing transformations.

One of these transformations – perhaps the most important – was the emergence of African nationalism from the long history of material, moral, and philosophical struggle in the Eastern Cape. In this transformation, diverse African polities were gradually drawn together within a Christian ethic of egalitarianism (cf. Chapman 1993, De Kock 1993a). It is one of the more interesting ironies of South African history that while the millenarian message of Christianity was ultimately betrayed by Europeans in the exclusion of all Africans, including 'civilised' converts, from the Union of South Africa in

1910, the subversive potential of the Christian ethic continued to undermine the moral authority of white rule. In this study, I try to look more closely at the pre-eminent centre of conversion and education in the Eastern Cape, the Lovedale institution, in terms of its contribution to fashioning narratives of identity for African people. After identifying particular tropes within which subjectivity was defined, I examine examples of the way in which some African subjects themselves subverted, internalised, or rewrote imposed narratives of proper identity. I also look at the narratives of missionary heroism found in the writings of Robert Moffat and David Livingstone, as well as the beginnings of an African story of *national* emergence within the beckoning modernity of the late Victorian world.

Were the barbarians in need of civilising, or were the civilisers the true barbarians? As the paradoxical semantic irresolution of the title implies, this question deconstructs itself because it relies on an unsustainable polarity. Yet it is just such a dualism which provided the context for the tortuous labours of the mission fields, and set the constraints for an emerging African solidarity in the face of European imperialism in southern Africa. It is therefore within this paradox that the subject begins to define itself, although it is only possible to do this outside the suppositions about people and their lives – also implicit in the title – that so wrenched the history of the nineteenth century. The forgotten links between the nineteenth and twentieth centuries, in this view, relate to the *colonial* unfolding of the South African 'race relations' story, which prepared the ground for twentieth-century apartheid. There is a larger plot, a greater range of characters, and more ambiguous forces at work in this story than the less finely orchestrated, Gothic tale of apartheid's horrors in the popular conception. And it is perhaps necessary to consider this larger colonial plot again so that its sequel can be more richly understood, so that, for example, one may disabuse many English-speaking South Africans (and their international counterparts) of their liberal innocence, or remind many black South Africans of their historical involvement in colonial processes, and of the need to bring that involvement into conscious memory, so that our newer narratives of identity will at least be rooted in, and germinated by, a profounder sense of a shared past.

# 1

# DISCIPLINARY INTERSECTIONS

Any study wishing to explore the discursive procedures by which a 'civilising' colonialism in nineteenth-century South Africa[1] sought to inscribe[2] orthodox forms of subjectivity in 'barbarous' Africans, must have recourse to the assiduous attempt by missionaries to create a universal regime of truth. The attempt by missionaries, particularly, and by the colonial administration at the Cape generally, to re-invent the lineaments of African subjectivity prepared the ground for momentous cultural struggle. This book describes some of the ways in which an aggressive colonising discourse[3] was appropriated and contested by Africans, even as they were marked and changed by it. The study deals with civilising discourse in English and with the appropriations of this discourse by Africans in textual forms of English.

My approach falls within the ambit of what has come to be known as postcolonial analysis, since it seeks to describe across a gulf or *post* of both time and epistemology some of the conditions of possibility for a peculiarly *colonial* discourse. Implicit in this *post*, then, is both a temporal and an oppositional element: the intervening century has seen, in the development of ideas and in the cultural politics of anticolonialism, a revision of the founding assumptions of colonialism. Said describes this process as 'the massive intellectual, moral, and imaginative overhaul and deconstruction of Western representations of the non-Western world' (1993:xxi). Postcolonial analysis has, however, not really gained much of a foothold in South Africanist socio-cultural discussion, nor was it employed very much as a conceptual tool of resistance in the years of apartheid.[4] My sense of the need for such a study therefore derives from the conviction that certain foundational aspects of a culturally embedded colonising discourse in nineteenth-century South Africa need to be established on a broader scale than has been attempted before. This could not be done without some straddling of disciplinary boundaries. Historians have long been working on the colonial archive in its material sense as a repository of events that are supposed to have occurred. Many postcolonial literary scholars, on the other hand, have become accustomed to the poststructuralist turn, in which the universalising humanism of the knowing Western subject – whose voice is strongly evident in the colonial archive – has been contested as a fiction contingent upon an order of signs which themselves serve particular interests. The fictions of Western humanism, in the postcolonial view, have been embodied in signifying economies whose assumptions of immanent truth need to be decentred and destabilised, in keeping with the notion, drawn from poststructuralism, of the deferred nature of meaning in language. The potential for cross-disciplinary engagement between history and this kind of theory would therefore seem to be self-evident, but the literary and the historical have generally not been allowed to converge in the field of South African cultural-historical debate. In other words, there has been little systematic attempt either by historians (and indeed by specialists in the social sciences in general), or literary-cultural scholars, to read what is thought of as the broader historical *record* as a cultural construct, although significant advances in this direction have been made in recent work by certain historians, cultural anthropologists and postcolonial critics.[5] Literary-cultural scholars in southern African studies who work within the interrelated paradigms of postmodernism, poststructuralism and postcolonialism have tended to restrict themselves to talking about *literary* texts, or more broadly defined *cultural* objects (which may include events such as funeral orations where political and contextual elements assume greater importance than formal qualities[6]), but such scholars have generally not felt inclined to extend their particular reading skills to the larger textual manifestations of social history.[7] This study aims to provide just such a reading, although within carefully circumscribed areas.

If literary scholars have tended to locate their work within generic categories of literature, historians and more general readers have often found what is thought of as literary theory inaccessible, dense, and even pretentious. Part of the reason for this perception among historians has been the tendency in literary-critical work of a theoretical nature to adopt a high level of assumed understanding and to disdain careful explanation of its procedure. In the memorable formulation of one of the most impenetrable cultural analysts, Gayatri Spivak, 'plain prose cheats' and 'clear thought hides' (in De Kock

1992a:40). Despite the danger of such hiding and cheating, though, my own rhetorical situation is defined by a desire to reach a broader readership, and by the positioning of my research between literary theory and socio-historical enquiry. I therefore feel obliged to explain theoretical notions afresh to this more diffuse audience without making too many assumptions about shared procedure. I shall, therefore, return to key theoretical terms and their explanation. But first, some comments on the role and place of theory are needed. Why bother with difficult, and perhaps unnecessary, abstractions in the first place?

In the South African case, theory is more than a convenient but dispensable aid for entering the subject of colonial history. In my view, theory should not be an eager appropriation, in a typically 'colonial' way, of impressive and abstruse 'international' ideas in order to confound and impress one's fellows in the antipodean backwaters. The point is simply that certain developments in recent thought about founding assumptions in all language-based systems of knowledge have made it impossible to proceed without considering the way in which such developments affect the revision of history. The very conception of knowledge and its production has changed to such an extent that all disciplines in the social sciences have been forced to reconsider how objects of knowledge have come into existence. This is why it has become a commonplace to say that postmodernism invites, promotes or makes inevitable the collapse of disciplinary boundaries (see for example Pool (1991:313) in anthropology; Elphick (1992:17) in history). In a more specific way, 'South Africa' can be regarded as a condition whose very historical *making* is derived partly from the creation of a certain kind of *colonial* knowledge about Africans, Europeans and the land, as I shall argue in the course of this book. Understanding nineteenth-century South Africa as a colonial order *in these terms* (that is, in meta-terms which relativise the founding constructs of colonial knowledge) requires the use of *post*colonial forms of understanding.

Framed in this way, theoretical premises inhabit the subject in a material and immediate sense. 'Theory' is thus anything but 'a baggage of abstract learning, out of touch with real life ... talking about real life at a level of abstraction, by people who are incomprehensible, endorsed by institutions' (Spivak in De Kock 1992a:39). The notion of decolonising knowledge, which is germane to theories based on the idea of postcolonialism, relies on an enquiry into Western ways of objectifying and domesticating its Others and their worlds from a central point of humanist influence (Europe). It involves the recognition that language was employed within larger configurations of power and influence, as discourse, to gain mastery over the worlds of Europe's Others. 'South Africa' is a case in point. To understand the constitution of the country as a particular configuration of differential relations involving land, power and culture, one needs more than the materialist version of history in which relations and forces of production and their articulation in social classes are explained. One needs, in addition, an understanding of the very framing of the material dynamics of history within the signifying economies of representation. In this regard, the cultural anthropologists Jean and John Comaroff (1988:6) have remarked that, in historical sociology, 'there remains a tendency ... to explain processes of domination in terms of political and economic forces ... realpolitik is given precedence over ritual, material factors over the moral suasion of the sign'.

It is not my intention merely to reverse the hierarchy suggested by the Comaroffs and favour representation as a determining factor above political and economic forces. The historian Clifton C. Crais (1992b:100) remarks that the issues of 'definition and difference, language and identity' are at the centre of both 'the colonial encounter' *and* postmodernism. For him, the question is whether historians can 'secure a beachhead' between what he characterises as the older social history and the new linguistic turn. Crais sees the answer as a concession to postmodernism that 'language does not faithfully reflect an objective social reality, while at the same time insisting that while discourse is constitutive, it is not determinative'. The main problematic, he says, is to move 'away from a history of experience and towards a history of the consciousness of experience'.

Another historian, Mary R. Anderson (1992:571), argues that while 'meaning' encompasses both mental processes of understanding as well as 'external' experience, the history of meaning is prior to the history of experience. This, she argues, is because experience is itself shaped and limited by the inherited, already constituted world of meanings in which and from which it is constructed. Both Crais and Anderson appear to agree on the minimum condition that no experience of 'history' is unmediated by structures that inhabit language and culture, and that the consciousness of experience is an important dimension of historical enquiry. Crais rightly emphasises the relevance of both material and representational forces in the making of history (see Marks 1993), while Anderson, following Derrida, introduces the caveat that 'consciousness' is never fully 'present' and should not be treated unproblematically as a category. The material-representational relation is one

I have relied upon in this book in that I cite established versions of 'material' history for a necessary grounding of ideas about the politics of identity. The two realms, 'representational' and 'material', should not be regarded as separate. Signification tends to saturate matter and assign meaning to things in various ways: it inheres, for example, in practices such as the disciplinary procedures at Lovedale which I describe in Chapter 3. The external world is apprehended conceptually, through discursive frames of 'knowledge' in which both material and linguistic forms of signification play a part. 'Theory' is integral to an understanding of such processes.

# I

I have suggested that a postcolonial perspective is helpful in understanding how agents of Western enlightenment sought to restructure the lives of autochthonous South African people in the nineteenth century. This is because the 'post' in postcolonial implies an undoing of the putatively universal categories which were at the heart of colonialism. I have also suggested that postcolonialism derives from poststructuralism in certain important ways. Clearly, then, the use of these terms should be elucidated before they can be assumed as implicit in the context of this book.

When scholars try to explain postmodernism, which is often taken to be a more broadly applicable category than poststructuralism (but which nevertheless derives from poststructuralism in important respects[8]), a frequent point of departure is the conception of the human subject in Western metaphysics. This is because the Renaissance-humanist movement assumed a coherent and unified subject in its own image, and projected the idea of such a subject as norm on to the Others of the New World. What is thought of as colonialism is thus fundamentally related to a certain conception of subjectivity, while the 'post' theories in their turn have argued against the falsifications inherent in Western representations of the subject.

An interrogation of colonial impositions of subjectivity is a prominent procedure in the novels of J.M. Coetzee. Writing about Coetzee's novel *Dusklands*, Stephen Watson (1990:41) has characterised the novelist's representation of colonialism as 'the projection of a certain mental aberration located exclusively in the divided consciousness that is a special feature of Western humanity'. Watson adds that the colonising project of the West was set in motion when '[Western man] embarked upon his Cartesian project of separating subject from object, self from world in a dualism which privileged the first of the two terms and thereby assured his domination of nature and any other obstacle he might confront'. For Watson, such dualism is inherent in colonialism, since 'the alienation that entered modern philosophy with Descartes translates itself, in the field of action, into a will to power whose appetite is voracious, limitless, precisely because there is an unbudgeable void at the very heart of it'. Colonialism is an expression of this void: 'Just as Western people conquer nature in an effort to conquer their own self-division, so they cannot desist from enslaving other human beings who necessarily confront them as that Other, alien and forever threatening'.

This synoptic description helps us to understand the position of the uniquely confident Victorian subject (usually white and male) who believed it was a God-given mission to subdue and Christianise Africa, and who made such an effortless division of the world into the civilised and the savage in a subject-object framework. Within the traditional humanist conception of subjectivity, a belief in transhistorical truth made it possible to think of culturally determined categories such as 'civilised' and 'savage' as unmediated and literally God-ordained. Colonial forms of knowledge (that is, the knowledge marshalled as a legitimating rationale for colonisation) depended precisely on a notion of the masterful Western subject as a repository of truth and immutability.

In contrast, the revolution of knowledge in the twentieth century culminating in the 'post' theories overturned the idea that subjectivity could exist outside of historical, ideological, cultural, psychological and linguistic determination. 'The humanist position tends to see the individual as the agent of all social phenomena and productions, including knowledge,' writes Brenda K. Marshall (1992:87). 'It is this unified, rational, controlled subject of humanism which leads to a questioning of the notion of the subject by contemporary theorists.' Histories of the development of a revised approach to subjectivity in the 'post' modes generally cite Ferdinand de Saussure as a figure of key importance. Saussure proposed a model of structural linguistics which suggested the arbitrary nature of linguistic reference by emphasising that language is a *differential* network of meaning and that there is no self-evident, 'real' or 'natural' link between the signifier and the signified which subjects could take as a privileged relation (Norris 1982:24). This is because, understood as a system of differences, language has no absolute referents or positive terms. A linguistically-based system of meaning is thus without a centre; it is inherently unstable, always unfinished, and subject to error and reversal. 'Language is in this sense *diacritical*, or dependent on a structured economy of differences which allows a relatively small range of linguistic elements to signify a vast repertoire of negotiable meanings' (p.25).

These general insights are developed in different ways in postcolonial literary-critical positions in which there is a critique of the self-privileging Western subject (author) who pre-constitutes his or her 'object' of writing (the African, Maori, Aborigine etc.) in terms which seek to foreclose the play of difference. Such a 'deconstructive' position is also generally taken to be a major revision of Cartesian dualism, which places subject and object in a relationship of antagonism, and in terms of which, as Watson's argument suggests, colonialism was conceptually framed. 'In the framework of the postmodern moment, neither the observer (the subject) nor the observed (the object) are autonomous entities; rather, they are culturally constituted, culturally interpreted, and mutually referential' (Marshall 1992:49).

The generalised notion of 'discourse' adopted in postcolonial theories is therefore derived from the broad notion that human subjects are embedded in greater contexts of signification, which they help to create but which are also constitutive of their subjectivity. In approaches based on the idea of discourse in such terms, there can be no *originary* sources of truth (such as the Bible) or universal categories which purport to be derived from such 'truth'. What is taken to be 'truth' in such transcendental terms will be seen variously as the ideological 'interpellation' of the subject, or a 'logocentric'[9] device of fore-closure to be deconstructed, or the discursive expression of particular interests masquerading as general wisdom. As suggested earlier, critics in the post-colonial moment straddle an historical divide: they offer critiques of concrete historical instances of logocentric closure (indeed, they are frequently the colonial Others or their descendants who feel compelled to speak back from what is sometimes called a 'space of difference'), and in doing so they employ aspects of the 'post' theories to assert a *disidentificatory* self-expression, or to help dissolve the deeply embedded residues of colonialist discourse which remain long after formal colonialism has departed. Perhaps the most celebrated example of such work is Said's *Orientalism* (1978), in which the Western world's construction of the Orient as Other in powerful and multiple operations of discursive imperialism is laid bare. The postcolonial field of cultural-literary analysis is, however, wide in range and scope.[10] This study has been conducted in the desire to make visible some aspects of the discursive ordering of colonialism in South Africa, and it takes as a general basis ideas about the human subject such as outlined above.

## II

Postcolonial approaches are not without their own problems, some of which relate to a continuing vigilance about presuppositions and an awareness of the strategic historicity of the 'post' mode (see Parry 1987; Slemon & Tiffin 1989; Sangari 1987; Spivak 1990; Carusi 1991a; Van Wyk Smith 1991; Ahmad 1992; Chrisman 1993). Such theories do not present themselves as one position or one side of an argument, but as a range of critical strategies in diverse contexts sharing some presuppositions. A problem which needs to be addressed briefly here, since it relates to the construction of material in this work, is the variously articulated debate about the concept of *binarity*. The identification of binarity as a mainstay of logocentric procedure – the deceptive assumption that oppositions adequately convey the presence of referents beyond the indeterminacy of signification – is one of the main facets of poststructuralist theory. This aspect of Derridean critique is peculiarly problematic for the scholar of colonialism who draws, to some extent, on Frantz Fanon's much earlier theory of 'Manicheism',[11] which I discuss in Chapters 2 and 3. Fanon perceived a particular kind of binarism as the major force of colonialist psychology in *The Wretched of the Earth* (1961), in which he declared, 'The colonial world is a Manichaean world' (1961:31). Fanon described the colonialist imperative to reduce the colonial Other to a negative term in a system of Manichean binaries succinctly when he asserted that the 'native' in the colonial scheme of things represented 'not only the absence of values, but the negation of all values'; he was the 'enemy of values', the 'absolute evil', the 'corrosive element', the 'depository of maleficent powers' (pp.31-32). In this study, I have identified and described Manichean frames of reference and description constitutive of colonialist discourse, and I have tried to show how even the subversion of orthodox discourse tends to be formulated from within the Manichean perspective.

The adoption of an approach which recognises the operation of a binary system of meaning and value, however, runs the risk of preconstituting its own object of study and replicating such binary closure in the name of academic research. The fact that one describes a binary scheme of representation, perceived to have operated in the past, means that one runs the risk of becoming implicated in the process by which, according to Spivak (1976:lix), 'each term in an opposition is after all an accomplice of the other'. In some of the best recent work on colonialism in various disciplines, one finds admonitions against the closure inherent in theories which posit an enduring moral and descriptive antagonism between coloniser and colonised in binary terms. In history, for example, Elizabeth Elbourne (1992:2) cautions against making the converts of missionary Christianity appear as 'the duped and agentless victims of processes beyond their control', since this approach has the effect of 'occluding agency'. Although many people were to some extent victims, Elbourne writes, there should also be a recognition that 'mission Christianity was used constructively by many individuals seeking positively to reconstruct a broken world' (p.2). Similarly, historian Richard Elphick (1992:16), following the Gambian missiologist Lamin Sanneh (1989; 1993), offers a non-binary model of 'translation' (which he aligns with a post-modernist orientation) as a way of explaining Christianisation in southern Africa. Elphick avers that 'two systems of thought do not "collide"; rather, real people negotiate their way through life, grasping, combining, and opposing different elements which the scholar (but not necessarily the actor) assign to different origins'. For Elphick, 'differences over meaning involve struggles for power, but ... power relations are multiple, widely diffused through society, and often do not correspond neatly to the "big" divides of class vs. class, nation vs. nation, or sex vs. sex'.

Elphick also emphasises 'mutual incomprehension, selective hearing, and struggle over meaning' (1992:15). These features compel one to question monolithic models such as a theory of class struggle, which foregrounds the broad processes of domination at the expense of local and individual struggles over meaning. In a similar spirit, the Comaroffs (1991:7) comment that in studies of the great evangelical encounter in Africa, the implicit question 'Whose side were the Christians really on?', which underlies much early work, reduces complex historical dynamics to the 'crude calculus of interest and intention, and colonialism itself to a caricature'. Once the motives, intentions, and imaginings of persons living or dead are allowed to speak from the historical record, the Comaroffs write, it 'becomes impossible to see them as mere reflections of monolithic cultural structures or social forces' (p.10). This is especially true of the colonial encounter, and of the civilising mission in particular. Yet, the writers note, historians and anthropologists may be accused of not having paid sufficient heed to those voices – not having done justice to the complexities and contradictions on either side of that encounter. 'They are robbed of any real internal dynamism or agency, any organizational complexity or cultural variation, even as they are drawn into the embrace of the modern world system' (p.10).

The Comaroffs insist on a subtle interplay of mutual influence and counter-influence between missionaries and their African interlocutors (see Comaroff & Comaroff 1991:170-97). What emerges from their approach is a denial of any easy-to-hand binary model of 'the' missionaries against 'the' Africans, evident for example in the approach of Nosipho Majeke (Dora Taylor) in *Role of Missionaries in Conquest* (1952). It can be argued, following those who advocate a less monolithic approach, that such one-to-one models run the risk of replicating the essentialism inherent in colonialist attempts to foreclose heterogeneity.

This argument has been made by literary-cultural critics as well. One example is the criticism of Arun P. Mukherjee (1991:28), who questions the tendency of postcolonial literary critics to 'perform several homogenising functions which produce an essentialised "native" who is devoid of race, gender, class, caste, ethnic, and religious markers'. Mukherjee (p.30) points to postcolonial theory's ability to '[lock] us into binary oppositions of coloniser/ colonised, domination/resistance' and argues that this 'monolith created by the unitary discourse of the postcolonial theory stands in place of the plurality, heterogeneity, and specificity of literatures subsumed under the unitary name assigned to them' (see Gates 1987; Slemon & Tiffin 1989; Ashcroft *et al.* 1989; Thomas 1994). To a certain extent, all these criticisms relate to relatively recent academic practice in which the experience of autochthonous people, or of the various players in colonial situations, are unwittingly reappropriated (and therefore recolonised) in reductive frames of reference, often by metropolitan scholars.

In historical writing about religion, in particular, there has been a gathering swell of reaction against binary models which assume that Christianity was little more than a tool of imperialism, and that it is best analysed within the context of colonial imposition or capitalist machination. Scholars such as Sanneh (1989; 1993), Richard Gray (1990a), Elphick (1992), Elbourne (1992), Paul Landau (1992), Norman Etherington (1994), Terence Ranger (1994), to name only the more obvious, have argued for the shift characterised by Ranger (1986:10) as one from 'the unpeopled structures of political economy to a primary concern with experience and consciousness'. This shift entails a move away from large models of explanation, and towards history 'from below' rather than history based on 'official', state, imperial or other more customary sources. It is often concerned with oral or otherwise 'ordinary' evidence of individual people whose experience contradicts clumsy social theories or dualistic schemes. It emphasises the diverse, individual experience of Christianity and the special role of conversion in the reconstruction of identity during traumatic, and transitional, historical epochs. Overall, it seeks to emphasise the role of African agency in the colonial process, a process that it refuses to simplify in terms of the tendency in older scholarship to seek 'monocausal' explanations or to detect imperial conspiracies behind even the most localised interactions.

The approaches characterised here as a general shift are themselves diverse, and they offer rich perspectives within a new style of revisionism which takes issue with an earlier, often Marxian, programme of scholarly revision. Yet they run the risk of underspecifying the extent to which missionaries, administrators, and other colonial agents can still be perceived to have worked within the parameters of a resilient and capacious civilising discourse, despite many internal differences among themselves, and in spite of the fact that Africans responded creatively and unconformingly to the colonising thrust. In particular, it seems unwise to ignore excellent research such as, for example, that which is recorded in D.M. Schreuder's 1976 article, 'The Cultural Factor in Victorian Imperialism: A Case Study of the British "Civilising Mission"', simply because it does not share the newer emphases. Schreuder's article was important because it questioned still earlier scholarship which characterised British imperialism as 'reluctant'. Schreuder insisted on the 'more expansive, energetic and belligerent cultural roots of British nineteenth-century colonial activity' (p.283). He produced a large body of evidence relating to the Cape to support his thesis that the 'administrative mind' in the colonial periphery consciously sought to conduct 'social engineering', drawn from what he describes as 'cultural hubris' and 'civilizing zeal', within a dynamic thrust of the 'master-culture of the nineteenth century' (p.284).

We have learnt to become wary of such sweeping claims, yet a reading of Schreuder's article shows a sensitivity to differences and a great respect for evidence. Schreuder says that it would be 'quite wrong to suppose uniformity in Cape administrative practices towards African groups', but that diversity at the micro-level of districts does not alter the 'apparent overall pattern of thought-idioms at the macro-level of "ideology" – the ideas general to the administration, the suppositions and values common as denominators of its cultural beliefs and attitudes' (p.288). He goes on to cite a large body of evidence, drawn from a diverse range of contexts in the Cape, to support the argument that both the earlier and later nineteenth-century administrative policy in the Cape shared the desire to 'undermine chieftainship and political authority; to encourage a labour supply; to provide a secure market for Cape commerce; and to "civilise" pagan tribesmen – in short, to "integrate" Africans into the colonial society, partly as consumers and producers, even more as agricultural labourers and a potential working class on the public works and mines' (p.290).

In Schreuder's argument, a 'combination of territorial advance and cultural conversion' (p.291) was widely regarded as a panacea for the development of the colony, particularly in the era of Victorian imperialism.

To advance arguments like the above is not to claim that such colonising aspirations were successful in reality, or to imagine that they were deployed as a conspiracy. Even Schreuder argues that 'Failure awaited most of these schemes, disappointment clouded most of these high Victorian hopes of Progress' (p.303). Similarly, Frederick Cooper (1994:1529) reminds us that 'Recognition of the much greater power of the Europeans in the colonial encounter does not negate the importance of African agency in determining the shape the encounter took'. A recognition of the large body of evidence pointing to a *generally* articulated civilising discourse does not, in my view, necessarily amount to a misrecognition of African insurgency, or an assumption that colonial processes are reducible to the effects of such a discourse alone. Nor does it imply a view of colonial interaction framed entirely within a coloniser-colonised, domination-resistance mould. Yet to underspecify the enormous *aspirations* of colonising discourse, and its considerable institutional afflatus, is to forget that agency, disavowal, conversion, appropriation, negotiation and creation occurred *within* the constraints of what Schreuder calls a 'belligerent' civilising mission.

One does need to consider carefully Cooper's (1994:1517) warning of 'The risk ... that in exploring the colonial binarism one reproduces it'. Cooper sees the difficulty as being able to 'confront the power behind European expansionism without assuming it was all-determining'. For him, the binaries of coloniser/colonised, Western/non-Western run the risk of constraining the search for 'precise ways in which power is deployed and the ways in which power is engaged, contested, deflected, and appropriated' (p.1517). Perhaps the better approach is to differentiate between binarisms in their primary operations as historically embedded discursive effects, widely employed by colonisers themselves, and sceptical appraisal of the ambit of such binarisms – appraisal that does not underestimate the range and scope of such dualistic schemes in their *historical* sense, nor imagines that the experience of colonialism itself is in any way reducible to the effects of these binaries alone. In terms of this study, for example, how does one deal with the perception that evangelists, administrators and others of a colonialist persuasion in the nineteenth century themselves adopted relentlessly binarist categories of knowledge? For a scholar to review missionary-colonial writings now and not come up against the leaden insistence on certain elementary tropes derived from the civilised-barbarian dyad is hardly conceivable. Certainly, the heterogeneous range of voices in the record will not fit into dualistic conceptual schemes. But an equally inescapable perception is that reductive coercion into just such schemes of reference is precisely how missionaries and their colonial fellows in general conceived their relations with African subjects (see Bolt 1971; Brantlinger 1986). In my reading of missionary documents and books (of which only a small percentage are explicitly discussed in this work) I was struck by the near-stupefying tenacity of Manichean description. Everywhere I looked I came across missionaries doing precisely what Mukherjee sees Western literary scholars doing: reducing heterogeneity and plurality to a binary scheme in which one term predominates and determines the other. I therefore do not wish to underrate what I regard as evidence of the Manichean basis of missionary discourse (Chapters 2 and 3). However, it is one thing to describe the *attempts* by missionaries and others to enforce a coercive narrative of identity on people, and quite another to argue that such a narrative adequately reflects the experience of colonial interaction. Indeed, I have found it invigorating to look at the ways in which people who have been institutionally colonised (such as pupils or former pupils who have willingly gone through the rigours of a Lovedale education) nevertheless subvert from within the terms by which their identity is supposedly defined, in a manner which is strikingly similar to deconstructive practice (Chapter 4). Likewise, it has been a revealing exercise to examine the possibility that missionaries deluded themselves in their insistence on particular terms of reference regardless of major discrepancies between their African experiences and their evangelical or imperial narratives (Chapter 5).

I have sought to present, therefore, a description of civilising discourse in a general and introductory manner which includes the characterisation of Manichean binarism as its own foundational aspect. Disavowing 'foundationalist' history (see Prakash 1992) surely implies that earlier instances of such narrative capture should be exposed and their effects probed. This book therefore proposes that it is important to examine, in a more broadly based manner than an examination of 'literature', or empirical 'fact' alone, what is perceived as a discursive edifice which itself had a tremendous will to power and an enormous essentialising impetus. It is precisely in the interstices of this discursive order and the semi-conforming responses of its agonistic[12] subjects that hybrid forms of colonial identity emerged. In order to describe this discursive monolith (if I am allowed its existence) which in its institutional operations played an important, if limited, role in identity formation, I characterise it in terms of its *own* essentialising bias, which is not the same thing as offering an analytical model of colonialism in essentialising, binary terms. Such a paradoxical process, described in deconstructive criticism as the 'double gesture' (Jay 1992:56; 64-71), means that one inhabits a vocabulary in order to render it problematic. Eagleton (1990:24) captures this sense of paradoxical articulation when he argues that 'Sexual politics, like class or nationalist struggle, will thus necessarily be caught up in the very metaphysical categories it hopes finally to abolish; and any such movement will demand a difficult, perhaps ultimately impossible double optic, at once fighting on a terrain already mapped out by its antagonists and seeking even now to prefigure within that mundane strategy styles of being and identity for which we have as yet no proper names'.

# III

The project to describe the representational character of missionary-colonial discourse strikes me as important because the subject has not been dealt with at all comprehensively from the point of view of cultural analysis. There is very little scholarly work on South Africa in which a general introduction to the representational basis of colonialism is offered, and scant scholarship which reads history as a cultural 'text' (see Biersack 1989), attending to the cultural ordering of history as well as the historical ordering of culture. The best work in this area has emerged from history and cultural anthropology. The appearance in 1992 of Crais's book, *The Making of the Colonial Order: White Supremacy and Black Resistance in the Eastern Cape, 1770-1865* (1992a), and the Comaroffs' *Of Revelation and Revolution* in 1991 were the first works in which questions of representation and the cultural negotiation of identity in relation to nineteenth-century South Africa were treated broadly and seriously.

Whereas the Comaroffs' emphasis falls on the 'anthropology of missions' (1991:7) and a broad cultural analysis of the 'colonization of consciousness and the consciousness of colonization' (p.xi), and whereas Crais's work is aimed at a comprehensive account, incorporating questions of representation and identity as well as the material forces of history, this book, considerably more modest in scope, seeks to describe the making, in the nineteenth century, of a discursive orthodoxy by *literary* means as a basis upon which identity was negotiated and reformulated in ongoing cultural exchanges between Africans and Europeans. I believe that missionaries in the nineteenth century, and more particularly those whose institution, Lovedale, I examine more closely, were crucial agents in the construction of a literary basis for self-apprehension by those regarded as Other in the particular colonial milieu of the nineteenth century. As I argue in Chapter 2, many Africans in the Eastern Cape were impelled by large-scale military defeat in the first half of the century towards a realisation in the second half that some concession to orthodox forms of the civilising mission, particularly the prospects held out by missionary education, was necessary in order to advance beyond peasantry and serfdom. Lovedale is particularly important because of the role it and its later outgrowth, Fort Hare University, played in the education of African intellectuals in the Eastern Cape who went on to establish nationalist movements such as the African National Congress (see Williams 1970).

Framing the subject in such terms means, however, that the more usual disciplinary limits of 'literature', 'English', and 'history' have to be breached. The representational contexts in which subjectivity was negotiated in colonial South Africa in the nineteenth century are, I maintain, far broader than the category of 'literature' will allow, yet 'English'[13] as a cultural factor in the making of contexts of subjectivity is too important to be ignored. I have therefore tried to go beyond the customary limits of studies about 'English in Africa' (the title of a journal which has traditionally published articles on South African literature in English) and regarded as potential texts for analysis the colonial archive as a whole. I have, however, been compelled to select exemplary texts and to contain the archival material within the demands of my particular arguments. The point nevertheless is worth making that whereas the disciplinary English study may look at the *results* of colonisation in the form of 'black literature' in English, this book wishes to describe, broadly, some of the *prior* representational processes in which colonial subjectivity was negotiated, and some of the representational modes in which colonising discourse was appropriated and redeployed.

My engagement with history is also not entirely standard, since it does not pretend to offer strictly diachronic and meticulously detailed empirical research on a micro-area of study. My emphasis on 'some' of the processes involved in a deeply complex area of history implies that I shall argue for a certain degree of discursive synchrony in an otherwise extremely diverse history. Areas of historical focus are Glasgow Missionary Society and Free Church of Scotland archival material, archival documents relating to the Lovedale institution in the Eastern Cape between 1870 and 1890, the African newspaper *Imvo Zabantsundu* in the 1880s and other newspapers, and certain selected book-length narratives which set the context for, and describe, the 'rise' of the 'New African' (by Robert Moffat, David Livingstone, John A. Chalmers, Tiyo Soga and John Knox Bokwe). In some cases I rely on well researched historical accounts in order to formulate ideas about representational contestation. For example, in Chapter 2, in which I seek to describe very generally the broad patterns of discursive 're-making' as evidenced in the Eastern Cape and, more particularly, by the rise of the Lovedale institution, I rely on a range of established historical narratives about general patterns of events (without trying to reinvent such history) and suggest that a representational orthodoxy supplemented this history in important ways. Drawing on Foucault's theory that the individual subject's relation to power is 'agonistic', I try to demonstrate the general discursive parameters within which African subjects were drawn into missionary-colonial orthodoxy in the Eastern Cape. My claims are not absolute, in that different time-and-place contexts will show different patterns of missionary agency and African response, but I do claim to identify some particularly widespread discursive problematics that can be typified as generically 'colonial' in the broader South African context.

An important element in my motivation is precisely to suggest a strong discursive basis for colonial orthodoxy in a general sense. It is fitting to recall Jean and John Comaroff's proposition (1991:17) that despite the postmodern insights about indeterminacy which we often use so profitably in unpicking colonial certainties, (South African) history presents us with a reminder that in material social relations, reductive orthodoxies have often succeeded in imposing themselves over time and distance. How is it, the authors ask, that 'history keeps generating hegemonies that, for long periods, seem able to impose a degree of order and stability on the world'? How do relatively small groups of people often 'succeed in gaining and sustaining control over large populations and in drawing them into a consensus with dominant values'? The Comaroffs turn to a carefully theorised conception of Gramscian hegemony, which they see as moulded within cultural-discursive terms, to answer their question.

My project has partly been to characterise as discursive the surprisingly persistent hegemonies described above, and I find the Eastern Cape example particularly suggestive. By its very nature, this book suggests that the instances discussed are drawn from a more general, and totalising, Victorian order. It was in the nature of the colonising ethos to adduce the Other to the Same, to subsume the particular and the heterogeneous under the general and the known. My argument claims to suggest instances, in cross-section, of this broader colonising process, much in the same spirit as Said (1978:14) when he describes the 'persistence and durability of saturating hegemonic systems like culture' and argues that 'nearly every nineteenth-century writer ... was extraordinarily well aware of the fact of empire'. Said, who in *Orientalism* had to deal with a vast documentary archive, writes, 'There still remained the problem of cutting down a very fat archive to manageable dimensions, and more important, outlining something in the nature of an intellectual order within that group of texts without at the same time following a mindlessly chronological order' (p.16). Said here relies on a relation between the general and the particular which I have found helpful in framing my own subject. Said describes his position as a fear, on the one hand, of 'a coarse polemic on so unacceptably general a level of description as not to be worth the effort', and, on the other, of 'so detailed and atomistic a series of analyses as to lose all track of the general lines of force informing the field, giving it its special cogency' (p.8).

Such 'special cogency' is remarkably similar to the Comaroffs' sense of the 'hegemonic'. Hegemony is an indispensable concept because it offers the analyst a way of understanding precisely the 'general lines of force' (Said) and the 'consensus with dominant values' (Comaroff) by which culture is entailed in power. I have found particularly illuminating the exposition of hegemony offered by the Comaroffs (1991:21), who explain culture as 'the shared repertoire of practices, symbols, and meanings from which hegemonic forms are cast – and, by extension, resisted'. Alternatively, they argue, culture can be seen as 'the historically situated field of signifiers, at once material and symbolic, in which occur the dialectics of domination and resistance, the making and breaking of consensus' (p.21).

My methodological emphasis on general and representative cultural orthodoxies, backed up by documentary sources in particular instances (which I regard as representative), relies on an understanding of colonial processes of subjectification as a widespread, generalising endeavour in which a certain hegemony emerged from an order of cultural signs and practices. No study that I am aware of has regarded the South African colonial order as a discursive event. Certainly, no literary study has gone backwards, behind the colonising forms such as the written novel, poem, play, essay, etc., to establish the existence of a discursive field within which English was entailed in the cultural dimensions of colonial power.[14] English as a discipline has also generally disdained serious consideration of its *own* emergence out of the bloody, unequal colonial distribution of power, preferring to affiliate itself with European modernism and the supposedly enlightened view of art above politics (see Morphet 1994). Nor has any historical or other study that I am aware of devoted primary attention to colonialist discourse on its own terms, and not as an adjunct to material history. The instances of colonialist discourse and its resistance that I cite in this study are seen in relation to this larger context, this indisputably powerful system of naming which is implicit in the term 'colonial' and its understanding in the first place.

The emphasis on discourse makes a further qualification necessary, namely the use of the terms 'colonial' and 'colonialist' and their reference in particular instances of citation, in this book, to *missionary* colonialism. Given this study's focus on signification and representation, I have found missionaries an inevitable subject. One may argue that the sovereign role of missionaries was the cultural reproduction of particular forms of representation, and the painstaking, cross-lingual cultivation of a receptive space in the (hegemonic) sphere of consensual evangelisation. Missionaries were pre-eminently agents of cultural influence and change. Other colonial agents, such as administrators, traders, farmers, and settlers in general, attended to the material facets of the colonial encounter, but missionaries were destined to transform the coercive processes of colonisation into the cultivation of 'civilisation'. Although the cultural agency of missionaries was always aligned with Christianity and Commerce as the three C's (see Bosch 1991:305; Bundy 1988:37-40), theirs was the domain in which signs were most assiduously contested and the imperialism of a European version of Christian truth most forcefully practised. John Comaroff (1989:680-81) has reminded us that 'colonialism did (and does) not exist in the singular, but in a plurality of forms and forces'. Similarly, there are various refractions of 'colonial discourse', 'missionary discourse' being one of them. Comaroff proposes that the separate but interdependent purveyors of colonialism were the state, which emphasised the politico-legal aspects of British rule; the settlers, whose domain was the socioeconomic dimensions of race relations in a new agrarian society; and the mission, which traded in the signs and practices of what Comaroff calls 'bourgeois European culture' (although by all accounts missionaries were frequently less than bourgeois). Despite the variation in articulation, the substance of the colonising project, over the long term, 'was all of these things, in proportions determined on the battlegrounds of history – the bodies and societies, the territories and cultural terrains of South Africa, white and black' (p.681).

Following this argument, my argument relies on a similar understanding of the part-whole relationship of missionary discourse to the broader discourse of colonialism of which it was a constitutive part. The sense of a wider colonial interaction is argued by Crais (1992a:94-95), who describes as one of a series of 'colonial paradoxes' the fact that the reproduction of a 'civilised' patriarchy in the Eastern Cape depended on 'barbarous' practices: it became increasingly clear to both the British colonial elite and to many bureaucrats, Crais avers, that economic growth in the colony would ultimately rest not on free labour, but on its opposite: 'Counter to their most cherished ideals, economic growth and human progress depended on subjection and the violence which accompanied the denial of freedom ... what was already clear by the end of the 1820s was that the contradiction of the "barbarous" basis of "civilized" colonial life had become an anxious issue for the nascent British colonial elite.' Njabulo Ndebele (1987:219) writes that colonial subjects 'soon discovered that the newly promised freedom was premised ultimately on the subject's *un*freedom ... the very concept of freedom came to be standardized ... according to the specification of imperial powers'. As my title implies, 'civilising' the 'barbarians' was a deeply paradoxical process involving the construction of the Self as well as the Other in a manner that rendered ironic the cherished ideals and certainties of an Enlightenment left behind on the shores of Europe. Missionaries, although only a part of the 'civilising' process, played an important role in holding back conscious suggestion of such irony by stabilising and legitimating, in the name of a Christian God, the unstable signifiers of 'civilisation'.

# IV

The shape of this book is related to an examination of various modes of textual contestation, and it does not always adhere to a strict chronology. Chapter 2 offers a broad focus on the general process under description, while Chapters 3 and 4 seek to provide particularly suggestive instances of this process. In Chapter 3 the study turns to a discussion of discourse pertaining to Lovedale in its founding phases and, more particularly, during the highly successful era of Dr James Stewart. In Chapter 4 the book explores the manner in which this discourse was 'mimicked' – internalised, re-appropriated and subtly undermined within the constraints of colonial orthodoxy – in the person of John Tengo Jabavu and his newspaper, *Imvo Zabantsundu*. Whereas Chapters 3 and 4 deal with particular examples of missionary narratives of identity and counter-narratives, Chapter 5, like Chapter 2, again seeks to establish broad characteristics of an enabling colonialist orthodoxy, but in Chapter 5 this is regarded via a discussion of book-length narratives rather than the more dispersed everyday forms of representation such as the sermon, the classroom lecture, the dialogue or the newspaper report (traces of which are examined in Chapter 2). My narrative develops towards a culmination in the figure of Tiyo Soga, whom I deal with at some length in Chapter 5 as a prime embodiment of agonism as a form of response to missionary discourse and its effects. I must emphasise at the outset, therefore, that this book does not offer a strictly diachronic, exhaustive account of missionary and other forms of 'civilising' colonialism. My choice of focus is methodologically consistent, in that I look at similar themes in different representational media. Chapter 5, while returning to the time introduced in Chapter 2, offers thematic progression in the sense that it shows how missionary colonialism was consolidated in the most influential medium of the time, the book. The progression in argument, therefore, is from general representational presuppositions and the making of colonial orthodoxy (Chapter 2), to the example of Lovedale's institutional discourse (Chapter 3), to counter-discourse in *Imvo* (Chapter 4), to the formal apotheosis of missionary colonialism, the book-narrative (Chapter 5). Similarly, I do not pretend to offer a geographically complete account. Many of my examples are drawn from the Eastern Cape, but in Moffat and Livingstone I take examples of missionary discourse from the northern Cape and beyond. I claim that Moffat and Livingstone's books set a general imperial context for southern Africa, as a result of their influence, which overrides geographic particularities. Further, I argue that the emergence of the 'New African' in the Eastern Cape – particularly this figure's narratively shaped 'rise' in book form – is not unrelated to this more general context of missionary colonialism, which, in the nineteenth century, was undergirded by the universalising ethos of the imperial book.

However, to talk about books and textual objects in terms of a more general notion of textuality means that one's own study cannot escape the implications of textuality. My focus on *narratives* of identity and on the constructed nature of colonial discourse must also apply to narratives of history in general, since all such textual assemblages represent a contemporaneous history in the making, a running story of the distant or immediate past in the present moment of apprehension. I have already argued, earlier in this chapter, for a relationship between the 'textual' and the 'material' facets of history which recognises the discursive basis of historical depiction. What is pertinent here is to question the status of my own representations of the past. Clearly, any work which draws on theories of textuality cannot pretend to offer foundational or unassailable versions of truth about the past when the status of transcendental truth beyond signification is itself brought into question.

Two points can be made in this regard. First, this book examines narratives of what are taken to be facts and not unmediated facts themselves. In this sense, it is a study about how other historical subjects sought to make sense of their own present realities in discourse, and how such discourses appear to have been integral to broader configurations of power. Second, despite the recognition that history is both discourse and event, one does not necessarily have to subscribe to a hopelessly relativistic position of absolute undecidability. The very relation between reality and discourse is such that while reality is *dumb* (it contains no stories of its own making, it is inchoate), reality also only exists as such (as the *concept* of reality) in relation to the ceaseless human activity of interpretation. When one talks history, then, one talks in a discursively constituted linguistic order of human interpretation about a past whose traces are partially evident in prior discursive events ('evidence' generally consists in verbal accounts, earlier interpretations). For Tony Bennett, 'the past as traces already in discourse (the historic past) acts as the referent for the historian *as if it were* pre-discursive' (in Jenkins 1992:12), and within this qualified sense, certain rules of reliability and credibility serve to enhance a historical narrative's purchase on extra-discursive reality. For clearly, in my view, there is always *some* purchase on reality in a historical account, even if that connection is no more than a recognition that a certain story has been told in a certain way about an ascertainable event. It is surely not a necessary consequence of theories which use the prefix 'post' that reality is denied an independent existence. This straw man is all too often conjured up in rhetorical broadsides against a practice of writing perceived as irresponsible. As Marshall (1992:171) notes, 'there is no project afoot in postmodernism ... to suggest that there is no past, no "real" historical referents'. There is, however, 'an insistence that those referents are only available in the present through textualized forms'. In my understanding, it is in the conjunctions of ascertainable events (by sensory evidence, by multiple perception, by significantly concurring accounts) and their appropriations in verbal discourse that the 'linguistic turn' in history should make itself most valuably felt. In this view, it is not necessary to adopt the attitude that there is no such thing as *truth* in the ordinary sense of the word. Unexceptionable truths, such as the fact that these words are printed on paper, abound in our everyday lives. It is only when dealing with large philosophical claims to truth about people and their supposedly intrinsic nature, about the allegedly essential attributes of races, nations or individuals as conveyed by forms of representation, and about the character of events in time, that a great deal of awareness is necessary in relation to the semantic interface between such claims and their referents, and about the degrees of reflexivity these claims exhibit.[15]

Rather than opt for an entirely relativistic position of undecidability in accordance with a hard view of poststructuralism (that any positive description is an essentialisation supporting particular interests), one can argue, like Paul Jay (1992:70), that it is naive to believe deconstructive thinking can ever be deployed in an idealised and pure form without political interest. How deconstructive thinking is used, Jay says, is ultimately determined by the politics of each critic (p.71). What, otherwise, would the point be of a 'postcolonial' criticism, if not to define a political interest (anticolonialism, revealing the discursive belligerence of colonialism), and to formulate a 'non-foundational, ethical political discourse that can matter' (Jay 1992:52)? In this sense, my own representations of particular facets of the colonial process in the nineteenth century in specific, and arguably representative, instances, are written against the grain of that history's own legitimating terms. Nevertheless, even though much of the writing in this book works to contradict the surface import of other, colonialist, writing (thereby safeguarding itself from claims to objectivity), there are important interpretative turns in my argument in which I fashion my own literary tropes to reconfigure the history under discussion in terms opposed to and different from its surface narratives. Here I am happy to declare my interest as politically and historically relative to my view of an ethical political discourse which is *post*colonial in both the temporal and oppositional senses of the word.

In such an argument, one might then ask, what distinguishes the ethical value of one account from any other? More specifically, what distinguishes the colonialist or imperialist view of South Africa's history from my own? It is here that one can, I believe, claim certain affirming values. Not all accounts are equal. The ones examined in this book, for example, patently exhibit discursive closure of a decisive nature. Narratives such as my own, which seek to reveal the historical contingency and the literary constructedness of earlier attempts to pass discourse off as reality, must by extension claim a greater degree of discursive reflexivity. In the absence of positivistic values, they can arguably claim a lesser degree of foreclosure. But even in their positive claims, narratives such as my own may be said to have the (unfair) advantage of a metacritical awareness never available to the historically embedded subjects who feature in this study. That is, one has the advantage of hindsight and review along with developments in theories of knowledge and historiography (which are also historically embedded). This advantage may be unfair, but it is mitigated by the sheer violence (ascertainable) and the mendacity of the colonial process in South Africa.

I must also emphasise that I do not regard my interpretation of African response to missionary orthodoxies as a case of *speaking for* or *giving voice to* the African subject from a position of critical objectivity, an act which is generally recognised as problematic (see Alcoff 1991). I am able to comment on African response because Africans affected by missionary colonialism have in fact voiced their own positions. I have found examples of such expression in archival sources. My work has been to review critically the degree of discursive mediation, subversion or mimicry which is evident in these texts, but this remains a critical act. It is not 'intercultural truth'; it does not seek to cross boundaries of culture and capture, in description that is 'entirely valid' (Van Wyk Smith 1991:29), features of 'otherness'.[16] Instead, this is criticism which reviews narratives of othering and then discusses the way in which those affected by such narratives have written counter-narratives in response to such manoeuvres.

If this book tells a story, then, it is the story of how a colonial order partly based on evangelical colonialism (despite the many contradictions between missionaries and other colonial agents) seeks to rewrite the cultural precepts of identity for people made subservient by war and imperial expansionism, and how some of the colonised people internalise these texts and begin to rewrite them in an emergent narrative of African nationalism. In this sense, it is a story of conquest, yearning for a reconstructed world, and betrayal. The African elite who readily assimilated missionary education in the hope of joining the millenarian society implicit in the promise of civilisation and Christianity, and who looked eagerly to the fulfilment of grand humanitarian ideals associated with the name of Victoria and formulated in the face of settler colonialism and Boer hostility, were ultimately betrayed as the 'liberal' Cape Colony was drawn into the first version of South Africa in 1910. While this study cannot hope to cover such expansive areas of history, the narratives of identity proffered by missionaries and the counter-narratives discussed here occur within this larger story of colonial duplicity which, if not consciously or maliciously formulated, nevertheless worked to savage effect in the name of 'civilisation'.

# 2

# THE MAKING OF COLONIAL
# ORTHODOXY

Your cattle are gone, my countrymen!
Go rescue them! Go rescue them!
Leave the breechloader alone
And turn to the pen.
Take paper and ink,
For that is your shield.
Your rights are going!
So pick up your pen.
Load it, load it with ink.
Sit on a chair.
Repair not to Hoho.
But fire with your pen.
              *– I.W.W. Citashe (1882)*[1]

In the latter part of the twentieth century – most intensely in the 1970s and 1980s – English-speaking literary scholars, critics and writers in South Africa could be found arguing about the relationship between art and politics. These debates, variously articulated in response to divergent impulses, generally saw traditionalists arguing against the corruption of form and high standards in literature by the increasing prevalence of revolutionary sentiment, while more radical scholars criticised their opponents for refusing to allow the political role of literature (in this debate, literature in English).[2] However, few participants in this argument seemed to recall or argue the more fundamental point that, to an important extent, the orthodoxy of English as a dominant

medium of educational discourse in South Africa, and the institutionalisation
of this discourse (by which English 'literature' is privileged as an area of study),
was won by blood.[3]

By this I mean that the ascendancy of English as a principal medium for
social empowerment among many black South Africans was secured in the
nineteenth century on frontier battlefields by colonial soldiers who resorted to
scorched earth tactics to decimate their 'savage' enemies (Mostert 1992:1130).
For Africans in the nineteenth century, the link between 'culture', 'English'
and revolutionary turmoil was more than a matter of polite debate. The
ultimate consequence of, for example, the Frontier Wars in the Eastern Cape
between 1779 and 1878 for the Xhosa was that the locus of socio-cultural
empowerment shifted from an autochthonous sphere to the politically
compromising colonial milieu. War, attrition and the loss of land often meant
that the only avenue open for advancement in the new colonial order was the
European-led mercantile economy, or peasantry, while the educational
infrastructure supporting the new system was largely in the hands of
missionaries (see Hunt Davis 1969; Mills 1975; Cobley 1986; Bundy 1988;
Mostert 1992; Crais 1992a). Africans aspiring to social elevation in colonial
society had little choice but to embrace Protestant values which were
embedded in the exalted medium of English and promoted in missionary
education. 'English' in this sense was the bearer of a cultural and intellectual
regime in which the dominant values, drawn from Enlightenment thinking
but corrupted in the deferred colonial context (Bosch 1991:302-13), were
progressive individualism, modernisation, capitalism, and ultimately racism.[4]
At the end of the twentieth century the relationship between English and
social empowerment is still complex and fraught with the implications of
colonial history, but many have lost sight of the bloody genesis of this link,
and the need continually to gauge the relationship between English in its
disciplinary guise and its role in broader relations of power (see Dunton 1993).

The process of what is sometimes called the 'Westernisation' of black
South Africans is extremely complex, and I have emphasised the element of
warfare for the sake of perspective. The colonisation of people in what only
later became known as an entity ('South Africa') was achieved by ink as well
as blood, in the irruption of a powerful new order of representation which ran
parallel with outbreaks of war. My suggestion is therefore that a violence of
similar proportions to that of warfare was committed on the epistemic[5] level by
the powerful repressions, the far-reaching censorship and the iron hand of
what historians Robinson and Gallagher (1961:7) call the 'Victorian world

mission'. The vehicle of this 'world mission' was an English which bore terrible certainties and was seldom tolerant of alterity. It was a language of closure and myopia, yet it represented an empire which could cause great turbulence for those who would not respect its insistence on orthodoxy.

I have chosen to concentrate largely on the Eastern Cape 'frontier' area because of its singular importance in the history of cultural contestation in South Africa (see Crais 1992a; Mostert 1992:228), and because developments there are, I believe, illustrative of the wider theatre of struggle between European cultural agents and indigenous South Africans in the nineteenth century.[6] At stake in the struggle on the 'frontier' was nothing less than the nature of reality, the proper forms of social life, and the highest questions of morality, religion and philosophy. Wars were waged on the ground, policies were framed in Cape Town and London, and the 'eager feet' of missionaries (Orr 1975), driven by the spirit of evangelism, were busy in the 'interior', but the greater context of all this activity was an emerging narrative in which the unequal struggle between different orders of signs was slowly resolved in favour of colonial hegemony, where the greater power ultimately lay, even though resistance and transformation could never be comprehensively managed. The term 'frontier' is problematic (Legassick 1980) and I use it here to suggest both a geographical and cultural contact zone (Pratt 1992:6-7) where forms of knowledge and identity were contested at the same time as wars were fought for land and physical control of the environment. Frontiers are 'uncharted spaces of confrontation – spaces in which people fashion new worlds by negotiating hitherto uncommunicated signs' (Comaroff & Comaroff 1991:13).

The argument that physical and representational wars were coterminous is well illustrated by an historical anecdote in R.H.W. Shepherd's tome on Lovedale, *Lovedale South Africa* (1940:400), where he records that some of the lead type of the Lovedale mission press (then at Tyumie) was melted down to make bullets during the War of the Axe (1846-47). It is an open question which form of lead was ultimately more persuasive in forcing traumatic and momentous change on the Xhosa and other people in the nineteenth century. Perhaps the lesson of the anecdote is that both kinds were responsible, each answering different exigencies. What seems clear, though, is that the lead of printing type was an enduring and consistent agent of change.

The issues raised by representation *vis-à-vis* the history of frontier conflict in the Eastern Cape (let alone the rest of southern Africa) are highly complex and potentially boundless. To delimit my subject and to avoid the obligation to re-establish 'material' history, I rely on reliably researched, existing accounts for a *context* of events (not an unquestioned history of facts) in which to survey the shape of missionary narrative and the representational procedures of a civilising colonialism. Although the vastness of written archival sources is daunting, there are strong thematic correspondences in much of the literary material on missionary work and 'culture contact', so that a degree of generalisation is necessary. This is so because the efforts of missionaries to 'civilise' African people, particularly in the Eastern Cape, were founded on the imperative to force multiple, heterogeneous forms of social organisation and belief in non-Christian communities into a new, Christian mould. This was a reductive and generalising mission driven by the need to impose the history of the Same on what was regarded as Other.[7] Ultimately, the process was designed to enforce an orthodoxy of identity. This means that traces of verbal and written forms of representation available to modern researchers can be scrutinised as examples of this broader process.

Although the laborious processes of missionary teaching over generations in the face of resistance and opposition in some cases, and gradual acquiescence in others, cannot be captured in the shape of a seamless or monolithic narrative of events, it is reasonable to assert that between, say, 1800 and 1880, substantial progress was made by European agents in rupturing the autochthonous belief-systems of Xhosa and other communities. The early history of missions is not a straightforward success story (see Williams 1959), but the argument remains that even in the first three decades of the century, when converts were hard won and scarce, the mission station 'occupied a critical interstice in the colonial encounter in which Africans came to better understand the material and intellectual consequences of colonial expansion' (Crais 1992a:101). There is, in addition, a degree of symmetry, on the one hand in the decline of African power in the Eastern Cape in the nineteenth century as the Hundred Years' War on the frontier dragged on, and, on the other in the gradual increase in the success of an institution such as Lovedale, along with the general encroachment of the European mercantile economy. Hunt Davis (1969:58), whose work looks specifically at the impact of education in the nineteenth century, characterises the broad process of change as a growing dependence on the European economy brought about by loss of land, the destruction of political independence, and the impact of military defeat. Hunt Davis (1969:288) writes that the early educational work of the pioneer missionaries, along with their other attempts at acculturation, made little headway, but in the second half of the century, rapid changes among the Nguni removed African unwillingness and unreadiness to accept what the missionaries were offering. In the last quarter of the century, 'a generation of Africans reached adulthood which included many (the middle sector) who accepted Western culture, or much of it, as the norm'. They sought to conduct their own lives in what they considered a 'civilised' manner and also were anxious to acculturate their fellow Africans. They thus gave major support to schools, churches, and other institutions of Western civilisation.

These 'rapid changes' among the Nguni owed their existence to the interlocking efforts of missionaries and other agents of the 'civilising mission'. Modern South African historians generally assert the complementary role played by these various players. Colin Bundy in *The Rise and Fall of the South African Peasantry* (1988:37), for example, writes,

> Missionary enterprise, ultimately, was concerned to transform social institutions and practices that were alien or incompatible with capitalist society into ones that were compatible, and hence to encourage a total change in the world-view of the people in whose midst they lived ... the mission societies and their most influential spokesmen sought consciously to restructure African societies along lines that would attach them securely to the British capitalist economy.

Bundy's view is supported by the evidence of Charles Pacalt Brownlee, for example, who as Secretary for Native Affairs in 1876 declared, 'We have ... a higher mission to discharge towards the barbarous tribes on our borders than to govern them simply from disinterested motives'. For Brownlee, who grew up in a missionary family and spoke fluent Xhosa, the *mission* of civil society in the Cape was 'to elevate them and enlighten them, and raise them in the scale of civlisation', and, in his view, 'the missionaries are the agency by which people are enlightened and educated' (in Schreuder 1976:287).

The history of mission education during the course of the nineteenth century and the gradual transformation of agro-pastoralists into subjects of a new capitalist order has been well documented and need not be researched anew (see Du Plessis 1911; Bruwer 1988; Bundy 1988; Crais 1992a). It is within this more general context that an enquiry can be conducted into the part played by the cultural agents of civilisation and their major weapon: literacy and the representation of a Utopian realignment of the world, backed by greater military and social power. On a conceptual level, however, it strikes me as imperative to consider how one views the processes involved in the making of a cultural orthodoxy in which colonial relations would eventually be forged. Here, one needs to consider how identity is constituted and by what means it is permeated by currents of influence and power in the world in which individual subjectivity is enveloped. What does it mean to talk about processes of 'subjectification'? Indeed, can one adequately discuss colonial processes without such a conceptual footing? How are subject positions negotiated in times of change and conflict? Once a basis for understanding such processes has been established, I shall review some of the procedures by which administrators and missionaries sought to reconstitute the subjectivity of 'barbarous' people in the Cape, and take a critical view of concrete instances of missionary representation. Finally, I shall discuss the effects of such cultural acts on subjects by looking at some of the broad, known responses to the general processes under description.

# I

Compelling insights about the operations of social power on individuals are offered by Foucault in his essay, 'The Subject and Power' (1982). Foucault presents a general description of the modes by which individuals are made subjects. One may also see his theory as a description of the relation between orthodoxy and oppositionalism within relations of power.

On the question, 'why study power?', Foucault (1982:777) answers that his work has tried to deal with 'modes of objectification which transform human beings into subjects'. The question of power emerges because 'the human subject is placed ... in power relations which are very complex' (p.778). In delineating common characteristics of struggles against power, Foucault suggests that they are what he calls 'struggles against the government of individualisation'. For him, 'What is questioned is the way in which knowledge circulates and functions, its relations to power. In short, the *regime du savoir*' (p.781). Describing his subject as a 'form of power' rather than any particular institution, Foucault writes that such power 'applies itself to immediate everyday life which categorises the individual, marks him by his own individuality, attaches him to his own identity, imposes a law of truth on him which he must recognise and which others have to recognise in him'. It is a form of power which, in Foucault's view, 'makes individuals subjects'. Two meanings for the word 'subject' are given: subject to someone else by control and dependence; and tied to one's own identity by a conscience or self-knowledge. Both meanings suggest a form of power which 'subjugates and makes subject to' (p.781).

The cultural transmission which occurred in the nineteenth-century Cape Colony arguably involved a 'government of individualisation' in which a circulation of knowledge was integral not only to imperial-colonial relations of power (bringing African subjects under colonial power), but also (and perhaps more importantly) to the making of new conceptualisations of individuality – the 'form of power which makes individuals subjects' and in which subjects themselves recognise a new 'law of truth'. This seems a crucial idea in any theory of cultural 'power', namely that such power can never be entirely coercive (although it does rely to a large extent on military force to provide space in which it may then operate). It is a power which is made effective, in a manner similar to the working of Gramscian hegemony, by the voluntary furtherance of such a 'law of truth' by the subject being acted upon. Foucault's argument goes on to deal precisely with the paradoxical nature of power relations, since the bringing into play of power relations 'does not exclude the use of violence any more than it does the obtaining of consent'. Indeed, he argues that the exercise of power 'can never do without one or the other, often both at the same time' (p.789).

If consensus and violence are effects of power, the principle of power is to be found in the idea of 'a total structure of actions brought to bear on possible actions … a way of acting upon an acting subject or acting subjects by virtue of their acting or being capable of action'. At the most abstract level of description, this is 'a set of actions upon other actions' (p.789). Foucault gives his abstraction force by harnessing the idea of government: 'To govern, in this sense, is to structure the possible field of action of others' (p.790). Then, to my mind, comes the crucial qualification: Power is exercised only over free subjects, and only in so far as they are free. Where the determining factors saturate the whole, Foucault writes, there is no relationship of power. Slavery is not a power relationship. Instead of a 'face-to-face confrontation of power and freedom, which are mutually exclusive', a much more complicated interplay is discerned. Freedom may well appear as the condition for the exercise of power, and its precondition, Foucault writes, since freedom must exist for power to be exerted. Without the possibility of recalcitrance, power would be equivalent to a 'physical determination'. The distinction between slavery, a non-negotiable form of domination, and power, a far more complex *relation* between apparently free subjects, allows Foucault to develop a refinement in his theory of how subjects exercise their relation to power in a paradoxical manner:

> The relationship between power and freedom's refusal to submit cannot, therefore, be separated. The crucial problem of power is not that of voluntary servitude (how could we seek to be slaves?). At the very heart of the power relationship, and constantly provoking it, are the recalcitrance of will and the intransigence of freedom. Rather than speaking of an essential freedom, it would be better to speak of an 'agonism' – of a relationship which is at the same time reciprocal incitation and struggle, less of a face-to-face confrontation which paralyzes both sides than a permanent provocation. (p.790)

I regard the notion of agonism as crucial in understanding the apparent contradiction inherent in a missionary institution, such as Lovedale, presenting its education as a free choice, but playing a 'belligerent' cultural role in power relations, as Schreuder might describe it. Lovedale did this by promoting as knowledge a particular government of individualisation. No one was ever coerced into enrolling at Lovedale, but the pressure to be educated was such that missionary knowledge was widely desired. The concept of agonism also allows for the idea that while many people may have been influenced by a typical, missionary-induced 'law of the subject', they were not necessarily submissive to it in the fullest degree. My postulate is that a relationship of agonism existed, incorporating elements of freedom and coercion, in which the 'permanent provocation' of 'incitation and struggle' could never be reduced to mere domination.

Further, Foucault's analysis makes it clear that relations of power consist of actions upon other actions and, more particularly, the *structuring* of the possible field of actions of others in the widest sense. For my purposes, this analysis means that 'cultural' power or the exercise of power in a cultural domain is integral rather than peripheral to a general theory of power relations. In the 'structuring' of the possible field of actions for others, the cultural content of action is of great significance, if culture is understood to imply precisely *forms* of human beliefs and practices, and the signs related to them, which are constitutive elements of any 'field of action'.

Arguably the most important means of structuring a field of action in the cultural domain is through representation. Writing about concepts which play a role in the New Historicism, Louis A. Montrose (1989:16) writes that representation plays a role in 'form[ing]' and 're-form[ing]' social subjects as conscious agents. Montrose argues that 'Representations of the world in written discourse are engaged in constructing the world, in shaping the modalities of social reality, and in accommodating their writers, performers, readers, and audiences to multiple and shifting subject positions within the world they both constitute and inhabit'. Montrose's formulation clearly owes a debt to Foucault, but his proposition extends the argument to encompass the role played by a regime of signs in such a process. Particularly relevant is his explanation of the project of New Historicism, which, he says, 'reorients the axis of inter-textuality, substituting for the diachronic text of an autonomous literary history the synchronic text of a cultural system ... the newer historical criticism is *new* in its refusal of unproblematised distinctions between "literature" and "history", between "text" and "context"; new in resisting a prevalent tendency to posit and privilege a unified and autonomous individual – whether an Author or a Work – to be set against a social or literary background' (pp.17-18).

Montrose's points may seem passé in an international scholarly environment where socio-political claims upon literary study are already strong. But the point bears emphasising that there is often an artificial distinction between the 'text' and its 'background', and between 'texts' and 'history'. In an approach such as suggested by Montrose, the area of enquiry must be broadened to encompass a more thoroughgoing sense of 'historicism', and a more precise notion of what it means to talk about the 'subjects' of history/textuality. For Montrose, the term 'subject' suggests an 'equivocal process of *subjectification*: on the one hand, shaping individuals as loci of consciousness and initiators of action – endowing them with *subjectivity* and with the capacity for agency; and, on the other hand, positioning, motivating, and constraining them within – *subjecting them to* – social networks and cultural codes that ultimately exceed their comprehension and control' (p.21).

In Montrose's formulation, therefore, processes of subjectification incorporate the representational transmission of 'cultural codes' which reinforce 'social networks'. This notion of subjectification, in which individuals are both shaped and constrained, is helpful when read alongside Foucault's theory on how individuals can be seen as 'agonistic' subjects of power. In these terms, one may view the historical experience of the Eastern Cape as a complex field of relations involving interdependent military, social and cultural components. Within the broad processes of colonial contestation, one may propose an interdependency of consensus and violence in which the missionary's cultural role extends the military one by the missionary's cultivation of a receptive space among African subjects for the promotion of Western modernity, which in turn makes the subject society vulnerable to division. Indeed, as Majeke (1952:20-24) forcefully argues, the missionary role can be seen to have deepened existing divisions to the benefit of the colonial incursion. In terms of cultural operations, missionaries acted upon, say, Nguni subjects by preaching Christianity and evangelising on an apparently consensual and voluntary basis. However, the ideology supporting their evangelism (an ideology which the receiving subject had to accept as 'true' were s/he fully to become a new, Christian subject) depended on a rigid framework of missionary knowledge – a new 'law of truth' and sense of self as a 'locus of consciousness' in Montrose's sense. Further, missionary 'knowledge' inscribed a typology of the Other which, as will be seen, was severely repressive and served to constrain subjects within cultural codes which were difficult to challenge.

The missionaries who arrived at the Cape in the late eighteenth and early nineteenth centuries were, however, not unique in their views of 'barbarism' and 'heathenism'. These notions – part of an international language of European modernity in which the world was divided into civilised and savage (see Pratt 1992; Mason 1990; Mudimbe 1988; Dickason 1984; Sheehan 1980; Dietrich 1993) – derived from a wider context of ideas. This context needs to be explored briefly here, since it underlies ideas and debates about the role of missionaries and of the civilising mission in the nineteenth century.

# II

The subject of colonisation in Africa leads immediately to the history of slavery, the very idea of which remains in some senses an archetype for the subsequent history of interaction between Europeans and Africans. Philip D. Curtin (1964:6) writes that in the later 1780s all European nations together exported about seventy-five thousand slaves a year from West Africa. About half these were carried by British merchants. The slave trade itself occurred within a greater context of Eurocentric and ethnocentric thought about the differences between European and African people (see Bolt 1971; Lovejoy 1983; Miers & Roberts 1988; Manning 1990).

Implicit in eighteenth-century thinking (and the thinking which made slavery possible) was the notion of a 'Great Chain of Being'. Eighteenth-century classifications of nature, such as Linnaeus's *Systema Naturae* (1735), as well as the older Biblical distinction between Ham, Shem and Japhet (Dietrich 1993:28-29; Adhikari 1992), shared the assumption that race and culture were closely related (Elphick & Giliomee 1989:526). There was never much doubt that Europeans were at the top of the natural scale of being. Voltaire and Rousseau suggested that black people were naturally inferior to Europeans in mental ability. David Hume argued in 1742 that 'there never was a civilized nation of any other complexion than white' (in Curtin 1964:42).

Edward Long, a resident of Jamaica, provides an example of what was in all likelihood a very common view of Africans. In 1774 he wrote that Africans were 'brutish, ignorant, idle, crafty, treacherous, bloody, thievish, mistrustful, and superstitious people'; they were also inferior in 'faculties of mind' (in Curtin 1964:43). By the late eighteenth century – when the missionary invasion of the Cape interior was only beginning – the argument that slavery should be abolished throughout the world was regarded as an advanced, highly liberal position to hold. The abolition measure was passed in Britain in 1807, but illicit trade continued for long afterwards.

The literary convention of the 'noble savage', which flourished in the last three decades of the eighteenth century, remained a convention and did not form a rationally supported affirmation in the debate about 'savage life'. Humanitarian thought was not principally interested in the black person as such. Rather, the aim of the humanitarians was to eradicate what was perceived as an evil trade in human flesh. Despite opposition to slavery, evangelical thought was steeped in standard conceptions of relative human worth. John Wesley, for example, employed the terminology of 'savagery' in a moral lesson – as an example of the influence of unrestrained original sin on corrupt mankind. For him, African culture was degenerate, showing the lot of common man without Christianity (Curtin 1964:53).

Such an adverse opinion of African culture was common among prominent anti-slave trade spokesmen. There was a common assumption in the eighteenth century that non-Western civilisations represented earlier stages in human progress, frozen into immobility while the European world advanced. This idea also derived from a conception of the progress of humankind via the stages of hunting, pastoral, agricultural and commercial activity. Alternatively, this schema was arranged as savagery, barbarism and civilisation. In such an ordering, Africans were often assessed as 'barbarous' rather than 'savage'. Lack of civilisation was equated with a lack of culture, and Africans were seen as malleable and oppressed people who would accept with gratitude whatever might be done for them (see Guy 1983:353).

This, in summary, was the context of ideas in late eighteenth and early nineteenth-century Britain, and it was from such an intellectual milieu that missionary thought took its main premises. Clearly, 'humanitarian' thinking was severely circumscribed by the more general belief that Africans were an inferior race. This supposed fact was based on erroneous but nevertheless scholarly theories of physical causes of inferiority (Comaroff & Comaroff 1991:98-107). Further, British discussion of Africa in the early nineteenth century took its departure from the eighteenth-century image of Africa.

In view of this, it is not surprising to detect in John Philip's classic statement prefacing his *Researches in South Africa* (1828:ix-x) many of the assumptions described above. Philip declared that while British missionaries who ventured beyond the borders of what was then the Cape colony, were 'everywhere scattering the seeds of civilization, social order, and happiness', they were also, 'by the most unexceptionable means, extending British interests, British influence, and the British empire'. Philip shrewdly detected how the missionary's rupture of autochthonous communities in the Cape opened the way for total acculturation: 'Wherever the missionary places his standard among a savage tribe, their prejudice against the colonial government gives way; their dependence upon the colony is increased by the creation of artificial wants; confidence is restored; intercourse with the colony is established; industry, trade, and agriculture spring up; and every genuine convert becomes the friend and ally of the colonial government.' For Philip, this was a cause for celebration, since it represented 'triumphs of reason over ignorance, of civilization over barbarism, and of benevolence over cruelty and oppression'.

Philip's view was the ameliorative vision of an humanitarian. Given the constraints of the general ambit of thought in his time, he could not be expected to go any further than advocate *humane* 'salvation' for people whom he was unable to regard as anything but 'barbarian'. In Philip's view, racial difference was commensurate with a lack of the master civilisation in whose discourse Philip's writing found its audience and meaning. This was an unexceptionable and quite conventional view to hold.

There are similar assumptions in the writings of the liberal poet and journalist Thomas Pringle. Describing the Xhosa ('Kafirs' or 'Caffers' in the terminology of the day) in *Narrative of a Residence in South Africa*, Pringle asserts: 'They are *barbarians*; but not *savages*, in the strict and proper sense of the term' (1834:414). Speaking of the treatment of Makanna (Nxele), a diviner who opposed the colony's alliance with the chief Ngqika (Gaika) against Ndlambe, another chief, Pringle writes: '… it is melancholy to reflect how valuable an instrument for promoting the civilisation of the Caffer tribes was apparently lost by the nefarious treatment and indirect destruction of that extraordinary barbarian …' (p.439).

What today may strike one as remarkable naïvety in the assumptions about uplifting 'barbarians', became in the Victorian era a customary brand of certainty about the 'Victorian world mission' and the 'manifest destiny' of the Western world (Robinson and Gallagher with Denny, 1961:7; Bosch 1991:298). This world mission involved what Ronald Hyam (1976:49) calls 'a general conviction that the British had reached the top of the ladder of progress, and that it was their duty to improve the lot of others'. This conviction is aptly captured in Lord Palmerston's grand statement, 'Our duty – our vocation – is not to enslave, but to set free; and I may say without any vainglorious boast, or without great offence to anyone, that we stand at the head of moral, social and political civilisation. Our task is to lead the way and direct the march of other nations' (in Hyam 1976:49). J.H. Newman, speaking in 1852, asserted that Western civilisation 'has a claim to be considered as the perfect representative society and civilization of the human race, as its perfect result and limit, in fact' (in Hyam 1976:50). Hyam concludes that 'ideologically the Victorian desire was to improve the rest of the world by a programme of Christian regeneration to spread civilisation on the British model, since this was the only – and God-ordained – perfection open to mankind' (p.52).

However, cultural suppositions in the Cape in the nineteenth century – especially the first half of the century – were varied and did not always derive from a homogeneous colonial ethos. As Andrew Ross (1986) is at pains to point out, the Cape Colony of the early part of the century (as opposed to the later 'South Africa') was a little known and rarely discussed entity in Britain. It was regarded as poor and of meagre commercial interest. There is, according to Ross, scant evidence of what could be called a positive policy towards South Africa during the first half of the century (p.11). Ross makes useful distinctions between the various levels of colonial involvement, lest scholars see a general 'conspiracy theory' where none exists in an explicit sense, as Dora Taylor, writing as Majeke (1952), tends to do (see also Cochrane 1987:37). The early governors of the Cape were old fashioned Tories in the soldierly mould who were accustomed to autocratic rule. As traditional high Tories they were opponents of the values of liberalism and urban humanitarianism (Ross 1986:27). For the British authorities at the Cape, says

Ross, no general plan existed to 'convert' heathens across the eastern frontier. Indeed, Ross argues, the opposite is true (p.29). British governors and administrators at the Cape often regarded the efforts of philanthropists with suspicion.

In addition, the early Protestant missionary figures generally came from a different class than governors and administrators. The evangelical movement in England (or the Evangelical Revival as it is generally known, which spawned the many missionary campaigns to South Africa and elsewhere) was primarily a layman's movement. The majority of evangelical activists were from the lower middle class or the skilled working class, later to develop into a new lower middle class that came into being in the developing towns and cities. These skilled people were a group significantly influenced by evangelical Protestantism (Ross 1986:38). This is not unimportant, since the coupling of Christianity and 'civilisation' was also a personal creed for many missionaries based on their own experience.

Transplanted on to the Cape soil, this personal experience of self-discipline and energetic industriousness often resulted in a misreading of culturally divergent practices as indolence, and a widespread myopia with regard to the heterogeneity of people encountered by evangelists. But missionaries were nevertheless committed to 'civilising the natives' and offering them the means of participation in the supposed benefits of their civilisation, whereas colonists, settlers and administrators had a far less Utopian attitude to Africans. The administrators were concerned with day-to-day government, while settlers saw in Africans a source of cheap labour. It is thus only by taking what Ross calls a 'long view' that the missionaries can be seen as conscious allies of the Cape authorities (1986:36).

However, not all scholars take such a mild view of the collusion between missionaries and colonial authorities (R. Ross 1982:210-11; Saayman 1991:27; 32; Cuthbertson 1987), and I believe one must ultimately insist on the 'long view' of African and South African history, since in the end the motives of authorities, settlers and evangelists dovetailed in the promotion of European control and dominance in all spheres of life. Certainly missionaries were the champions of an humanitarian attitude to autochthonous South Africans. One has to remember that slavery was not finally abolished at the Cape until 1838 (Armstrong & Worden 1989:167), and that this emancipation made the settlers extremely antagonistic towards missionaries in general (evangelical leaders in England such as Wilberforce and others in the 'Clapham Sect', virulently hated by South African settlers, were instrumental in pushing for the abolition of slavery). Indeed, throughout the century, some missionaries were seen as 'protectors' of black interests within the more immediate political scenario and within the given fact of European dominance. But the longer view insists that these differences are ones of accent and emphasis. The more sophisticated philosophical position of evangelical philanthropy, and the rabid prejudice of Grahamstown settlers and their champion, Robert Godlonton (editor of the *Graham's Town Journal* and author of titles such as *A Narrative of the Irruption of the Kafir Hordes*, 1836), implicitly shared the assumptions of 'civilised' superiority drawn from eighteenth-century scholarly thought (see Mostert 1992:593-99).

Jean Comaroff and John Comaroff (1988:6) express this ultimate sense of an all-embracing colonialism succinctly when they write, 'In Southern Africa, nonconformist missions, the vanguards of empire, conjured up new maps, new systems of relations, new notions of time, production and personhood. From their very first encounters with native communities ... they sowed the state of colonialism on which the colonial state – and a far more enduring condition of dependency – was founded'. Donovan Williams, in his comprehensively researched doctoral study, *The Missionaries on the Eastern Frontier of the Cape Colony, 1799-1853* (1959), writes that even 'liberal' attitudes quickly wore thin in the difficult circumstances in which the missionaries worked. 'It required but the studied rejection of Christianity,' he writes, 'the hardships of life in Kaffirland and the recurring frontier wars which impoverished and tried patience, to make those who had come prepared to save by persuasion, and who were wont to see the Kaffirs as potentially equal in every respect to the European, gradually to change their outlook to one which recognised alleged inferiority and which sanctioned coercion' (p.173).

Williams quotes a letter in which the Wesleyan missionary John Ayliff wrote in 1835: 'They are now reaping the reward of their iniquity ... They have rejected the Gospel which was benevolently sent unto them ... and now they have the sword' (p.173). Antagonistic as they may have been, the interests of the settler, the missionary, and the governor coincided in cases when European dominance was threatened, such as during the War of the Axe when Lovedale was used as a barracks, and the much-vaunted instrument of modern learning, lead type, was hastily melted down to make bullets. After this war, Sir Harry Smith, who was in the habit of demanding that vanquished Xhosa chiefs kiss his feet (Peires 1981:165), had the following to say to his defeated adversaries:

> Your land shall be marked out and marks placed that you may
> all know it. It shall be divided into counties, towns and
> villages, bearing English names. You shall all learn to speak
> English at the schools which I shall establish for you ... You
> may no longer be naked and wicked barbarians, which you will
> ever be unless you labour and become industrious. You shall be
> taught to plough; and the Commissary shall buy of you. You
> shall have traders, and you must teach your people to bring
> gum, timber, hides etc. to sell, that you may learn the art of
> money, and buy for yourselves. You must learn that it is money
> that makes people rich by work, and help me to make roads. I
> will pay you. (In Peires 1981:166)

It is here, in the conjunction of an imperial-colonial military humiliation of
the Xhosa and the ideas of cultural transformation central to the efforts of
missionaries, that the 'long view' of ultimate complicity between the different
agents of British imperialism, and the discursive regime founded in 'English',
becomes clear. While making chiefs kiss his feet was a show of arrogance alien
to the style of missionaries, Smith nevertheless articulated in a classic way the
British desire to 'remake' autochthonous South Africa in the image of
'counties, towns and villages', with English as the medium of a mercantile
economy in which individual ownership would supplant the pastoral-
agricultural system of the Xhosa. The work ethic had to be instilled in
otherwise 'naked and wicked barbarians', and Smith made it quite clear what
the position of the Xhosa had to be in the new hierarchy: servants with the
desire for money to buy things in the European economy. In the 1850s,
another governor of the Cape, Sir George Grey, elevated Smith's subdue-and-
civilise intentions to the status of official policy in the Grey Plan (Hunt Davis
1969:214), by which substantial financial support was given to missionary
education as part of a project to 'civilise' the African – in Crais's description,
an attempt at 'colonization of the mind' (1992a:200) – so that peaceful
conditions might prevail on the frontier.

Missionaries in the Cape Colony and beyond were therefore deeply
involved in the overall policy of colonisation as the three C's – Christianity,
Commerce, and Civilisation (Bosch 1991:305). As the Western economy
drew in more Africans, so missionary education became increasingly
important. But this education involved an act of considerable epistemic
dislocation. It was centrally implicated in consolidating, in representational

forms, the modes of othering which Africans had to negotiate in order to achieve the social and cultural empowerment of education. In this education, English was both a means of transmission and a state of ideality – the place where 'civilisation' was cultivated. This process was only indirectly related to *literature* as such; English literature was but one form of the greater ideality in which morality, philosophy, Christianity and aesthetics were definitively universalised in the image of a little island north of Africa. One work of English literature, *The Pilgrim's Progress*, was partially translated into Xhosa by the first ordained black minister, the Reverend Tiyo Soga (Shepherd 1940:145), and had a strong influence on mission educated Africans of the Cape Colony and beyond. 'Literature' therefore had a clearly defined, but circumscribed, role in the attempts to colonise consciousness and to recreate cultural forms.

# III

Given the conceptual basis of subjectification expounded earlier, and the historically specific context in which acculturation took place, one can begin to view the general representational procedures by which African 'barbarians' were othered, and to take a more concrete view of the typical processes of representational contestation. An intensive process of metaphorical description in English was to culminate in a reification of representational forms, which African people would have to negotiate in the course of missionary education – and, by implication, in colonial society at large.

This examination must begin with the question of figuration or representation itself. It needs to be recalled that the period under review bears the marks of an attitude to language and to the idea of 'truth' formed by the rational empiricism of the Enlightenment Age of Reason, and buttressed by the implicit certainty of God's plan for the world (Bosch 1991:263-67). The intellectual benefits accruing from philosophy of figures such as Nietzsche, Freud or Wittgenstein were not available to writers in the early nineteenth century. Neither can one expect an appreciation of the 'contingency' of language and of being so eloquently described by pragmatist philosopher Richard Rorty. However, we need to recall Rorty's sense of contingency to appreciate the status of the language used in attempts to attach a new government of individualisation to subject people in the nineteenth-century frontier context.

Rorty's argument, in two essays, 'The Contingency of Language' (1986a) and 'The Contingency of Selfhood' (1986b), relies on Wittgensteinian and Nietzschean notions about language and truth. The central idea in Rorty's argument is that there is no essential truth 'out there', only what Nietzsche called a 'mobile army of metaphors'. To say that truth is not out there, Rorty writes, 'is simply to say that where there are no sentences there is no truth, that sentences are elements of human languages, and that human languages are human creations' (1986a:3). For Rorty, truth cannot exist independently of the human mind 'because sentences cannot so exist, or be out there'. The world is out there, but descriptions of the world are not. The suggestion that truth, as well as the world, is 'out there', is for Rorty 'the legacy of an age in which the world was seen as the creation of a being who had a language of His own'.

Rorty captures very ably the tendency in missionary writing and thinking to profess a 'God with a language of His own', whose vocabulary of 'Truth' coincided with their own. The 'contingency' of language had no place in their mental outlook, and usually they did not recognise that their 'truths' about human nature were a particular configuration of historically embedded metaphoric description rather than intrinsically or essentially true in a way that could be tested by objective criteria. The temptation to look for criteria, Rorty writes, 'is a species of the more general temptation to think of the world, or the human self, as possessing an intrinsic nature, an essence'. That is, it is the result of the temptation to 'privilege some one among the many actual and possible languages in which we habitually describe the world or ourselves' (1986a:3).

Such privileging leads to an encrustation of metaphor, or, in Rorty's words, 'old metaphors are constantly dying off into literalness' (1986a:6). When the language of a man such as James Stewart, Lovedale principal between 1870 and 1905, is examined, such metaphor encrustation is abundantly evident. In a volume entitled *Lovedale South Africa: Illustrated by Fifty Views from Photographs* (1894:15), Stewart articulates the classic metaphor of dark and light: 'And that is just what we labour for – a day in the future when the Dark Continent shall be a continent of light and progress, of cities and civilisation and Christianity.' Stewart, writing at the close of the century, was distilling the gathered terminology and metaphoric stasis of a century's 'work among the heathens'. His language (here embellished for the London audience) reveals many of the preconceptions which operated throughout the century, and which were enforced as 'education' on the subjects of missionary endeavour. His language may therefore provide an insight into the kind of orthodox discourse used to influence identity and create new forms of subjectivity.

After introducing the light-darkness idea almost as a literal 'fact', Stewart exerts his language even further:

> [The] new religion took [the African] by the hand and led him out of a land of thick darkness, gloom, and horror – filled with malevolent shades and dreaded spectral powers – and brought him into the clear, sweet light of a simple belief in a God of goodness and love, such as Christianity reveals. (p.43)

It was this kind of general mythology about a journey from dark to light which, scholars now believe, served to mask other journeys taken by what Tim Couzens (1980), and Jordan K. Ngubane (1971:5) before him, have called 'New Africans'. These other journeys were a departure from agro-pastoralism and a cattle economy to peasantry and subservience in the mercantile economy (Peires 1981 & 1989; Bundy 1988; Mostert 1992); from oral culture within the Nguni tradition to the literary culture of English Protestantism and a few centres of literary patronage (Kantey 1990:vii; Mphahlele 1980; Sole 1977); from sovereignty over communal lands to large-scale loss of land and of independence. Throughout the century, the Christian metaphoric overlay served to obscure these other, not necessarily salubrious, social processes.

Indeed, the 'Christianise and civilise' credo explicitly called for an 'overlay' of a different kind: a comprehensive re-making of social and cultural modalities of identity. This depended on a conception of the Other that was often xenophobic in its intolerance of difference. In missionary writing, difference was swiftly transcoded into idleness, vacuity, degradation (for example, marriage rites, circumcision rites, etc.) and then metaphorically recast as 'low' and 'fallen' states, or as 'spiritual slumber'. Sir Harry Smith's invective quoted above against 'wicked barbarians' aptly captures the manner in which a metaphoric trope, derived from cultural xenophobia, acquired in the South African colonial context the force of orthodox declaration. Such orthodoxy was backed by the new authorities in the spheres of government and education, and ultimately by the military policy of 'fire and sword' (Peires 1981:135), or, in the words of Hunt Davis (1969:37), the 'normal manner of "clearing Kaffirs"': burn their homes, destroy their crops, and run off their herds'.

Drawing on Lacanian psycho-linguistic theory, Crais (1992a:129) makes the observation that a 'discourse of condemnation situated around a chain of signifying dichotomies' was part of a process of 'symbolic inversion'. From the end of the 1820s, Crais writes, 'Africans were increasingly represented as libidinous, uncontrolled, lazy and disrespectful of established authority'. The settler, in turn, became what the African was not. 'In this topsy-turvy process the African became the "Other". In the transition from an imaginary order – the settler "sees" or "imagines" himself in the African – to a symbolic one, the Other emerged as signifier around which a colonialist discourse was born.' The identity of the colonialist was, in this view of things, intimately bound to that of the Other. Crais (1992a:150) argues that 'the central point is that settlers depended on these negative assessments in their definition of self'. Similarly, the Comaroffs (1991:86) argue that 'Africa became an indispensable term, a negative trope, in the language of modernity'.

In retrospect, one may look at a composite of representational practices by which European cultural agents helped prepare the ground for what they considered a re-making of the African Other. In the process, they consolidated their own sense of self in the African 'wilderness', locking their identities into a perpetual Self-Other antagonism whose effects remain evident today. In the terms introduced earlier in this chapter, these practices involved a new government of individualisation enforcing altered conceptions of value, labour, time and space. The key role of representing the new order in terms of Western subjectivity fell to missionaries. It was the work of the mission to stress the signs and practices of European culture. This was done, in my argument, by the assiduous construction of a colonial 'text' for self-apprehension: a text that depended on the new edifice of literacy in English, and that exhibits all the selections and exclusions characteristic of narrative in general.

The composite of practices I am arguing for was clearly no conscious or general conspiracy. Its constitutive elements tended to be haphazardly although intensively applied, and a remarkable concordance can be discerned when one reads the documents relevant to the period, despite the absence of any politically co-ordinated overall plan. 'New Africans' did not simply emerge. They developed over decades of intensive representational realignment in which missionaries sought to inculcate altered forms of subjectivity and modified cultural practices.

The foundation of all missionary work was the 'reduction' of African languages to a written orthography (the verb 'reduction' is telling, and it has unproblematically remained in use in modern scholarship[8]). The printing press accompanied the missionary as his foremost weapon of civilisation from the earliest of times. Van der Kemp, first missionary of the London Missionary

Society and a pioneer figure in South African missionary history, carried a small printing press when he arrived at the Cape in 1799 (George 1982:59). Another early missionary, John Ross of the Glasgow Missionary Society, transported a Ruthven press to the Cape in 1823, along with a supply of type, paper and ink (Shepherd 1940:62). John Bennie, who was to lead the efforts at 'reducing' and learning Xhosa, wrote: 'On the 17th [December 1823] we got our Press in order; on the 18th the alphabet was set up; and yesterday we threw off 50 copies ... a new era has commenced in the history of the Kaffer nation' (in Shepherd 1940:62-63). Bennie was describing the founding of the first mission press, later to become known as Lovedale.

The printing press made it possible to realign an entire cultural order. In the argument of Mike Kantey (1990:vii), 'one of the most important effects of these early mission presses was to reduce a rich and diverse oral tradition to a few centres of literary patronage' (see Peires 1979b; Switzer 1983), although many would argue that the oral tradition was never so simply 'reduced'. The realignment brought about by the printing press was the beginning of a very large process. The press would serve as the basis for a strong literary role in the cultural conversion of people. Meanwhile, cultural codes for the establishment of new forms of identity, to be transmitted by 'church, school, [and] printing press' (Mphahlele 1980:31), would touch on almost every aspect of living. Housing, clothing, forms of labour and agriculture, modes of belief and worship – in short, almost every daily cultural practice – would be affected by the representations of missionaries.

A juncture in the history of the nineteenth century which allows one a comprehensive view of the insistence and strength of these new practices and representations is the response by several missionaries, from a range of missionary societies, to a circular by Sir Harry Smith in 1848. The circular invited missionaries to give him their views on the best methods 'to inspire in the Bantu a desire to cultivate their lands by ploughing and to induce them to follow habits of industry, the first steps to civilization and equally so to their embracing of the Christian Faith ... to see the necessity of wearing clothes ... the use of money ... of establishing schools on such a footing as would ensure hereafter teachers from among themselves ... of all things His Excellency requests ... English to the exclusion of the Kafir dialect' (Government Circular, 17 April, 1848, signed by Richard Southey. In Du Toit 1963:17).

Prior to this circular, a teacher named Adolphus Schaller from Diep Rivier in Wynberg had sent a memorandum to the governor entitled 'On the Condition and Improvement of the Moral Character of the Kaffir People', in

which he advocated the introduction of agricultural schools. Schaller wrote
that by such a system 'many valuable members of society might be formed
from the native population, the hitherto ungovernable passions of the Kaffir
people, arising from ignorance, superstition, and poverty, would be
transformed into habits of industry and economy' (Cape, G.H. 22/3,
Memorandum, March 16, 1848. In Du Toit 1963:18).

Taken together, Schaller's opinion and Smith's request reveal a great deal
about the kind of thinking current in the 1840s (see Harington 1980:95-129).
Clearly, half a century of missionary effort had not reversed the condition of
Africans to the satisfaction of colonial agents. Yet Smith and Schaller still
maintain the desire to refashion Africans entirely. Smith envisioned a
'bourgeois revolution' (Legassick 1993:345) to turn the Xhosa into what he
called 'real Englishmen' (in Mostert 1992:769). The reductive paradigm of
Schaller, in which 'industry' and 'economy' are juxtaposed with 'ungovernable
passions' and 'ignorance, superstition and poverty', is typical and became an
entrenched trope in the colonialist discourse of the nineteenth century.
Fanon's 'Manicheism' in colonial relations suggests itself very strongly in these
sources. Caught in what JanMohamed (1985:63) calls the 'vortex' of
Manichean thinking, missionaries – particularly the Scottish Presbyterians so
dominant at Lovedale – were committed to transforming existing African
culture.[9] In doing so, they would be effacing the alterity perceived through the
Manichean model. In Crais's words (1992a:95), the projection of relations
between black and white as a Manichean struggle came to 'dominate every
facet of the colonialist mentality … emerging in the world of the Eastern
Cape'. The key elements of the commitment to efface alterity are present in
Smith's terms in his circular: cultivation of land, wearing clothes, using
money, using English.

The importance of agriculture in colonial relations was related to the
perception that the pre-capitalist subsistence mode of production had to give
way to commodification of land and labour. JanMohamed (1985:60) observes
that in Kenya the British 'systematically destroyed the native mode of
production'. For JanMohamed, this means that 'the Europeans disrupted a
material and discursive universe based on use-value and replaced it with one
dominated by exchange-value'.

On the discursive level, agriculture and clothing in the Eastern Cape
represented a symbolic 're-dressing' of both the land and the person which was
coterminous with the transformation of precapitalist modes of production into
capitalist ones. JanMohamed (1985:64) writes further that 'we can observe a

profound symbiotic relationship between the discursive and the material practices of imperialism: the discursive practices do to the symbolic, linguistic presence of the native what the material practices do to his physical presence …' There is great emphasis in the various responses of missionaries to Sir Harry Smith's circular on the key discursive markers of dress and agriculture (and one can assume that in their persistent verbal representations to Africans in the mission fields, there would have been an equally persistent emphasis). One respondent, Wesleyan missionary William Impey, betrays a rankling frustration at the intractability of both the land and the people:

> Universal history teaches us that no people have ever become civilized or risen in the rank of Nations until first *concentrated in Societies and invested with personal and indefensible rights in the soil*. Neither of these ingredients are to be found in the present state of Kaffir society. It is notorious that the Population of Kaffirland is one of the most scattered imaginable, and although there is a sort of legal possession which the Kaffir holds of his plot for cultivation, yet it is not of that definite kind which gives *value* to the soil and results in improvement. The whole of Kaffirland is in fact one vast commonage where every man lives as he likes, takes temporary possession of any unappropriated ground and excepting the effect which habit and continued residence may create has no other tie to the country in which he dwells. The scattered state of the population presents insuperable difficulties in the way of all appliances of government and civilization, as well as of moral and religious instruction … (William Impey to Sir H. Smith, Mount Coke, 22 October, 1850. In Du Toit 1963:88-89.)

Impey went on to advocate the use of 'despotic authority' and the 'strong arm of power' to achieve the aim of 'concentrating people into societies' so that they may be governed. He was not to know that in less than a decade an act of national suicide by the Xhosa (the Cattle Killing of 1856-57) would to a large extent reverse the condition he complains of and make substantially more people dependent on the European economy and culture than was previously the case. But in this piece there is a strong sense of outrage at the simple fact that the Nguni lived under a system of migratory agro-pastoralism in which land was held communally and generally regarded as pasturage rather than

agricultural property (Peires 1981:161-69), although missionaries also tended
to ignore the fact that the Xhosa did in fact cultivate land (Lambourne
1992:7). A scene such as Impey's 'vast commonage' was a desert, because it
'lacked definition and defied surveillance' (Comaroff & Comaroff 1991:175).
The land was a 'wilderness' to be turned into a 'fruitful field' (Comaroff
1985:138) or an Edenic garden that would eventually exclude the African
(Grove 1989:169, 186). Impey was clearly irked by the lack of systematic
organisation of people and land along European lines. Like other missionaries,
he wanted to institute a different order of land usage, one in which intensive
cultivation of crops would replace cattle farming. The cultural relativity of the
difference between these practices was not recognised. The European model
reinforced classic Protestant values of virtuous industry, hard labour and
frugality, while the more relaxed Nguni style filled the Europeans with the
kind of revulsion associated with nightmarish inversions of cherished values.

Such revulsion is clearly evident in comments such as that of Lovedale's
James Laing and James Weir:

> We observe with regret that, instead of purchasing clothes,
> many of the Kaffers with great avidity give their money for that
> disgusting red paint with which they bedaub their bodies. To
> prohibit the sale of this article might perhaps interfere with the
> principles of Free Trade, but all who seek the improvement of
> the Kaffers may rest assured that no general change for the
> better has taken place so long as this barbarous custom is
> extensively practised. (James Laing and James Weir to Richard
> Southey, Lovedale Missionary Station, 6 June 1848. In Du Toit
> 1963:63)

In similar vein, the Methodist missionary A. McDiarmid took the opportunity
of a governor's audience to express his desire to recode the personal, and
therefore moral, appearance of Africans:

> But a far more serious hindrance is the introduction again of
> red clay – or ochre – among them. Large sums of money are
> now given for what renders them so filthy, and checks
> incipient improvement as surely as frost destroys the tender
> bud. (A. McDiarmid to Richard Southey, Burns Hill, 17 May
> 1848. In Du Toit 1963:60)

James Read snr, in his enthusiasm to re-dress his mission subjects in a Scottish image, seems to have been quite impervious to the absurdity of his experiment with kilts:

> The wooden spade has already given way to the English iron one, also the earthen for the iron Pot, the oxhide Coross to the English blanket, and but few women are to be seen without the blue Handkerchief on their heads. This is a beginning. If the men could be induced to wear the Scotch Kilt in the first instance it would be a great deal gained. I once got a dozen made, and gave them to the Caffres, who wore them, and afterwards took to trousers ... generally the first Symtems [sic] of religeious [sic] impressions were the change in their clothing. (J. Read Senr. to Sir H. Smith, Philipton, 25 June 1848. In Du Toit 1963:68)

Notwithstanding the unintentional quaintness of Read's picture, his point that a change in clothing generally accompanied a conversion to Christianity is important. This point is borne out by many missionary writings. In particular, the symbolic dividing line between red clay and European clothing became the standard means of representing Christianised or 'school' people as against the 'red' people. This symbolic division became the central image in the story of Ntsikana, known as the first 'New African' literary figure.

Ntsikana, composer of the still famous 'Great Hymn', has been celebrated in subsequent writings as the 'first Christian convert among the Kafirs' (Bokwe 1914:1). He has also come to be regarded as the 'first individualized black poet' (Gray 1979:171; see Gérard 1971:24-26) as a result of the fame attached to his hymn, 'UloThixo omKhulu, ngoseZulwini', or 'He, the Great God, High in Heaven' (Kunene & Kirsch 1967:II,7). By the time the story of Ntsikana's conversion began to be recirculated in the writings of later generations of black converts, a crucial element of the story was the juncture at which Ntsikana has a mystical revelation (a vision of bright rays of light shining on his favourite ox) and then throws off the trappings of heathenism: 'As they neared home, they came to a small river. Here Ntsikana threw aside his blanket, plunged himself into the water and washed off all the red ochre that painted his body' (Bokwe 1914:11-12). Clearly, the cultural coding of dress played an important part in marking off forms of identity and giving symbolic and recognisable form to the choices which were being presented to people.

The other crucial 're-dressing' of the environment centred on the form of dwellings. Missionary writings are full of references to the desirability of square as opposed to round houses. Wesleyan minister Henry H. Dugmore, responding to Sir Harry Smith's circular in 1848, wrote:

> Could they be induced generally to abandon their grass huts, and adopt a kind of dwelling more favourable to habits of cleanliness, it would greatly tend to promote the use of European apparel. It would indeed, almost render it *necessary*. Their huts are so low, and so hot and smoky, that European Clothes can scarcely be borne in them; and the loose kaross, and squatting posture seem an almost necessary accompaniment to their habitation. The use of walled houses would necessitate the use of more clothing, at the same time it would enable the wearer to preserve it in a way that is impossible in a Fingo hut. (Henry H. Dugmore to Col. McKinnon, Chief Commissioner, 30 June 1848. In Du Toit 1963:73).

Commenting on the missionary obsession with square dwellings, Kate Crehan (in Bundy 1988:37-38) relates it to 'certain key elements of capitalist society' (the notions of private property, the individual as the basic unit of society, and the nuclear family), and argues that the 'African house expressed values that were quite alien to those that the missionaries saw as so crucial. It did not cut nuclear families off from one another, privacy within it was virtually impossible, it did not manifest the owner's industriousness', nor did it mirror the notions of social order and hierarchy as did square buildings. Jean Comaroff (1985:143) has remarked that the 'rationalisation' of African community structures required the 'geometric grid of civilization' with the four-sided figure as the 'key shape in the spatiovisual construction of the West'. For Crais, the landscape was 'reshaped ... in the language of private property' (1992a:82; 137-38).

Missionaries were therefore involved in a comprehensive attempt to re-make the forms of culture they encountered. Their particular role was to saturate the mission fields with signifiers of Western subjectivity. Through the introduction of a new order of representation, they sought to refashion the very environment in which the Nguni people of the Eastern Cape lived, or, more precisely, to refashion the understanding and perception of that environment and of the manner in which subjects interacted with it. African pastoralist cultivators in the Eastern Cape were compelled to negotiate their identities in terms of this colonial order of representation. Caught between the socially ascendant view of themselves as unclean, idle, negligent, indecent and licentious (Crais 1992a:133), and the ideal proposed for them of Christian salvation in newly forged and rigorously Protestant forms of culture, people affected by the widespread 'civilising' enterprise faced difficult options. As suggested, this difficulty was compounded by a context of war coupled with the dispossession of land and social power. It is precisely in this link between the material war for land and power, and the representational war for 'correct' cultural conceptions of identity, that English as discourse can be seen to have affected notions of the self, the body, space, time, the land, and the abstract realms of beauty, godliness, philosophy and morality (see Lambourne 1992; Crais 1992a:103; 121). Missionary discourse in its various forms never achieved the status of absolute hegemony, but was resisted and negotiated (Crais 1992a:220; Hofmeyr 1991:634; 1993; Kunene & Kirsch 1967:I,10-11). In addition, as noted by Crais (1992a:83;104) and Jean Comaroff (1985:2; 11; 129; 150), the message of evangelical Christianity offered ambiguous scope for conformity as well as resistance. Nevertheless, the significance of the missionaries lies in the fact that, however ambiguous or partial their reception might have been, they set the terms and prescribed the forms, in conjunction with other agents of colonialism, in which ongoing dialogues about selfhood and identity would be conducted. From the start, missionary subjects were 'compelled to fight on the linguistic and conceptual terrain of the whites' (Comaroff & Comaroff 1991:307). How did the Nguni (and others affected) respond to this?

## IV

Janet Hodgson, in her major work of doctoral research, *Ntsikana: History and Symbol; Studies in a Process of Religious Change Among Xhosa-Speaking People* (1985), suggests that religious change among the Xhosa occurred gradually as a result of contact with missionaries and socio-cultural disturbance in general. She demonstrates how this change was incremental and that, to a large extent, it was mediated by two prophet figures, Ntsikana and Nxele, in such a way that the new cosmological concepts were seen as appropriate to a traditional framework of beliefs. Ntsikana's 'conversion' was seen among the Xhosa as a 'Damascus' experience not directly connected with missionaries (p.183). However, the importance of Nxele, particularly, was that he both conformed to Xhosa custom and was seen as representing a link with the white source of power (Hodgson 1985:112; Peires 1989:32-33). Both figures demonstrate the turbulence in the symbolic world occasioned by the coming of the Europeans and, more particularly, war with the Europeans.

One of Hodgson's premises is that words can be 'carriers' of change, and that religious symbols have the power to shape both culture and society (1985:52). However, she argues that members of a group who have their sense of reality firmly integrated with their socio-cultural experience will not be open to any serious shift in their understanding of 'ultimate reality' (cosmological belief) unless significant socio-cultural disturbance occurs (p.53).

Such disturbance began to happen in earnest during the frontier war of 1811-12. Peires (1979a:53) writes that the second and third frontier wars (1793 and 1799-1803) must be counted as Xhosa victories, but that Xhosa ascendancy on the frontier was broken decisively following the British decision to retain the Cape after 1806. Peires notes that the 'total war' of 1811-12 was a shattering experience for the Xhosa, since their own methods of warfare were less bloody and aimed not at the destruction of productive resources, but at their acquisition and absorption. The Xhosa would absorb their defeated enemies into their own society (as was the case with the Khoikhoi), but in war with whites they were killed and expelled. 'Old fears must have been reawakened; the whites were not people like other people, they were *abantu abasemanzini*, the people from the water, associated with all the mystical power of the sea. For the first time, the full power of the colony's immense technical and material resources was revealed' (Peires 1979a:54).

Peires argues that the expulsion of the Xhosa created problems which the chiefs were unable to solve, and that in the years immediately following 1812, political leadership passed from chiefs into the hands of prophet figures. The two prophets who came to assume prominent profiles were Nxele, and to a lesser extent in the more immediate context, Ntsikana, whose reputation as the 'first African convert' grew large only after his death.

Both Nxele and Ntsikana tapped into the perceived new European sources of power, but in different ways. Nxele's early preaching followed the missionary example of criticising Xhosa custom. He caused a stir and drew the attention of Ndlambe, a Xhosa chief whose dynastic rival was Ngqika (with whom Ntsikana aligned himself). Nxele rose to power and was treated like a chief (Hodgson 1985:103). After the expulsion of the Xhosa across the Fish River, Nxele began calling himself the younger brother of Christ, and his path began to diverge from missionary influence. Nxele then initiated a thaumaturgical event in which the need for nationalistic unity and new sources of power was transformed into symbolic action. According to Isaac Wauchope's rendition (1908:34-35), Nxele ordered his people to kill all dun-coloured cattle and proceed to a particular spot on the coast near East London. Nxele prophesied a mass resurrection of the dead, who would drive the whites into the sea.

The resurrection did not occur, but Nxele's reputation was not damaged (Peires 1979a:57). Nxele was captured after leading a suicidal attack on Grahamstown in May 1819, of between nine and ten thousand men, believing he had reduced European firepower to water (Hodgson 1985:210). More than a thousand Xhosa lay dead on the battlefield after Nxele's force was routed, and a defeated Nxele was sent to Robben Island for life imprisonment. He died after trying to escape in a boat which capsized (Mostert 1992:491).

Ntsikana represents the opposite pole of Xhosa symbolic reaction to the coming of the whites (see Odendaal 1984b:4). Peires argues that Ntsikana's thought developed towards Christianity rather than away from it.[10] After Ntsikana's mystical conversion experience (described earlier), he joined forces with Ngqika and set up as Nxele's rival (Peires 1979a:59). Ntsikana developed a small following during his lifetime, but the seed he planted would, in succeeding generations, yield 'New African' figures: Christians trained by missionaries and fully 'Westernised'. Of Nxele and Ntsikana, Peires concludes that their different revelations 'were simply alternative permutations of the same stock of concepts, deriving from the necessity of fusing Xhosa religion with Christianity in order to formulate a new world-view capable of comprehending the irruption of the Europeans' (p.61).

Peires describes how the traditions represented by Nxele and Ntsikana came to represent the two major directions taken by Xhosa society:

> The spiritual heirs of Nxele from Mngqatsi the rainmaker, through Mlanjeni to Nongqawuse, prophetess of the cattle-killing disaster, and beyond, found traditional techniques increasingly helpless against European power … At the same time the seed Ntsikana planted had, through the efforts of men like Tiyo Soga, son of one of Ntsikana's converts, flourished, and Christianity was well and truly planted among the Xhosa as an African religion brought not by the missionaries but by Ntsikana. Today the wheel has come full circle as young Xhosa

turn towards the nationalism of Nxele rather than the humility
of Ntsikana. (1979a:61)

Peires here sums up very briefly what was presumably a long and painstaking
process. More particularly, the transition from Ntsikana's 'African'
Christianity to a form of Christianity in Western cultural dress can be traced
over the generations in the story of the Sogas (see Odendaal 1984b:6).

Ntsikana's chief disciple was 'Old' Soga, who was a leading councillor of
Ngqika (Hodgson 1985:340). Soga continued Ntsikana's practice of holding
prayers twice a day and he attended church on Sundays, yet he also functioned
in his traditional role as headman and was made a councillor of Tyhali,
Ngqika's son. Hodgson writes that as a 'bridge between old and new', Soga
'came under constant pressure from the conflicting demands of competing
cultures, but he resolutely held firm to Ntsikana's path of evolutionary change
while remaining a Xhosa patriot, much to the missionaries' fury'. She adds,
'The mission station people were expected to take over the whole Western
cultural package, the symbols of the new including loyalty to the British
Crown. Soga played a leading part in the Frontier wars of 1834-35, 1846-47,
and 1850-53, and this led repeatedly to angry confrontation with the
missionaries.'

'Old' Soga was caught in the historical dynamic which forced a gradual
acceptance of Western cultural codes. During a colonial reprisal for a Xhosa
attack in the war of 1834-35, he was forced to flee to a cave, whence he
watched his homestead being burnt. As a result of this loss, Soga had little
choice but to adopt new methods of securing a livelihood. He was the first
Xhosa to use a plough, the first to irrigate his lands, and the first to market his
crops (Hodgson 1985:342). Indeed, in Soga we see how the inculcation of new
cultural codes was an agonistic process. Hodgson relates that Soga was forced
to break with tradition, since in Xhosa society a strict division of labour
regulated that men were responsible for cattle, while women worked the fields.
The missionaries introduced the plough, but the plough demanded male
labour. Accepting this reversal of traditional roles therefore implied a deep
break with the past. Missionaries also set up irrigation systems and created
watercourses, which meant that there could be less dependence on rain and
that crops could grow even in times of drought. 'It was [the missionaries']
belief that the change from a pastoral to an agrarian way of life would be the
means of "settling" the Xhosa and changing their "lazy habits"' (Hodgson
1985:342).

After the destruction of his homestead, Soga approached government agent Charles Lennox Stretch and complained that his large family was starving (see Le Cordeur 1988). Stretch declined to give assistance, arguing that Soga had the means to obtain cattle by working his lands. Stretch told Soga to get seed and plant vegetables to sell to the soldiers at Fort Cox. A few months later, Soga returned to Stretch with his hands full of coins. He had grown peas, onions, barley and potatoes. He had then sold his vegetables to 'Johnny the Redcoats' (Chalmers 1877:6; Hodgson 1985:342-43).

Soga's action so impressed the then Colonel Harry Smith that he arranged for a plough to be given to Soga, and for Khoikhoi workers to be hired from Kat River with oxen and gear to assist him, at government expense (Hodgson 1985:344). Soga was an important transitional figure. He had political power and wealth, but as a disciple of Ntsikana he had already broken certain ritual and social ties and established himself on the fringe of the mission community. Now Soga contradicted the ethic of sharing and communalism by insisting that his followers, whom he paid for working on his lands, should pay him for food. It was only because Soga had great authority that he was able to remain connected with both worlds (Hodgson 1985:345). As Hodgson argues, this ethic of work and the production of a cash crop went hand in hand with the teaching of the missionaries, creating new wants and smoothing the way for the acceptance of the Western way of living.

Writing in the 1870s, John A. Chalmers (1877:7), the biographer of 'Old' Soga's famous son, Tiyo (the first African to be ordained as a minister), saw the process in the following terms:

> Thus a new era dawned at Soga's village; the sneezewood spade gave place to the crooked ploughshare; the oxen, which hitherto had galloped for the amusement and fame of their owner over the plains above the Chumie mountain, were now yoked to a willing team, and ploughed the virgin soil; the brook which had babbled for ages, undisturbed in its onward flow, was now made to irrigate his fields and crops – silent emblems these of a still greater power which was secretly at work, and is destined yet to revolutionize the moral wastes of Southern Africa. By the gift of the plough the Government, which had begun to conquer, showed that it desired to achieve this more lasting victory over barbarism, indolence, and poverty.

It took a generation beyond 'Old' Soga before widespread absorption of Western forms would take effect, in the person of Soga's son, Tiyo. Tiyo Soga occupies a 'model' position as a total convert who became a minister and a missionary after an education at Lovedale and in Scotland (see Chapter 5). Sol Plaatje was a similar case (see Willan 1984). Tiyo Soga was given a scholarship to Lovedale in 1844, only three years after the seminary had set up on its new site in 1841 (Shepherd 1940:95). He was later taken to Scotland where he studied theology. Tiyo's story is not an exact representation of the history of Xhosa conversion to Christianity within the tradition of Ntsikana. Ntsikana's own sons, Dukwana and Kobe, who predated Tiyo Soga, were absorbed into the new order at an earlier date (Hodgson 1985:348), and one would be able to find many other examples to defy a history of progressive and linear conversion. Tiyo Soga nevertheless stands out as a prominent figure in a gradual transition over generations occasioned by immense and traumatic socio-cultural disturbance consequent upon the loss of land, authority and independence. And while his father resisted total absorption into missionary life, Tiyo's life was sufficiently removed from the traditional stronghold for him to become Westernised to a much fuller degree. Odendaal (1984b:9) writes that 'Soga articulated some of the attitudes which had been generated on the frontier since the first contacts between black and white and was paving the way for thousands of literate and Christianised Africans, facing the same problems of reconciling the conflicting worlds of which they were part, who would follow in the next decades'.

Indeed, in Tiyo Soga we see the ultimate result of the Ntsikana tradition of response within the Xhosa to change in the symbolic order. In Saayman's words (1991:63), Soga 'wanted to be consciously African and Christian at the same time'. Although the religious tradition initiated by Ntsikana was seen as belief inspired by direct contact with God, unmediated by missionaries, Hodgson (1985:33) adduces evidence for the claim that Ntsikana was in fact influenced by missionaries (see Gérard 1971:27). Hodgson argues that Ntsikana's teaching, alongside that of Nxele, was a direct response to the need to make sense of a world changed beyond recognition by the coming of Europeans and colonisation. There were different ways of tapping the new power represented by the whites. On the one hand, thaumaturgical responses beckoned, based partly on Christian teaching, such as Nxele's call for the sacrifice of cattle to elicit the resurrection of the dead and the destruction of the whites. Alternatively, there was the more mundane possibility of eventual incorporation: joining up for mission education in the knowledge that in a world dominated by Europeans, Western education would become the new route to social empowerment. In other cases, depending on circumstances, there was the option of becoming a labourer in the white economy.

These were not so much choices as a history of available options. After the final, shattering thaumaturgical response, the Cattle Killing of 1856-57, and the Xhosa defeat in the war of 1877-88, few choices were open (see Peires 1989). As Hunt Davis (1969:58) argues, loss of land and military defeat produced an unavoidable dependence on the European economy. Mission education became an important bridge between the Xhosa world and the European economy. The trap was sprung: 'As for the Africans, the loss of land in the frontier wars compelled them to enter the labour market, while the wants which trade created led them to become wage earners in order to purchase desired goods. Furthermore, the missionaries encouraged African employment in the colonial economy as part of their efforts to impose Western cultural patterns' (Hunt Davis 1969:75).

Christianity promised 'a novel source of influence and control; the mission was a tangible embodiment of force – guns, water, the plow, the written word, and the underlying power that animated them – which professed its availability to all who would "believe"' (Comaroff 1985:150). It required only the discovery of diamonds in 1867 and of gold in 1886 to take South Africa into an industrial age with its voracious need for a labouring class. By the late nineteenth century, the majority of adult Nguni males were entering the wage-labour force (Hunt Davis 1969:89).

In this social context, it was the African elite – made up by the people who had most fully assimilated European culture – which provided leadership. Hunt Davis (1969:99) argues that, having witnessed the African defeats in the wars of the late 1870s, the new leaders realised that future African welfare depended on working within the framework of South African society, not opposing it. 'They found in the franchise clause of the Cape Constitution the needed opportunity for political participation. The political leaders' earliest activities centered around Lovedale, the Colony's foremost African school ... ' The elite in the later part of the century urged their countrymen to obtain an education, to participate in politics (through the limited franchise), to forsake war as a policy for defending their rights, to work hard, and to earn the respect of the Cape's European population through their efforts to improve themselves (Hunt Davis 1969:116; see Christie 1991:76; Molteno 1984).

And so the ground was prepared for the entrenchment of a new cultural and social orthodoxy. As the land was reshaped by a hundred years of war into constituencies of the Cape Colony, so the discursive world was recreated and new loyalties, new laws of the individual subject forged. Lovedale began to thrive, ranking as one of the best schools in the Cape. It was only in the late 1880s that several white schools, backed by heavy government aid, began to surpass it (Hunt Davis 1969:206). Certainly for black South Africans, Lovedale in the second half of the nineteenth and the first half of the twentieth century became a pre-eminent centre for black advancement. Noni Jabavu, granddaughter of John Tengo Jabavu, famous Lovedalian and editor of *Imvo Zabantsundu*, and daughter of Professor D.D.T. Jabavu, Lovedalian and Fort Hare professor, writes as follows about Lovedale in her memoir, *The Ochre People* (1963:20-21):

> The uncles [Roseberry Bokwe and Cecil Makiwane] greeted each other tumultuously. Apart from blood links they had other ties. They had taught at Lovedale together before I was born. In family albums I had pored over pictures of such things as the staff cricket team in which they had both played ... My mother too had taught at Lovedale with them before her marriage; all my elders were part of the net of people linked by professions, business, blood, and for many of them Lovedale was the *alma mater*, the cradle where they had shared a social and political background inherited from earlier generations of Bokwes, Jabavus, Makiwanes and others – tens, scores, hundreds, now thousands.

The 'thousands' of educated blacks were multiplied further by Fort Hare University, which grew directly out of Lovedale (Shepherd 1940). Monica Wilson, in her edition of Z.K. Matthews's autobiography, *Freedom for My People* (1983:127), gives some idea of the centrality of the Fort Hare-Lovedale tradition:

> Students who were at Fort Hare while Z.K. was teaching there have become prominent through Africa from the Cape to Uganda. There are those who have become leaders in their professions and who practise as doctors, lawyers, teachers, headmasters or headmistresses, inspectors of schools, journalists, writers, research scientists, and technicians of one sort or another. There are those who entered politics and

helped bring the independent African states into being, and who still hold office in these states. There are those in opposition, in prison, or in exile. Within the Republic there are those who hold office in one or another Bantustan, and those who were active in the ANC, the PAC, or the Indian Congress, most of whom are in prison, in exile, banned, or dead.

Wilson (1983:131-36) mentions scores of individuals who graduated at Fort Hare, including figures such as Nelson Mandela (1940), Oliver Tambo (1941), Robert Sobukwe (1946), Govan Mbeki (1937), Dennis Brutus (1947), Robert Mugabe (1951) and many others.

The subject of Lovedale as a 'cradle' for emergent black leadership and for the shaping of new generations in severely modified forms of subjectivity following the Frontier Wars is the subject of the next chapter. Suffice it to say here, in conclusion, that for the African elite in the second half of the nineteenth century, the struggle for selfhood, which their forefathers had initially fought on battlefields, was taken up at centres of learning such as Lovedale. It was a struggle to be conducted on borrowed terms, in a borrowed discourse. The leading 'school' figures of the second half of the nineteenth century, such as John Tengo Jabavu, became acculturated in Victorian-English style ('They were wedded to the Victorian way of life', writes Noni Jabavu in *The Ochre People*, 1963:157). Leaders such as Jabavu devoted their lives to seeking equality for their people along the lines of British constitutionalism and loyalty to the Crown of Victoria. The limited franchise introduced in 1853 at the Cape satisfied the claim of British constitutionalism to fairness, but this borrowed discourse finally saw African leaders deserted and betrayed in 1910, at Union. Then the counter-struggle began, which has seen a resolution only in the final 10 years of the twentieth century, to reappropriate power lost in the name of English and 'civilisation'.

# 3

## A SAVAGE CIVILITY

Take up the White Man's burden –
Send forth the best ye breed –
Go bind your sons to exile
    To serve your captives' need;
To wait in heavy harness,
    On fluttered folk and wild –
Your new-caught, sullen peoples,
    Half-devil and half-child.
        – *From Rudyard Kipling,*
*'The White Man's Burden' (1899)*[1]

The effective conquest of information leads to the
ultimate collapse of the Aztec empire ...
        – *Tzvetan Todorov,*
*The Conquest of America (1984)*

Literacy was at the core of colonisation in South Africa. It was implicit in the
frontier struggle between sharply contrasting modes of information and
comprehension. In this struggle, there were two main lines of conceptual
agency. On the one hand, the Nguni people of the Eastern Cape resorted to
thaumaturgy in an attempt to expel whites by cathartic apocalypse, while, on
the other, missionaries assiduously and laboriously exercised cultural
surveillance based on the pseudo-rationalism of a professedly revealed Truth.
As the historical record suggests, the thaumaturgical mode of response largely

ended in the Cattle Killing disaster of 1856-57, which in turn opened the way for significant growth of mission education and the teaching of mainly Protestant educators who propagated a discourse of metaphors masquerading as literal truth.

Literacy was the basis of what became an informing, knowledge-creating representational order. The larger object of literacy was a linguistic colonialism which placed 'English' and the values embedded in it at the apex of 'civilisation'. The linguistic/semantic/semiotic transformation implicated in literacy teaching was therefore at the centre of the broader colonisation of South Africa, and the great contribution of missionaries to the re-invention of the country and her peoples. For missionaries, literacy meant crossing the semiotic divide between languages and pursuing a dual goal: 'reducing' languages of the Other such as Xhosa into a written orthography so that the Bible could be translated into the semiology of a previously oral culture (in which symbols are regarded with great seriousness); and teaching subject people facility in English so that their assimilation into a master discourse could be effected. If, as Stephen Gray (1989:xix-xx) has suggested in another context, translation can be seen as central to the literary processes of southern Africa, then one of its sources is surely in missionary interaction, where large attempts were made to transcode orality into literacy. Although this was an incomplete, complex, and two-way process which was not necessarily dichotomous or evolutionary (see Gunner 1986; Hofmeyr 1993), it never-theless had deep and far-reaching implications. Anthropologist Jack Goody (1977:37) developed the theory that literacy – implying as it does a shift of emphasis from speech to writing – facilitated a transformation in cognitive procedures by which knowledge could more easily be reified.[2] 'Translation'[3] occurred not only between languages, however, but between the *forms* in which ideas would be expressed. In this chapter, I argue that Lovedale, along with other institutions and individual missionaries, not only established a widespread literate order incorporating institutional surveillance, but that in doing this it sought to 'translate' African subjectivity into excessively narrow limits of expression determined by Western literary forms of understanding. I shall argue that the formal, linguistic constitution of missionary behavioural prescriptions, although based on Christianity and the Bible, found expression within *literary* modes by which 'strange' data was domesticated for Western comprehension.

More than three decades ago, historian Donovan Williams (1959:218) asserted that the 'literary aspect of education' was integral to the overall strategy of missionaries. Williams noted the strategic motivation of 'native agency', by which literacy and Western education would be pursued in the Eastern Cape. All mission stations (in what Williams in 1959 still called 'Kaffirland') set to work to create a system of education, both inside and outside the mission station. 'The initial impulse involved a desire to create a class of Native preachers and teachers and for these special institutions were envisaged at some mission stations, either in Kaffirland or in the Colony, while the plan for the broader education of the Kaffir included not only these, but also elementary schools at all the missions and missionary outstations where both missionaries and Native Agents would teach' (p.219).

In *Towards an African Literature* (1973:37), A.C. Jordan describes the connection between literacy and Christianisation as central to the history of African education in South Africa. He writes,

> In all speech communities of the Southern Africans, what literacy exists is inseparably bound up with the Christian missionary enterprise. To be able to 'preach the Word' the missionaries had not only to learn the languages of the people, but also reduce these languages to writing. Translators, interpreters, preachers, and teachers had sooner or later to come from among the aborigines themselves. And so some of the apt converts had also to be introduced to the rudiments of modern learning through the language of the missionary body concerned. But since, outside of the missionary bodies, no one undertook to educate the Africans, acceptance of 'the Word' remained the only means of access to any form of modern learning, and literacy became the exclusive privilege of a few Christian converts and their progeny.

Jordan adds that the 'dawn of literacy' is to be associated, first and foremost, with the Glasgow Missionary Society, whose representatives 'reduced the Xhosa language to writing' (p.37).

Writing in 1877, John A. Chalmers describes missionary work in the contested 'Caffreland' *circa* 1820 as a 'perpetual round of preaching and teaching' (1877:18). He recounts that the Glasgow missionary William Chalmers taught a school of eighty pupils at Tyumie (the early site of Lovedale), but 'There was ... jealousy of the instruction, when [Xhosa parents] saw that their children were, one by one, renouncing their heathen mode of life'. The efforts of William Chalmers, who is reported by John A. Chalmers to have expanded his range by establishing four elementary schools at neighbouring villages, were being supplemented by other missionaries from various countries entering 'Caffreland', including Wesleyans, Congregationalists, Anglicans, Methodists, Roman Catholics and Lutherans (Etherington 1976:593).

The typical context of early conversion work is suggested by John Chalmers's citation of a 'quaint description of school work at the Chumie' (1877:18), which he contrasts with the 'very admirable system of Government-aided schools' in his own time (he was writing in the 1870s). The report he cites is from the minutes of a meeting of the Presbytery of Caffraria in January, 1840:

> The Presbytery proceeded to examine the schools of the district, and found present 150 scholars, of whom 65 were males and 85 females; 46 were dressed in European clothing. Of the whole, 52 read the Scriptures in their own language, and 15 also in English; 5 read the history of Joseph; 9 the account of the creation; 19 were found in the spelling book, and 65 were in the alphabet. Fourteen exhibited specimens of writing on paper, and 29 on slates; 14 also presented solved questions in simple multiplication. The more advanced were examined in natural history and in the Shorter Catechism.
>
> The Presbytery expressed their satisfaction with the number of pupils present, their approbation of the order and appearance of the scholars, and noted the improvement since their last examination. (Chalmers 1877:19)

Donovan Williams (1959:222), quoting the Minutes of the Presbytery of Caffraria of 1853, cites a similar record in which meticulous record-keeping of cultural transformation is reflected:

> The details contained in the Minutes ... give an insight into the part played by the translation of the Scriptures in Kaffir education at Lovedale. There were 49 pupils present for examination, of whom 17 were English. 16 pupils were reading the Scriptures in the Kaffir language. Five were reading easy lessons in English and two of these could also read the

Scriptures in Kaffir. One was reading easy lessons in Kaffir. Sixteen were spelling in English. Eight were spelling in Kaffir. Five knew the alphabet. Thirteen showed specimens in writing. Ten read in the British School Lesson Book, No. 4, and the same were examined in English Grammar, Geography and Arithmetic from simple addition to reduction. During the course of the examination the pupils sang various infant school rhymes and moral songs.

In these reports the surveying eye of the missionary projects his African subject into a context entirely stripped of any influence or significance other than the virgin ground of re-making. Such culturally exclusive surveillance was typical of African education in nineteenth-century South Africa.[4] However, rigorously exclusive as it may have been, missionary education opened many doors in the colonial economy. Cobley (1986:93) notes that graduates of missionary institutions 'could expect to escape employment in subsistence agriculture or wage labouring' and obtain salaried employment in jobs which demanded literacy, numeracy and facility with the colonial languages. Cobley describes Lovedale as 'the first and most important example' of 'native training institutions' (p.93). Other such institutions opened by the end of the century were St. Matthews (Anglican, near Grahamstown, set up in 1855), Healdtown (Wesleyan, Eastern Cape, 1857), Blythswood (United Free Church of Scotland, Transkei, affiliated with Lovedale and opened in 1877), Amanzimtoti (Congregationalist, American Board Zulu Mission, 1853), Inanda (sister institution to Amanzimtoti, 1869), Marianhill (Roman Catholic, Natal), and Morija (Paris Evangelical Mission, Basutoland). Important centres opened at slightly later dates are Tiger Kloof Native Institution (Anglican, Free State), Botshabelo (Lutheran, Transvaal), Kilnerton (Wesleyan, Transvaal), Grace Dieu (Anglican, Pietersburg) and Wilberforce (the African Methodist Episcopal Church School), among others (Cobley 1986:93-94).

At Lovedale, which was specifically set up to further 'native agency' through the training of African preachers, teachers and catechists (Shepherd 1940:88-91), a concentrated enterprise of literacy was begun. The Scottish pioneers of Lovedale, who led the way in making a literate order in the Eastern Cape, placed great importance on translating the Bible into Xhosa. For many years, the Bible would be a primary teaching text. As early as 1826, John Bennie, known as 'the father of Kaffir Literature', printed at the old Lovedale site *A Systematic Vocabulary of the Kaffrarian Language in two Parts; to which is prefixed an Introduction to Kaffrarian Grammar* (Shepherd 1945:4). William Boyce (Wesleyan) in 1834 produced the first grammar of an African language in South Africa with his *Grammar of the Kaffir Language* (Williams 1959:226). Shepherd (1945:5) reports that in 1830 missionaries extended their collaboration at a meeting at Buffalo (the present-day Kingwilliamstown) 'for the purpose of fixing rules for writing the language', taking Bennie's system as the basis. Further, missionaries of the London, Wesleyan and Glasgow missionary societies again met at Buffalo to consider co-operative effort in translating the Bible (Shepherd 1945:6). After the destruction of the Lovedale press in the war of 1834-35, the Wesleyans with their press at Mount Coke began to take a more prominent role in the translation of the Bible (Shepherd 1945:6; Fast 1991:8).

These details illustrate the intensity with which the literary aspect of colonisation was pursued. The early efforts of translation, lexicography and grammatical analysis broke through the relative linguistic homogeneity of the Nguni people and opened the way for institutions such as Lovedale to take the semiotic invasion much further. Lovedale, like many other similar institutions, would isolate its pupils and seek to remake their discursive identity. In this, language – more particularly, English and the forms it encodes – would be their main instrument.

# I

Lovedale has been chosen for particular attention here because, according to all accounts, it was for many decades the largest and most influential missionary educational institution in the country. Molema (1920:217) described Lovedale in 1920 as 'the largest mission station, perhaps, in the world, certainly in Africa', while Walshe (1970:8) comments, 'The most outstanding educational institutions such as Lovedale were ... directly instrumental in creating a new elite ... it was from [Lovedale] that the majority of African political leaders emerged for the whole of South Africa, giving expression to their peoples' new political consciousness'. Shepherd, writing in 1940, said that Lovedale 'is at present the most complete, the largest, and the most successful of its kind in the country, and the institution as a whole is probably the greatest educational establishment in South Africa, and that with the greatest range in scholastic operations, the utmost boldness in its plans and prospects, and the most perfect order in its organisation and administration' (1940:199). James Stewart, Lovedale principal between 1870 and 1905, provided more concrete evidence of Lovedale's pre-eminence in the work *Lovedale: Past and Present*. Here Stewart compiled figures based on inspections of 700 schools in the Cape Colony during the three years of 1884, 1885 and 1886. Lovedale was ranked first in numbers of pupils passing Standards III, IV and V. In the years 1873 to 1886 it came first in numbers of pupils passing the Elementary Teacher's Certificate. In other comparative tables Lovedale's lowest position was third (Lovedale 1887: 537-51).

During the Stewart years, Lovedale seems to have acquired an aura of exclusivity which is reflected in comments such as the following by Noni Jabavu (1963:28):

> We crossed yet another bend of the winding Tyumie and arrived on the outer edge of the campus of Lovedale, the missionary institution ... The great school had continued to grow. As the sun's rays beat down on it the place looked established, solid. As indeed it should, for it was a hundred and fifteen years old; a venerable age in a young country. When my uncles and aunts, and even older Lovedalians, talk about it, they generate an atmosphere that reminds me of a similar one in England among people linked by an old school tie.

Her father, D.D.T. Jabavu, writing about his father, John Tengo Jabavu, remarked in 1922:

> Those who knew Jabavu from his young days will agree that he was immensely benefitted by the subtle glamour of the Lovedale environment of the early eighties ... As he often remarked to the present writer, those were the happiest days of his life. For he was a vigorous youth placed by the Grace of God in congenial surroundings, the future holding out before him an infinite vista of possibilities. (Jabavu 1922:14-15)

However, Lovedale was not always so big, so popular and apparently so successful. There appear to be three distinct phases in the institution's nineteenth-century history. First, a modest beginning under the principalship of William Govan, who, in accordance with the earlier missionaries' philosophy, wished to offer a full classical education with tuition in Greek and

Latin, and whose aim was to 'raise' African students to complete equality with Europeans (Hunt Davis 1969:164). Second, there was the Stewart period, in which, according to Hunt Davis, a shift is discernible from the belief in mere cultural superiority to one in *racial* superiority, influenced by Darwinism (pp.172-73). During this period, the foundation established by Sir George Grey's plan in the 1850s and early 1860s for promoting 'peace' by supporting education (with particular emphasis on industrial education) coincided with Stewart's antipathy against the idea of classical education for Africans, and with his own preference for 'useful' (industrial) training. Under Stewart, Lovedale flourished and achieved wide renown, although the missionary message was ambiguously received. Third, there is the period beginning roughly around the 1890s which sees dissatisfaction with missionary paternalism culminate in the secessionist movement of figures such as the Reverend P.J. Mzimba, who started the African Presbyterian Church (Cuthbertson 1991:57-64).

During the first period after the opening of Lovedale as an educational institution in 1841, growth appears to have been slow and numbers small. In addition, the War of the Axe in the 1840s saw the institution closed down for use as a barracks, and Lovedale was not reopened before 1849 (Shepherd 1940:104-19). In the 1850s Sir George Grey instituted strategy for educating the Nguni, based on his New Zealand experience (Hunt Davis 1969:220). The Grey Plan dovetailed with suggestions by Earl Gray, Secretary of State for the Colonies from 1846 to 1852, for providing industrial education to 'civilise races emerging from barbarism' by turning them into a 'settled and industrious peasantry'. The anticipated result of such training was a docile and efficient labour force which would accept both European religious and political authority, as well as European social superiority. Lovedale added to its stature as the leading school for Africans by assimilating the special programmes of the Grey Plan into its course of instruction. Vocational training was begun, in which carpentry, masonry, wagonmaking, blacksmithing, and later post office and telegraph work were taught, while for women there was laundry work, sewing and dressmaking[5] (Stewart pamphlet, undated, Stewart Papers (hereafter SP) BC 106 D16:4). Masonry was later replaced by bookbinding and printing.

The inflow of government funds under the Grey Plan, in addition to its own resources, allowed the institution to retain vocational teachers and adopt a four-year apprenticeship programme. It also added a general education to its vocational programme. Apprentices would work at their trades during the day and then receive classroom instruction for two hours during the evening. While Govan remained principal, Lovedale's academic curriculum was seen as a primary concern. Govan wanted Lovedale 'to give a good English education, and also a higher education, including classics, mathematics, logic, theology etc.' (in Hunt Davis 1969:229). Initially, few Africans achieved the higher levels of education. According to Hunt Davis, only two out of sixty-two Africans took higher subjects in 1856, but by 1863 more Africans enrolled for advanced subjects. Nevertheless, Lovedale's high standards meant that its alumni generally fitted into the emergent African middle class (p.229). Although the Grey Plan ended in 1863, industrial education at Lovedale continued to thrive, while the lure of higher levels of scholarship would attract increasing numbers of African pupils.

An event in Lovedale's history which was to have important consequences was the disagreement between Lovedale's first and second principals, Govan and Stewart, which led to Govan's resignation and Stewart's assumption of the principalship in 1870. This difference is dealt with fully by Brock (1974:107-14) as well as Shepherd (1940:152-64) and only the salient features need outlining here. The dispute was based on the issue of Greek and Latin as teaching subjects, and, behind this, on the matter of an equal education for African and European pupils, following the highest standards, as opposed to a differentiated approach for Africans in which English was to be regarded as a 'classical' language. Brock (1974:111) explains that where Govan aimed to train 'an African elite who could compete on equal terms with Europeans in any sphere of life, Stewart, in accordance with the wishes of the [Foreign Missions] Committee, aimed to provide instruction especially tailored to African needs, with the particular object of producing African teachers and preachers'. The Free Church of Scotland Foreign Missions Committee considered submissions from both Govan and Stewart and pronounced in favour of Stewart, deciding that the classical languages 'should be sacrificed if they stand in the way of the pupils acquiring a thorough understanding of English' (Shepherd 1940:160).

Apart from the merits of the immediate issue between Govan and Stewart, the real dispute was philosophical, raising the question of attitude towards Africans and the real objective of colonisation. Govan was a missionary of the old school, writes Brock (1974:110), a true exponent of the 'principle of conversion'. Stewart's approach implied that the ideal of ultimate equality between African and European was impractical and that education designed mainly for Africans should be differentiated. While logic and practicability appear to have been on Stewart's side with regard to the teaching of Greek and Latin, his implicit denial of the ideal of equality raised the ire of educated Africans and was to have important implications for the kind of discourse Stewart would enforce at Lovedale.

Lovedale under Stewart began to show significant growth, and Stewart's own voice as leading spokesperson for the institution became confident and self-assured. In a paper read in 1878, Stewart was able to report a steady increase in numbers in the ten years between 1868 and 1877: Against 86 pupils in 1868, there were 380 in 1877 (pamphlet, SP BC 106 D1.1). In another pamphlet, 'On Native Education – South Africa', Stewart outlined the nature of an ideal educational grading for Africans as follows:

> The right lines of native education are then that it should be –
> (1) largely industrial, with a good general education up to at least Standard IV; (2) with a normal course of training for three years for a more limited class to afford the supply of qualified teachers for native village schools; (3) with opportunity under certain financial limitations for a much smaller class to go as far as matriculation; and (4) further, to any extent they may choose to go at their own expense, and on the same terms and privileges as Europeans. This last may be justified on the theory that education proceeds from above downwards, not from below upwards. A small educated class stimulates the ambition of those below; and specially does this hold good among Africans. (SP BC 106 D16, undated:6)

Indeed, Stewart's 'right lines for native education' corresponded closely with Lovedale's own programme. Lovedale's annual report for 1873, for example, set out the 'objects of the institution' as (1) 'to train as preachers such as may desire to enter the work of the ministry, and who may after considerable trial be found fitted, by their mental qualifications and general character'; (2) 'to train teachers for native village schools'; (3) to teach the 'various arts of printing, bookbinding, wagonmaking, blacksmithing, carpentering, general work, and to train a few as telegraph clerks'; and (4) 'to give a general education to those whose course in life may be as yet undecided'. In addition, the 'real' object was cited as 'spiritual results, and the formation of moral character' (Cory PR 242:3). The report indicated that in the 'educational' (non-industrial) department, three years were spent on the theological course, another three on the 'ordinary college course', and three years on the 'school department', beginning with 'the Junior Reader and Simple Rules in Arithmetic' (p.7).

Stewart's notion of education spreading downwards seems to have some basis in fact. Odendaal writes in *Vukani Bantu!* (1984a:6), 'The numbers of the new educated class had also by now [the 1880s] swelled to the extent that these Africans were identifiable as a distinct, well-established stratum of society'. He reports that by the 1860s the number of African converts throughout southern Africa had risen to approximately half a million. The number of people receiving an elementary mission education rose from nine thousand in the 1850s to a hundred thousand by the end of the century. The greatest concentration of pupils was in the Cape Colony (p.3). Lovedale was at the centre of this activity.

Supporting Lovedale's order of discourse was a regimented, hierarchical order of material disciplinary practices which was designed to combat the 'idleness' of the African (see Coetzee 1988b). The report for 1873 gives some idea of the daily routine. The earliest classes began at 7am, during which translation from English into Xhosa and Dutch was done for pupils at the lowest levels. At 8am all pupils assembled for worship and breakfast, while the 9am bell summoned classes to regular work. Pupils assembled for dinner at 1.15pm. At 2pm, or 3pm in the summer, all pupils not engaged in trades met for two hours for work in the fields or in the grounds about the institution (Cory PR 242:7-8). Pictures in James Stewart's *Lovedale South Africa; Illustrated by Fifty Views from Photographs* (1894:72-73) show neat groups of pupils in military formation, captioned 'muster for afternoon work', while a photograph in Shepherd's *Lovedale South Africa* (1940) – and on the cover of this book – shows the entire contingent of boarders in drill formation with Major W.L. Geddes, the boarding master, at the head.

Such a precise and orderly organisation of time and labour was certainly not unique to Lovedale, but a common feature of the more general Calvinist theological imperative to instil a stringent work ethic among pupils. It was a process in which the African body and mind were drawn into a precise network of control and surveillance. In the description of Crais (1992a:121), the European project in evidence here comprised an effort to 'control the time, space and cultural practices of an 'intimate enemy' and to seek to redefine the body of the African as a metonym of a dominated life'.

A rare insight into such a process at Lovedale is given by the hand-written nineteenth-century journal of one James Aitkin (undated), who worked at

Lovedale under Stewart. Aitkin describes with relish the regimentation of eating procedures:

> The labour involved in the boarding, not to speak of the discipline, of so many pupils of all shades of colour, must of necessity be onerous and heavy: yet everything is managed with a regularity and a clock-work precision which would not suffer by comparison with the daily duties appertaining to the best regulated military barracks. There are three meals per diem – breakfast at eight, dinner at one, and supper at six. Permit me … to invite you to take a look in at the evening meal. The 6 o'clock bell has just rung, and the boarders are taking their seats in the spacious dining-hall … At one end of the hall, on a dais, are placed, under spotless white covers, the tables at which the Europeans take their meals, the centre table of these being occupied by the boarding master, the members of his family and some of the staff. Mr Geddes sits enthroned at the head of his table and commands a full view of every individual in the dining hall. Noiselessly and without the least confusion or hustling, the pupils come trooping in and take their places, the higher class natives, or at all events those whose relatives can afford it, being seated nearest the Europeans and provided with somewhat more substantial fare than the other natives.

Corroborating Aitkin's observations, and giving material evidence for the spatial notions of elevation and descent, Victorian novelist Anthony Trollope wrote in 1878 that 'coloured boys sat below the Europeans', who dined at a 'high table' (p.217). Aitkin, meanwhile, went on to make a startling comparison between the material scene before him and an imagined feudal harmony in England, when the baron and his retainers 'all blythe and gay' sat down to meals in a spirit of contented regimentation. He continues:

> Every one being seated, Mr Geddes touches a little bell, and immediately perfect silence ensues. He then gives out a hymn … Following this a portion of the Scripture is read, after which a prayer is offered up … Thereafter the meal is commenced, small talk being permitted, but should any opportunity be

> taken by the boys of raising the voice to an undue extent, the
> boarding-master has simply to touch again his magic bell, and
> instant silence is the result ... Native waiters glide noiselessly
> around, attending assiduously to their duties and ever and anon
> whispering into your ear questions such as 'Some more half cup
> sir?' The food purveyed to the Europeans is ample, varied &
> well prepared ... Crushed maize with plentiful supplies of
> butter milk form the staple article of diet of the native pupils,
> meat being provided only occasionally ... In leaving the hall,
> as entering it, perfect order is maintained, the occupants of the
> several tables being dismissed in turn, an usher calling out the
> necessary word of command, which is simply 'Rise'. Some
> military drill has been imparted to the boys by Mr Geddes ...
> and this accounts in great measure for the method and
> precision which characterise the daily routine of the place. Mr
> Geddes has told them off into companies, and has taught them
> their 'facings' and other rudimentary parts of drill, with the
> result that on occasions such as church parade on Sundays,
> these fine manly young fellows may be seen marching to
> Divine service in 'fours' with all the aplomb of well-disciplined
> troops. (Cory MS 10,369:24-28)

For all Aitken's emphasis on 'blythe and gay' feudal companions, his narrative
points toward hierarchisation in every sense: seniority according to position,
race and means, which is manifested even in the content of food served. The
militaristic emphasis on strictly defined and carefully monitored order appears
to have served as a basis for everyday living at Lovedale. One can also assume
that it provided the physical counterpart for the discursive order enforced in
the institution's teaching.

## II

In discussing such an order of discourse from the point of view of the late
twentieth century, one has the advantage of sharing in theoretically
sophisticated scepticism about metanarratives and totalising discourses in
general. In a sense, then, the parameters of such an analysis are indicated by
the monolithic nature of the discourse under review on the one hand, and, on
the other, the availability (indeed the necessity) of discursive-analytic insights

to reveal the contingency of a discourse such as that employed by Lovedale in the nineteenth century.

It must be stressed that my approach here is a synchronic review of the typical discourse evident in the historical record of Lovedale in the nineteenth century, more particularly during the institution's successful years under Dr James Stewart, roughly between 1870 and 1890 and before the turbulence occasioned by the Ethiopian movement in the 1890s. I do not pretend to provide an historical narrative *per se*. Lovedale's history spans more than a century and is closely tied up with the dense and complex history of that period. As such, it is well beyond the purview of this study. However, in all the studies of Lovedale I have been able to find,[6] none offers a specifically discursive analysis of the institution's operations within the context of the nineteenth century. This omission is understandable in the light of the historian's primary socio-empirical objective, but it means that the historical narratives on Lovedale lack critical discussion of the way in which the institution and its operatives constituted themselves, their subjects and the broader world in language. An analysis thus conceived may go some way towards the kind of aim articulated by Homi K. Bhabha (1983:18) that 'the point of intervention [in colonial discourse] should shift from the *identification* of images as positive or negative to an understanding of the *processes of subjectification* made possible (and plausible) through stereotypical discourse'.

Postcolonial cultural critics implicitly depend on the premise stated baldly by Jean Francois Lyotard (1984:xxiv) as follows: 'Simplifying to the extreme, I define *postmodern* as incredulity towards metanarratives'. The term 'narrative' is employed here in the broader sense denoting encodations and protocols of discourse which constitute a regime of truth or, in the Foucauldian terms introduced in Chapter 2, laws governing or influencing individuality and subjectivity. The predilection for meta-narratorial control at Lovedale is evident, in the more obvious sense, in newspaper and book production, and, less visibly, in educational discourse. A short example of newspaper history should illustrate the more obvious case.[7] Lovedale operated several newspapers, starting with *Ikwezi* in 1844, which was terminated in 1846 after the outbreak of the seventh frontier war. *Ikwezi* was succeeded by *Indaba* in 1862, and by the jointly published *Kaffir Express* and *Isigidimi Sama-Xosa* in 1870. *Isigidimi* was controlled by the Lovedale missionaries, but it nevertheless reflected the opinions of the emerging educated African elite.

The needs of the African reading public led to the *Kaffir Express* and *Isigidimi* being separately published in 1873. In 1874 Elijah Makiwane became the editor (under European 'supervision') of *Isigidimi*. As such, he was the first African newspaper editor in South Africa. Makiwane was succeeded by John Tengo Jabavu in 1881. However, all did not go smoothly. The literate African elite soon became frustrated by the paternalism implicit in missionary control of *Isigidimi*, while Jabavu was warned by Stewart to be more moderate in his editorship. Stewart found it necessary to 'eviscerate' a 'very political' article criticising the then prime minister and governor of the Cape, and when Jabavu used *Isigidimi* to comment on election matters, sharp differences arose between him and Stewart (Odendaal 1983:103-104). Jabavu handed in his resignation in 1884, and started his own newspaper, *Imvo Zabantsundu* (Native Opinion), with the backing of sympathetic white politicians, in the same year.

In this account it appears that Stewart was intolerant of alternative narratives of 'native opinion' other than those sanctioned and approved by Lovedale missionaries. Further evidence of narratorial authoritarianism in the operations of the Lovedale Press has been convincingly argued by Peires (1979b:155-75) and Gray (1979:172-80). It can therefore be suggested that an institution such as Lovedale – along with so many others in the 'more powerful Victorian missionary movement' worldwide (Elbourne 1991:164) – stands as a stark example of what the postmodern argument would typify as denial of heterogeneity in that its discourse constituted a narrative 'that predetermines all responses or prohibits any counter-narratives' (Carroll 1987:77). Paraphrasing Bakhtin, Carroll notes that 'no representation, no narrative, and no theory can encompass and resolve such a fundamental conflict [that representation is always an open, unresolvable conflict of representations] without denying its own dialogic foundations and becoming authoritarian and dogmatic' (p.81).

Victorian discourse under the sway of 'manifest destiny' (Bosch 1991:298) was generally monolithic. Further, the roots of such thought lie in neo-classical conceptions of language as an apparently 'transparent medium for thought' (Coetzee & Attwell 1992:181). It therefore does not come as a surprise to find that Lovedale's typical discourse suggests authoritarianism and dogmatic certainty, nor do I wish to suggest that Lovedale was unique in this regard, although for my particular interest in Lovedale's educational preconceptions the point does need to be established and given concrete substance. First, however, a clearly elaborated approach towards the nature of the 'discourse' under scrutiny is needed.

Among the plethora of theories in relation to the nature of archival or 'empirical' writing[8] such as that evident in documents relating to Lovedale, I have found the work of cultural historian Hayden White especially useful. White has developed a theory for the contingency and *tropological* nature of all discourse which purports to be 'historical' or 'factual'. As a theoretician, White stands out prominently, along with Dominick LaCapra, for relativising the 'objective' quality of historical or factual writing. Their arguments have aimed at showing that conventional historiography often relies on a notion of representation which is implicitly grounded upon nineteenth-century theory. In this view, historiography must, as science and literature did, digest the lessons of a European tradition which includes Nietzsche, Derrida and Foucault, and which examines critically the founding assumptions of knowledge (see Kramer 1989:100; White 1978; LaCapra 1983; Alonso 1988). White has questioned the distinction between 'imaginative' writing (such as found in 'literature') and 'historical' or 'factual' writing. His interest to me in this study is that he suggests a way of looking at the representational suppositions of 'historical' documentation in the Lovedale archive. In his major work, *Metahistory: The Historical Imagination in Nineteenth-Century Europe* (1973), White set out to analyse the historical work 'as what it most manifestly is – that is to say, a verbal structure in the form of a narrative prose discourse that purports to be a model, or icon, of past structures and processes in the interests of *explaining what they were by representing them*' (p.2). That White's theory also applies to supposedly 'factual' writing is illustrated in his essay 'The Fictions of Factual Representation' (1978:121-34). Here White argues, for example, that

> all original descriptions of any field of phenomena are *already*
> interpretations of its structure, and ... the linguistic mode in
> which the original description (or taxonomy) of the field is cast
> will implicitly rule out certain modes of representation and
> modes of explanation regarding the field's structure and tacitly
> sanction others. In other words, the favoured mode of original
> description of a field of historical phenomena (and this
> includes the field of literary texts) already contains implicitly a
> limited range of modes of emplotment and modes of argument
> by which to disclose the meaning of a field in a discursive prose
> representation. If, that is, the description is anything more
> than a random registering of impressions. The plot structure of
> a historical narrative (*how* things turned out as they did) and
> the formal argument or explanation of *why* things happened or

turned out as they did are *prefigured* by the original description
(of the 'facts' to be explained) in a given modality of language
use: metaphor, metonymy, synecdoche, or irony. (1978:127-
28)

In this extract, all the constituent components of White's theory are
compressed into summary. White's schema comprises the *prefiguration* of
phenomenal data into linguistic modes of comprehension (metaphor,
metonymy, synecdoche, irony), the *reconstruction* of such data by means of
what he terms different modes of *emplotment* (romance, comedy, tragedy,
satire) and the *explanation* of the story so emplotted by various modes of
argument (White 1973:1-42). The basis of White's theory, namely the
prefiguration of data into linguistic modes, rests on Roman Jakobson's and
Kenneth Burke's theories of language and rhetoric, while his emplotment
theories rely to some extent on Northrop Frye's theories of literary archetypes.
The idea of linguistic modes is derived from a theory of tropes, elaborated in
the introduction to White's collection of essays, *Tropics of Discourse: Essays in
Cultural Criticism* (1978).

Here White proposes that 'Tropic is the shadow from which all realistic
discourse tries to flee' (1978:2). But the flight is futile, since 'tropics is the
process by which all discourse *constitutes* the objects which it pretends only to
describe realistically and to analyse objectively'. I wish to dwell on this aspect
of White's extensive theory of 'factual' or 'historical' writing, since I want to
demonstrate how in nineteenth-century colonial South Africa in general and
in Lovedale in particular a certain 'reality' was constituted in discourse which
functioned on the representational level – and within the orthodoxy of
English education as a means of empowerment in the colonial world – as a
significant way of influencing subjectivity.

White explains that 'tropic' derives from *tropikos, tropos*, Classical Greek
words for 'turn', 'way' or 'manner'. The word came into modern Indo-
European languages through *tropus*, Classical Latin for 'metaphor' or 'figure of
speech'. All these meanings, White argues, sedimented into the early English
word 'trope' and capture the meaning of the concept modern English calls
'style'. The idea of 'style' is especially apt for understanding that form of verbal
composition which, to distinguish it from logical demonstration on the one
side and pure fiction on the other, is termed 'discourse' (1978:2).

Relying on Harold Bloom's statement in *A Map of Misreading* (1975) that
'all interpretation depends upon the antithetical relation between meanings,

and not on the supposed relation between a text and its meaning', White proposes the 'ineluctable fact' that all texts intended to represent 'things as they are' fail in their intention: 'Every mimetic text can be shown to have left something out of the description of its object or to have put something into it that is inessential to what *some* reader, with more or less authority, will regard as an adequate description' (1978:3).

White points out that the etymology of the word 'discourse', derived from the Latin word *discurrere*, suggests a movement 'back and forth' or a 'running to and fro'. Discourse moves 'to and fro' between received encodations of experience and the 'clutter of phenomena' which refuses incorporation into conventionalised notions of 'reality', 'truth', or 'possibility'. In addition, White argues, it moves back and forth between alternative ways of encoding this reality, so that, in the final analysis, discourse is quintessentially a *mediative* enterprise (1978:3-4). However, White allows for the possibility of certain forms of conceptualisation *hardening into hypostasis* when he argues that the aim of some discourse is 'to deconstruct a conceptualisation of a given area of experience which has become hardened into a hypostasis that blocks fresh perception or denies, in the interest of formalisation, what our will or emotions tell us ought not to be the case in a given department of life' (1978:3-4).

It follows, therefore, that such 'hardened' conceptualisation is antithetical to the notion of discourse as a mediative enterprise acknowledging implicitly or explicitly its status as a figurative encodation of reality which must always be open to argument or contradiction. More specifically, data which is prefigured by one of the linguistic modes of informational comprehension (metaphor, metonymy, synecdoche, irony) tend, especially in cases of 'hardened' conceptualisation, to become 'formalised' in one or another type of literary emplotment (romance, comedy, tragedy, satire). In missionary discourse, which shows evidence of 'hardened' conceptualisation, all four kinds of plot are evident: romance (the heroic individual missionary on a quest in the moral wilderness), comedy[9] (successful resolution of error and confusion by the awakening of understanding, and joyful social reunion under a kindly Godhead), tragedy ('fallen' states, particularly after an attempt has been made to commune with God), and satire (the representation of half-educated, 'book-knowledge' buffoons, whose pride and hubris have travestied the noble aims of missionary education).[10] Because the typical Lovedale discourse of the second half of the century tends to follow the general pattern of Manichean prefiguration in terms of dark and light, good and bad, civilised and barbarian, information tends to be coded in paired metaphors which do not evolve beyond their binary structure. This is in contrast to White's sense of progression, within historical writing at large, in linguistic modes of information, from 'an original metaphorical characterisation of a domain of experience, through metonymic deconstructions of its elements, to synecdochic representations of the relations between its superficial attributes and its presumed essence, to, finally, a representation of whatever contrasts or oppositions can legitimately be discerned in the totalities identified in the third phase of discursive representation' (1978:5).

The examples of Lovedale discourse which I examine in this chapter appear to be largely *arrested* in the metaphorical stage, although examples of metonymic and synecdochic representations are also evident. As a result, the discourse under review often tends to emphasise comedic resolutions, as these rely on a resolution of warring opposites characterised by binary metaphoric description. At the edges of the ideal comedic outcome, however, are the possibilities of backsliding or over-reaching pride, which respectively call for tragic/melodramatic or satirical emplotment. This very limited range of formal knowledge processing provided a particularly narrow ground for self-apprehension by pupils who were compelled to reproduce as learning such cognitive procedures.[11]

# III

The textual traces of missionary discourse in general and of that emanating from Lovedale in particular, though imperfect and incomplete, are nevertheless overwhelming in volume and suffocatingly repetitious. This is because, barring minor or major shifts in attitude and strategy among Lovedale missionaries during the nineteenth century, the dualistically conceived prefiguration of the world as a (metaphorical) battleground of good and evil, and the many subsidiary metaphors attendant upon this Manichean prefiguration, remain consistently evident in the textual traces under review. It is possible, therefore, to propose some general features of the 'translation' of African subjectivity in this material into particular formal emplotments.

By the very nature of their vocation, missionaries were always under a duty to *report back* to their sponsoring bodies. They therefore provide a pre-eminent example of entrapment within a particular mode of expression. Typical of neo-classical, empirical rendering of knowledge, their mission was never to discover heterogeneity, but always to confirm pre-existent notions of the nature of 'reality' which they regarded as objectively true. Examples of metaphorical troping become evident in reports of the early Lovedale operatives. What is striking here is that these reports are styled as *empirical* accounts of data from the mission fields and were received as such. In the *Glasgow Missionary Society Winter Quarterly Intelligence* of 1843 (two years after the opening of Lovedale seminary), the editor wrote:

> We have now before us several communications from Mr Bennie. Some of these are descriptions of native customs, well fitted to awaken deep feelings of Christian sympathy. The poor Kaffres are morally bound hand and foot with the most depraved customs and laws. So exceedingly impure and depraved are they that we are prevented from going into detail. (p.7)

In this extract, the editor explicitly acknowledges that the accounts he wishes to quote are *well fitted* to awaken Christian sympathy. To do this, they must satisfy a preconfigured notion of the African as a 'depraved' barbarian. Such is the conceptual overdetermination (and its corresponding figurative hypostasis) that the editor's comments rely on adjectival expression as a substitute for the raw information he finds too unpalatable for his readers. 'Depraved customs' and 'exceedingly impure' function as indications that the matter of the reports would, if published, offend good taste, but that the awfulness of the contents can be taken as read, given a shared prefiguration of 'strange' data. The actual quotation then offered (supposedly a 'mild' example of the impurity of Cape Africans) reads in part as follows:

> While conversing this afternoon with some natives, a man approached whom I had long known, but whom I had not seen for some time. I always thought him a fine-looking Kaffre. He used to be always well dressed and ornamented according to Kaffre costume. On seeing him to-day, however, he was so altered in appearance as to induce the belief that he must be seriously ill. He was in dishabile, his firm step and haughty mien were gone, and he looked ill. I asked what ailed him? 'During the late war,' said he, 'I killed a Fingo who had the igungu, and in the act of killing him I became infected.' His account of its effects on his system was one of subtle and

powerful poison. He spoke of himself as pained all over the
body down to his very toes. And yet the truth seems to be that
this poor child of nature is merely the victim of superstition.
He believes that he is under the influence of bewitching
matter, and that he will in consequence surely die. And such
are the effects of a belief such as this in dark heathen minds.
Poor sons of Ham, when shall the day dawn and the shadows as
to them flee away? When shall Ethiopia stretch out her hands
to God? (p.7)

This 'report' is divided into an 'empirical' observation and a subsequent
explication. The observation is rendered in descriptive prose presenting the
pathos of man fallen from health and dignity because he had killed someone
with the 'igungu', while the explication collapses all possible speculation
about the cause of this condition (if one were to accept the account as
reliable) into a want of Christianity and the captivity of 'dark heathen minds'.
The emplotment of the account offers the prospect of tragic delusion (fallen
from the dignity of his 'firm step and haughty mien' and reduced to
'dishabile'). The account as rendered is plainly a literary construct relying on a
pre-existent Western literary culture for comprehension and agreement. The
linguistic mode of information relies on a metaphoric opposition between
'dawn' and 'shadows', although the relation of the data about superstition to
the presumed essence of the account, 'dark heathen minds', might be styled as
synecdoche. The underlying metaphoric dualism implicit in the entire
passage, and explicitly figured in the juxtaposition of 'dawn' and 'shadows',
offers an instance of how otherness was informationally processed by
missionaries. The reporter's rhetorical purpose is satisfied by the confirmation
of a metaphorical-taken-for-literal opposition between 'light' and 'dark'. It
goes without saying that such figurations of events and conditions were
prejudicial to the people who were the subject of this metaphoric gaze, since
they were being objectified in terms owing allegiance to the emergent colonial
power increasingly affecting their lives in an adverse manner, and which
would also insist that its 'knowledge' be accepted as truth.

   Such metaphoric dualism appears to underlie missionary-colonial discourse
in its entirety. It provided a basis for the various narrative plots which
consistently totalised difference and heterogeneity as a function of the
Manichean dyad: good/evil; savage/civilised; heathen/Christian; indolent/
hardworking; slothful/diligent, and so on. It is within this dyadic discursive

frame that one finds the typical metaphors which function as dominant modes of comprehension underlying predictable emplotments of otherness and Christianisation.

Moreover, such reductive discursive operations occurred in a context of public debate which saw missionaries as the champions of African interests against a hostile settler population. This general context is well illustrated by an exchange reported in the *Christian Express* of 1 May 1876, in which Lovedale replied to charges in the *Port Elizabeth Telegraph* and the *Graaff-Reinet Advertiser*. The accusations related to comments by *Isigidimi* (sister paper to the *Christian Express*) on a highly publicised court case in which a European youth was accused of shooting to death three African children and wounding two. The *Christian Express* reported that the hostile papers published 'a long bill of accusations against Lovedale in particular, and against native education generally, and against a Kaffir periodical press in addition, as a special and permanent nuisance which should be abolished' (*Christian Express* 1 May 1876:1). In its response, the *Christian Express* wrote, in part: 'The *Isigidimi Sama-Xosa* has for two and a half years been edited very properly and very well too, by a "superior" native – *but under supervision of course*. The article in question was carefully revised every word of it, by a white skin and whatever blame there be, must fall on a skin of that colour' (p.1, emphasis added).

Two months later, the controversy flared again. This time the *Port Elizabeth Telegraph* was quoted with approval by the *Fort Beaufort Advocate* and the *Queenstown Representative*. In its riposte, the *Christian Express* of July 1876 enlisted the support of the *Alice Times*, whom it quoted as follows:

> The *Port Elizabeth Telegraph* after having received a sharp reprimand from the *Christian Express* a short time ago, for writing about things it did not understand, has again returned to the attack, if not with vigour, at least with as much spite as the occasion warrants.
>
> An article in the *Telegraph* of 23rd June, begins by lamenting the difficulty of obtaining an adequate, or suitable labour supply in Port Elizabeth; and the impertinence of well-fed, well-paid, and comfortably housed servants in that town … [the *Telegraph*] traces the evil to its source, and ascribes 'much of our domestic inconvenience in this respect to the high pressure rate at which the native servant girls are being educated at various institutions'. (*Christian Express* July 1876:1)

This view by the *Port Elizabeth Telegraph* allowed the *Alice Times*, clearly in sympathy with the missionary enterprise, to characterise the attacks against Lovedale as 'a singular instance of perverted judgment, and narrow-minded illiberal and un-Christian sentiment'. Further, it was argued that 'the common sense of the nineteenth century, to say nothing of its philanthropy and Christianity, demands that no race of people be consigned en masse to be hewers of wood and drawers of water, as the *Telegraph* would fain compel the Kaffirs to be' (in the *Christian Express* July 1876:1).

What emerges from this exchange, which is typical of the settler-missionary conflict of views in general, is that Lovedale was able to appropriate the high moral ground of liberal values – 'philanthropy and Christianity' – while sharing many of the presuppositions of the settlers about white superiority, as evidenced in the hasty assurance that *Isigidimi's* black editor worked 'under supervision of course'. But one can reasonably conjecture that in the eyes of black people who were seeking education to avoid precisely the servile status desired for them by the likes of the *Port Elizabeth Telegraph*, Lovedale and missionary education in general presented itself as the 'friend of the native'.

Though a 'friend of the native', Lovedale's views of the social and cultural universe from which its subjects emerged show the closure of a dyadic discursive framework and its repetitive plots, and one can only imagine the difficulties this narrow cognitive frame must have presented for pupils. For example, in the April issue of the *Christian Express* of 1878, the editorial had this to say about what it styled 'The African Social Problem':

> The social problem in South Africa is confessedly a difficult one, and its solution must necessarily be a work of time. The situation, in the case of the Kaffir [Xhosa] race, is something like this. Individually they have more or less an incapacity for persevering labour. They had rather live as they do, in mud hovels with enough to satisfy their animal wants, than make any systematic effort to better themselves in life – and somehow there is a wall of separation in habits, tastes, and everything else, between them and the English colonist, so that they fit into our social system nowhere. Socially they hang together on the clan-system. The individual has no rights, nor security of person and property, and therefore no motive to toil, where he cannot securely enjoy the fruits of his industry. The institution of chiefs is now only a curse, if as a cure for

anarchy it ever was a blessing. For many a day it has been only a gainful trade, in robbing and murdering the rich through imputation of witchcraft, and making the administration of justice an organised system of plundering the poor. (p.1)

For a more recent account which provides a picture of the very same society as that described above, but in sympathetic terms, one consults J.B. Peires's book, *The House of Phalo* (1981). The excerpt above is remarkable mostly for the conspicuous manner in which it subjects its data (clan living, chiefdom, communal land-holding, other cultural approaches to labour, alternative styles of housing) to a dualistic metaphorical value system. The lack of a specifically Protestant work ethic becomes 'an incapacity for persevering labour'; the absence of middle-class British life in brick and mortar houses is figured as 'animal wants' in 'mud hovels'. A minor aspect of a more comprehensive cosmological system (see Hodgson 1985:1-5) is figuratively transposed into 'robbing and murdering the rich through imputation of witchcraft'. The account depicts a society tragically trapped in social degradation, and hints, via the obvious binary implication, at the comedic resolution available to such 'fallen' barbarians in their 'hovels': a retreat from the errors of heathenism and an awakening to a God who happens to prescribe Western cultural habits.

The hypostasis of narrative evident in this piece goes some way towards explaining the missionary need to isolate its subjects in institutions where its regime would be unchallenged (see Etherington 1976). Only outright control of environment would serve the rigid strictures of a discursive system committed to remaking a strange world in its own image. This need is captured in the comments of the Reverend J.D. Don, whose observations upon visiting Lovedale appear in the January 1877 issue of the *Christian Express*. Don expresses his conviction that Lovedale possesses a 'great advantage' in having youths as boarders, living on the premises day and night, 'separated from adverse influences and subject to the rule of the institution for a whole term at a time'. The Lovedale teacher 'fights the devil at an advantage compared with his Indian comrade', Don wrote.

This desire for isolation to combat the devil at an advantage is set against the actions of the early London Missionary Society pioneer, Johannes van der Kemp, by Lovedale historian R.H.W. Shepherd (himself a Lovedale principal in the twentieth century). Van der Kemp did the reverse of what Lovedale was later to do: he lived among his Khoikhoi charges, adapted his dress, and took a slave for a wife. Shepherd (1940:11-12) notes with disapproval that Van der

Kemp 'did not teach his charges the dignity of labour' and that 'his marriage to a slave girl more than forty years his junior alienated sympathy that would have been given to missionary work'. Clearly, the Van der Kemp option was seen as aberration (see Enklaar 1988; Elbourne 1991).

This is made explicit by a *Glasgow Missionary Society* report of 1839, in which it is written that Lovedale should 'contain apartments for the Students, and that they should be entirely separated from general Kaffre society during the period of their studies'. The report conceives this as necessary to 'their success in study, and perhaps still more to their moral and religious culture'. The report warns, however, that this will require 'management', since robust young men 'previously accustomed to roving habits, and with a full vigorous constitution, would neither be willing nor able to sustain such confinement and protracted studies as are common in this country [Scotland]'. It is therefore proposed that the institution should have 'a piece of ground in the cultivation of which [students] will be required to labour under the direction of their tutor, or some one else appointed by him'. In this way, the report concludes, it is hoped that 'their health will be preserved, habits of industry obtained, a knowledge of agriculture acquired, which may through them be dispersed over the country' (*Glasgow Missionary Society Summer Quarterly Intelligence* (IV) 1839:10).

If the dyadic cognitive frame enforced a rigorous disciplinary philosophy encouraging representational dichotomies, what were the typical metaphors for education once inside the institution, and how was the educational experience of pupils plotted? Much can be gleaned from the writing of Lovedale's most illustrious leader, James Stewart, and from textually recorded advice given to Lovedale students during Stewart's years. Stewart's writings on the question of 'native education' suggest the prevalence of a narrative in which Africans are metaphorically characterised as an 'infant' race in the more general march of 'civilisation' worldwide, spearheaded by the Victorian Christians. Coupled with this very common metaphor – as in Kipling's 'half-devil and half-child' – is the notion of cyclicality in the progress of civilisation. As the Greeks and Romans were responsible for the transformation of the Anglo-Saxon savages, so Victorian Christians would transform the Cape Africans. The *Glasgow Missionary Society Summer Quarterly Intelligence* for 1839, for example, reported that English should be used as much as possible in teaching, since this 'would lay open the rich stores of English learning, and enable those educated at the Institution to pour forth on the native mind what they themselves drunk in from a foreign channel'.

This is seen as a renewal of the civilisational cycle: 'It was thus the literature of our own country grew up, amidst the intellectual acquirements of ancient Greece and Rome. And the day may yet come, when mighty nations on the continent of Africa shall look back with filial regard on these and similar attempts to nurse the infant mind of their early progenitors' (p.11).

The justificatory invocation of cyclicality, as if by some law of historical determinism the British could not avoid colonising Africa, begs too many questions to discuss here. But the idea that knowledge can be 'poured forth on the native mind', like the 1841 *Glasgow Missionary Society Autumn Quarterly Intelligence*'s comment that Africans should be enabled to 'drink at the English fountains of literature, science, and practical godliness', indicates a view of the African missionary subject as an empty vessel or *tabula rasa* common to educational discourse of the time. The infant metaphor miraculously swept away all earlier 'civilisation' of the Cape Nguni and implied that previous forms of culture were irrelevant, undesirable and disposable. It also allowed the emplotment of African 'progress' as an unproblematic line of growth from ignorance to knowledge within comedic parameters, which sees childlike confusion and error resolved by maturity and understanding. The strength of the infant metaphor and its acceptance by later generations of Westernised Africans is shown by the fact that its use is evident in the 1930s, almost a hundred years later. Couzens (1985:30), in his biography of H.I.E. Dhlomo, cites S.H.V. Mdhluli in his 1933 book, *The Development of the African*, as saying 'we are still beginning to crawl in this field of education'.[12]

One of Stewart's most explicit expressions of the 'race' of civilisation in which the African must of necessity be an 'infant' or a late starter, is in an address to the Lovedale Literary Society in which he roundly rejected the idea that there could be any possibility of 'equality' between black and white. Referring to what he called 'capacity for self-government, training, and power to advance in the arts of civilization', Stewart pronounced as follows: 'Starting as but yesterday in the race of nations, do you soberly believe that in the two generations of the very imperfect civilization you have enjoyed and partially accepted, you can have overtaken those other nations who began that race two thousand years ago, and have been running hard in it for a thousand years at least?' (Cory pamphlet, Lovedale 1884:27)

The wide ambit of the 'infant' idea allowed for the elaboration of subsidiary metaphors and a shift from comedic idealism to satirical ridicule. In a pamphlet entitled 'On Native Education – South Africa', Stewart made the startling declaration that 'the mind of the African is empty'. Presumably he meant that an 'empty' mind was consonant with the idea of an infant, and he went on to characterise in mocking tones the pretensions of an 'empty' mind suddenly stuffed with book-knowledge. Stewart frequently developed this figure as a satiric antitype of the properly educated person: a puffed-up, impertinent African child who imagines that a little book-knowledge constitutes real learning. In the pamphlet under discussion, he wrote:

> The mind of the African is empty, and he has a great idea of what he calls 'getting knowledge'. Hence his anxiety about instruction merely, apart from mental discipline and habit … there is the erroneous idea that manual work is servile toil, and mental work is supposed to elevate a man to a higher class … His desire, therefore, is to learn whatever the white man learns. This aspiration is very strong, no matter how slight the knowledge attained of any particular subject. Educational equality is probably looked at as a step to further equality. There is such an idea existing among a small and not very satisfactory class. Hence there is a strong desire, almost amounting to a craze, for Latin and Greek among a few, though the amount of knowledge gained of such subjects is, of course, useless. (SP BC 106 D16:3-4, undated)

Stewart's ideas on equality in education and his derisory attitude to the prospect of Africans seeking to learn Latin and Greek is in line with his educational philosophy and underlay the dispute with his predecessor, William Govan. But behind Stewart's professional tone in this passage there lurks the prefiguration of the buffoon, made obvious by the give-away sarcasm of phrases such as 'mental work is *supposed to* elevate a man to a higher class' and 'his anxiety about instruction *merely*'. Given the evidence of the many responsibly educated people who did emerge from Lovedale and who qualified for 'equality' by any measure, Stewart's extreme level of generalisation can only be ascribed to the captivity of his discourse within the arrested metaphoric characterisation of people as necessarily conforming to stereo-typed configurations (themselves a function of binary pairings: buffoon/responsible; education/'getting knowledge' etc.).

The implication of the infant metaphor was that Africans would always lag behind, and that the missionary-teacher would always lead them by the hand. Expressed otherwise, the Manichean dualism implicit in the missionary's every discursive act served the teacher's purpose because s/he also *presided over* what was conceived to be a temporal, developmental gulf presented by the reconstruction of reality done in his own terms in the first place.[13] Stewart said in a paper to the General Missionary Conference in London, 1878 ('Lovedale, South Africa'), 'The bridge is at once thrown over the chasm which separates the two states of barbarous heathenism and Christianity' (SP BC 106 D1.1:2). For Govan, first principal of Lovedale, the aim of missionary education was complete equality between Africans and Europeans, but the rift between Govan and Stewart meant that the goalposts were significantly shifted and the perceived aim of education became less easy to define. In his own writings, Stewart substituted as the end point of the Manichean divide (as the secular counterpart of salvation) an ideal far more nebulous than Govan's notion of equality, namely the attainment of what he called 'character'.

In a manuscript written by Stewart, presumably as an address to his staff, Stewart wrote that 'character' was mainly formed by the 'spirit and general influence of the place'. That, in turn, was made up of the 'thought, ideas, feelings and emotions which form the prevalent mood of ourselves and others'. Such feelings were as infectious, Stewart wrote, as typhoid fever. Only 'unity of aim' would allow the teachers to influence character (MS, SP BC 106 D4 (undated):1).

Stewart's fever metaphor, implying a rapid infection of 'character', is potentially misleading. Later in the document he qualified his understanding of the rigours involved in attaining this quality:

> To describe in detail the object of this place would be tedious and unnecessary here … Character I suppose will embrace it. The formation of character, the development of it till it is consolidated and the man or woman is fitted by his or her training for the work of this life and for the life beyond where all depends on character is the *true object* … And as character decides a mans [sic] fate in the life to come it also decides a mans [sic] real usefulness in this. We cannot set before us a simplier [sic] truer or better idea of our work than this. In so far as we secure this in those who come under our care we succeed. (pp.5-6)

From this it appears that Stewart's rather demanding notion of 'character' (depending as it does on culturally exclusive Protestant notions of worthiness) also had a utilitarian aim: 'usefulness'. 'Usefulness' appears to have been a stringent and, again, a culturally biased demand. Stewart at one point wrote about particular converts, 'Both were pure Kaffirs, – once ignorant, and troublesome, and *unprofitable to themselves and to others*, but very different men when they became Christians' (MS, SP BC 106 D3, undated:12; emphasis added). The demand for 'usefulness' was amplified in an address to the Lovedale Literary Society by the Reverend John Buchanan, entitled 'Ultimate Usefulness'. Buchanan formulated in a classic way the dualistically conceived narrative in which disaster (tragedy) or salvation (comedy) depended on the moral choice of pupils:

> There are two antagonistic forces now at work in this field of South Africa, already in stern contention for the mastery over the native races, sure to gather into yet greater strength and to close in yet deadlier struggle. These are the hosts of good and of evil, respectively. On the one side are ranged the following parties, viz.: (1) The truths and powers of Christ's Kingdom of grace ... (2) The elevating and stimulating powers of the Educational world, plied by enlightened, benevolent and earnest men. (3) The countless, nameless influences for good derived from continual friendly intercourse between the natives and a large community of civilized and Christian men. On the other side are ranged the principalities and powers of darkness, in two very distinct yet conspiring bodies; being each sufficiently formidable by itself; but, when combined, simply terrible. These are;- (1) The whole body of South African heathenism, with its gross superstitions, its idle habits, and coarse vices, *all* proud and defiant to this hour; (2) A wholesale importation of the evil agencies which have for long proved the curse of the civilized world ... Of all the constituents of this evil host, probably the most menacing to your own existence are *your* Native habits of sloth and idleness, and *our* low grog-shops ... (p.5)

The way to conquer this menacing host of evil forces, wrote Buchanan, was to 'rise' into usefulness. He declared that missionaries 'are telling us that our Natives must now rise out of their idleness, and ignorance, and sloth, and fit themselves to cope with the white man, if not in learning, yet at least in skilled activity and practical usefulness, or, they must eventually and soon sink out of sight, their name as well as nation disappearing as a rotten thing' (p.6).

Earlier missionary ideals of educational equality were here reduced to the capacity to live in the white person's world; if equality was out of the question (as Buchanan implied), then the African could at least be practically useful. It is interesting to note that despite the change in attitude towards the idea of equality, the earlier and later missionaries were still able to employ the same binarity in their discourse: the metaphoric construction of the world as bipolar, and the further prefiguration of this polarity as organic (growth from infancy to maturity) or, as in the example where Buchanan cites 'antagonistic forces', as military. In terms of the literary form in which such dualism was given expression, the sheer simplicity of the choice between 'rise' or 'sink' tends towards the reductive emplotment of melodrama, itself a sentimental combination of comedy ('rise') and tragedy ('sink').

In similar vein, Stewart in an address to the Lovedale Literary Society entitled 'The Experiment of Native Education', opened his penultimate paragraph with the pessimistic line, 'You may yet rise' (Stewart 1884:30). This came after a display of cultural chauvinism in which Stewart berated his youthful audience for supposedly imagining that they deserved to be regarded as the equals of whites. 'What single thing have you done as a race which the world will preserve, that you sit down contentedly and say we are as good as our white neighbours?' he demanded to know. ' Who first utilized steam and perfected the steam engine? Was he born on the banks of the Kei or the Clyde? Was his name James Watt or *Umpunga Wamanzi?*' (p.28).

Stewart's act of italicising the fictional name 'Umpunga Wamanzi' reveals a bitter residue of contempt for Africans who presume to be the equal of Europeans. Earlier in this same address, Stewart developed his ideas of 'character' and 'usefulness' in a comprehensive statement on what he regarded as an 'educated' person. The effect of this statement was to reinforce the very gulf he saw the missionary as bridging, since the requirements were both vague (in the sense that they were abstract) and formidably demanding. On one level, Stewart argued, a person is educated when 'he' is 'fitted' for the position he occupies (p.13). But this was only one level of education. There were more important dimensions of an educated person. A person is educated when 'he has stored his mind with serviceable materials to such an extent that he is able to make vigorous use of the knowledge he possesses' (p.14). Further, a person is educated when 'his moral powers have become so developed and experienced, that he has both a high and delicate sense of duty, and when his conscience also gives its sanction to what his understanding approves' (p.14). There was more: a person is educated when 'his will has been strengthened by discipline, the effect of which is such that he can act with decision; and bear the strain of difficulty and disappointment, and yet continue or hold on under this strain, in the belief that perseverance and fortitude will bring final success: and when Will and Conscience have been both so developed as that he recognises the importance of all action ...' (pp.14-15). If this was not enough to demonstrate to his pupils how far they were from the ideally educated person, Stewart added a final category: 'We say a man is educated when in addition, his mind has been so awakened that he can look on all that is beautiful and orderly in nature ... and feel that his doing so adds to his pleasures ...' (p.15)

The standards Stewart imposed here, gendered for male use only, were extremely demanding. His first category, that of being 'fitted' for one's position in life, would in itself have been a major accomplishment for African students crossing the enormous cultural divide and 'fitting' themselves for professions by passing examinations in English, in a strange and demanding milieu. But where, one may ask, were they to learn how to develop a 'high and delicate sense of duty', not to mention the intricate computations of Will, Conscience, Intellect and Taste which Stewart handed down as the definitive marks of education? It would appear that 'native education' under Stewart (and the evidence points to a strengthening of these attitudes after Stewart's time[14]) by its very discursive nature set goals which could have little effect but to perpetuate the gulf originally perceived by the missionaries as one between barbarism and civilisation. In effect, the difference underlying this 'chasm', once stripped of the metaphors constituting the 'truth' handed down as education, was little more than one between cultures. But since the Protestant culture of the missionaries was in a position of dominance, it was able to create the metaphors, assign meanings and rigorously seek to enforce them within institutional contexts such as Lovedale.[15]

# IV

Apart from black journalism (to be examined in the next chapter), and evidence of general reaction among the Nguni to the missionary project (see Fast 1991:94-168), there is little documentation on the way in which African pupils at Lovedale responded to the imposition of the Manichean discursive order which relegated them to seemingly perpetual 'infancy' in a savage comedy of manners. I have, however, examined some documentary evidence which indicates that the influence of missionary discourse appears, on the surface, to have been considerable.

An important qualification is necessary in this regard. Although the educated African elite appears from textual evidence to have largely internalised the discursive regime of the missionaries, it should be kept in mind that there existed what Shula Marks (1975:162-80), in a study of John L. Dube of Natal, calls the 'ambiguities of dependence'. Paraphrasing Marks, Cobley (1986:29) writes that 'the ability of these leaders to speak with different voices to different groups without fatally compromising their positions was the essence of their political survival in a society where the patterns of domination and subordination were so sharply defined, so racially stratified, and so brutally enforced, and was a practical expression of their identity as part of a class which was "structurally ambiguous"' (see Daniel P. Kunene's remarks in this regard in Kunene & Kirsch 1967:I,10-11).

One must therefore approach documents written in English for consumption by the missionary overlords with a degree of caution, regardless of the apparent submissiveness evident in them. Textual responses range from the desperate requests for certification, to outpourings of gratitude on ceremonial or formal occasions. An example of the first kind is a letter to Stewart from a pupil, Andrew Cindi, in which he pleads for 'religious certification':

Mafeking
22nd Mar. 1898

Dear Sir

I dont [sic] know whether I would be felicitating [sic] you by asking this.

Dear Sir please be merciful on me about what I am going to ask.

I ask only my Daily Soul's bread from you, which is the blood of Christ & Body.

I ask my religious certification to be received in the congregation I am at now.

They are called the London Congregational. Sir I am in great trouble of doubting my forgiveness from God the Omnipotent. As it is said in the bible that anything that Peter the apostle will hold it guiltful or sinful, it will be reckoned the same in heaven.

Then because I doubt the forgiveness from you so I doubt from God.

I'll prove that you have forgiven me by giving me my certificate I can't do without the Lord's supper.

My gilt [*sic*] is that I have been smoking Dagga & I never knew that it was sin. I found out afterward that you don't reckon it as tobacco, is therefore sin if you hold it sinful. In the name of God I ask you to read John the evangelist 20th chapter & 23 verse. I am sure that is a block to my forgiveness. Give my certificate.

I have much to say but I must see my forgiveness first.

Yours<br>Andrew Cindi

I can't live without Christ. You have the Celestial City's key. And please give it to me or let me in you don't know the day I'll be summoned at.

Let me in let me in let me in.

I am only sorry because I am short in English.

(SP BC 106 C252.33)

Notwithstanding the rhetorical exigency of making his point with as much pleading as possible, there can be little doubt of the writer's sense of desperation at the prospect of being excluded from the 'Celestial City', to which Stewart supposedly had the key. This letter suggests the emotional strength of the reductive dualism imposed on pupils in the form of stark moral choices. For Cindi to be left *outside* the realm of God's forgiveness (significantly, this is represented by Stewart's forgiveness) appears to have been a terrifying prospect. One can argue that his education (evident in his relatively fluent English) has succeeded in inculcating the orthodox *forms* of a Manichean discursive regime. In this case, the melodramatically exaggerated prefiguration of moral destiny as a choice between dark damnation or the Celestial City (the allegorical figure for heaven in Bunyan's *The Pilgrim's Progress*), indicates that Cindi at least knows he must submit to missionary forms of linguistic comprehension in making his request. He consequently expresses the feeling that he cannot conceive of himself as anywhere but outside or inside the grace of God and the missionaries. The desperation of his cry, 'Let me in let me in let me in' suggests that in this case, his own captivity within such metaphorical prefigurations – and the consequent forms of linguistic expression – perhaps goes beyond mere 'structural ambiguity' (suggested by Cobley) as a feature of African response to missionary teaching. C.J. Kros (1992) has argued in relation to R.H.W. Shepherd in the twentieth century that Lovedale principals wielded great influence in their ability to confer or refuse testimonials, or, as in this case, certification. Here indeed is the power of the Word in its local habitation.

Another strongly suggestive example of African response is a joint letter, signed by more than fifty students and former students of Lovedale, on the occasion of Stewart's departure on sabbatical leave to Scotland. This is a ceremonial joint letter and the sentiments expressed in it must therefore be regarded as a formal expression of gratitude. Written in painstakingly crafted longhand with near-perfect lettering, the letter reads in part as follows:

Lovedale 2nd May 1890

Sir,

We, the Undersigned, as representing Natives of different religious denominations of South Africa have heard of your intended visit to Scotland, and we feel it our duty to congratulate you on the prospect of having a short rest from the arduous duties in which you have been engaged for twenty-four years.

We hope you will have a pleasant voyage to Scotland, and that your stay there will be enjoyable to yourself and family, and beneficial to your health. Although we feel that your absence even for a short time will be a loss to us and those whom we represent, we cannot begrudge you the well-merited furlough you are now about to take.

We avail ourselves of this opportunity to express our high appreciation of your efforts to *raise our people*. Many of us have come under your direct influence, and we are glad to be able to state that we have been much benefited thereby. Along with others you have showed [sic] us the value of education – the value of a trained and disciplined mind – in the struggle for life; that education did not merely consist in knowing certain facts, but in qualifying the mind to perform the duties of life; you have taught us the great value of *time* [original emphasis], which you are aware is so little thought of amongst our people.

We think it right to testify also on this occasion, that those who say that education such as the natives receive at Lovedale makes them to be above what is called manual labour, are not correctly stating the true facts of the case. It has been your constant effort – for which we are most thankful – to shew our people that all labour is necessary and noble; and we may here state that as a result, those who were amongst the first in point of rank in their classes while at Lovedale, thought nothing of going to the fields during ploughing or reaping season and doing other work of that class when necessary. We would distinctly state that those who have gone out with any feeling of being above manual work, have not received that idea from being trained at Lovedale. We hope you will excuse our dwelling so much on this point, but we feel it our duty to acknowledge the influence of your teaching in this direction, for we think its value to us cannot be over-estimated.

From the signatures you will see that the good you have done for Africa is not only appreciated by those who have come under your immediate influence, nor only by parents of pupils who have been at Lovedale, but by all classes. You have done much to make us better understood in the Colony and in Scotland. You have especially done much to restrain those who were inclined to be too impatient with our failings,- who were *expecting too much from a people just emerging from a state of barbarism*. We feel that in your influence there has been a protecting element, if we may express it, and it gives us great pleasure to have an opportunity of acknowledging it.

In connection with this we think it right to point out that we felt that you were on the one hand restraining those who were expecting too much, and leading them to sympathize and help us; while at the same time you did a great deal to show us that there was much which *even in our present state* we could do for ourselves; and encouraged us to hope that if we embraced the opportunities for advancement offered in places such as Lovedale, *we might rise in the scale of civilization.*

The influence you have exerted has not only been within the Colony, but also outside of it. Our people have testified to this, and to the confidence they have reposed in you, by sending their children to be under your care from Basutoland and beyond, from Natal, Free State, Transvaal and Bechuanaland. We need hardly state that no more sympathetic testimony could be given by our people.

(SP BC 106 C252.22.
Unless otherwise indicated, emphasis added)

The letter is signed by many prominent Lovedalians, including the Rev P.J. Mzimba, Elijah Makiwane, Isaac Wauchope, John Knox Bokwe and B. Soga. The name of Mzimba heading the list of signatories is interesting because it was the same Mzimba who in 1898, eight years after signing this letter, resigned from the Free Church of Scotland to form the secessionist Presbyterian Church of Africa. Mzimba was only the second African, after Tiyo Soga, to become a Free Church of Scotland minister in South Africa. He was minister of the Lovedale Church at the time of his secession, but became alienated from the white clergy in Kaffraria, whose paternalism and discriminatory practices he resented (Cuthbertson 1991:58). Mzimba's position is therefore not as clear cut as one might imagine from a mere reading of this letter. The letter, combined with the knowledge of Mzimba's later secession, suggests that a relationship of agonism may have persisted between successful Lovedale subjects such as Mzimba and the Lovedale missionary order itself. Further, it appears that the dualistic prefigurations of Lovedale discourse provided a framework for both assenting and dissenting responses. It is difficult to imagine that Mzimba would entirely abandon the beliefs enunciated so emphatically in the above letter upon his secession. It is possible that secession provided the opportunity to interpret a 'rise in the scale of civilisation' among Africans more freely, and in an administratively independent manner, without the effects of discriminatory paternalism.

The letter must also be allowed its share of rhetorical exigency. But there is an emphatic assertion of Manichean dualism in which Africans and Europeans are situated at opposite ends of a value-spectrum. The signatories appear not only to accept, but indeed to wish to underline their allegiance to, this order of understanding. Many of the stock conceptions reappear: education being more than mere book-knowledge; the dignity of manual labour and the acceptance that men should labour in the fields, contrary to Xhosa custom; the 'value of time', meaning an attitude of employing time 'profitably', in contrast to the 'slothfulness' of unschooled Africans; and the idea that 'patience' must be exercised and that too much must not be expected of a people 'just emerging from a state of barbarism'. The idea that 'we might rise in the scale of civilization' is a direct reflection of the reductive emplotments in which the moral choices of Africans were projected as simplistic allegories of salvation in terribly earnest, though structurally comedic, form. It seems hard to believe that the letter-writers would cynically repeat these ideas simply to flatter Stewart. One can therefore propose on the basis of the letter that, among the leading subjects of Lovedale education at least, a large degree of willing subjection to the orthodox *forms* of missionary narrative is discernible. A crucial point in this regard is made by the Comaroffs (1991:311): that the 'spatial, linguistic, ritual, and political *forms* [of] European culture' made up the context within which agreement and disagreement, subjection and rebellion took place. 'Colonised peoples ... frequently reject the message of the colonisers, and yet are powerfully and profoundly affected by its media. That is why new hegemonies may silently take root amidst the most acrimonious and agonistic of ideological battles' (p.311). So much more, one may add, would hegemonies take root in the case of apparent consensus such as expressed in the letter under discussion. One is also reminded of the significance some critics, who propose a psycho-linguistic theory based on the work of Jacques Lacan, accord to the 'symbolic order', in which the unconscious is seen to be structured by language.[16] I do not wish to recode my argument in this terminology, but such an approach would also find, in the adoption by the letter-writers of the linguistic forms of missionary discourse, a significant degree of subjective influence.

Other correspondence makes it evident that among converted, 'school' Africans, a strong feeling of warmth and gratitude prevailed in relation to Stewart and Lovedale. The expression of this warmth often conveys a sense of pride in the institution, but the discursive markers showing acceptance of Lovedale's metaphors are prominent. One joint letter dated 1896 and signed by many hands, 'on behalf of the Colonial and Natal natives and adherents of the Presbyterian church in Johannesburg', welcomed Stewart to Johannesburg and continued as follows:

> We know the great work you are doing at the Lovedale Institution, for the coloured races of South Africa. You have

had no doubt many disappointments in raising the Africans. They are people who have been for generations under the most degrading influences of heathenism, ignorance and superstition but you are teaching them the gospel ... The institution and your name is well known and has become famous throughout South Africa.

May God be with the great work of elevating the natives and may your sojourn amongst us in these parts be a blessing to all. (SP BC 106 C252.29).

Particularly noticeable in this and the other joint letter is the tendency to apologise for the supposed slowness or backwardness of the African. This suggests an internalisation of the dualistic metaphors of degradation and heathenism, ranged against elevation and salvation, and the reduction of the complexity and heterogeneity of African subjectivity to these melodramatic configurations of happy and sad endings.

Couzens (1980:117) and Odendaal (1984a:8) cite further instances where leading African figures such as R.V. Selope Thema and Elijah Makiwane uttered statements of a similar nature. The work of S.M. Molema, too, is full of such sentiments. This class of statement was the work of a relatively small elite group of educated Africans which formed the important middle class who would increasingly provide the leadership core of nationalist movements (Odendaal 1983:3; Walshe 1969; 1970:8; Crais 1992a:220-21;[17] Etherington 1976; Hartshorne 1992:222-23). Cobley (1986:98) in his work on black 'school' people ('kholwa'), comments that even among non-Christian and uneducated Africans there was a growing recognition of the relative economic prosperity achieved by the *kholwa* because of their success in adapting to colonialism. 'Although committed to their own beliefs and customs,' Cobley writes, such Africans began to look to the *kholwa* to learn their 'secular secrets of survival'.

Nevertheless, Cobley (1986:99-100) writes that the resilience of pre-existing African cultural forms among the *kholwa* remained strong despite the best efforts of church and school. 'In areas where tribal loyalties remained strong, social pressure often proved more telling than the moral strictures of the missionaries. Also, in times of personal crisis, such as illness, bereavement or crop failure, belief systems could easily become blurred, for example concerning the nature of the spirit world, and a range of remedies tried, whether mission approved or otherwise.' Other practises, such as the support of the extended family, were retained by the *kholwa* even as allied 'African' practices were discarded. This 'common sense' approach to cultural practices, Cobley writes, ensured that few Africans, even among those educated by the missions, learnt to regard their 'Africanness' in a wholly negative light.

That Cobley's portrayal of cultural syncretism is largely accurate is borne out by a reading of Noni Jabavu's *The Ochre People*, in which the co-existence of a Victorian influenced 'school' tradition and a Xhosa-based cultural milieu is poignantly conveyed. Jabavu herself was educated in England after attending day school at Lovedale (Jabavu 1963:29), and, as indicated in Chapter 2, she represents the third generation of Lovedale influence in her family. Yet she has the following caustic comment for people who assume Africans were merely imitators of the colonisers who influenced them:

> And [extended family bonds] seemed to me an example of how some of us moderns sometimes benefit from the effects of recondite things like the 'extended family' of olden days, whereas observers carelessly assert that 'Westernised blacks are but poor copies of the white man'. To this I and 'cousins' like these can scoff: 'How ignorant some observers and self-styled experts can be about "us kaffirs"!' Indeed how can they help being so, forced as they are by the present political dispensation to observe us from a distance which distorts and throws little light on our lives as we live them? (Jabavu 1960:56)

Jabavu's words here, as well as the qualifications introduced by the idea of 'ambiguities of dependence' among an African elite and Cobley's argument about the resilience of African customs, should be regarded as counter-arguments to the automatic assumption of orthodoxy under missionaries. What does emerge is that within the linguistic forms of information and comprehension most assiduously inculcated by missionaries, the marks of subjection are strongly evident. Slippage, resilience and resistance, such as noted by Cobley, may well have been more strongly evident in cultural practices outside the disciplinary, institutional ambit of surveillance, but one can assert that missionary discourse – exemplified here by the case of Lovedale and its influential teachings – was effective to a considerable extent in shaping new *modalities* of subjectivity among the 'school' elite. Such modalities, like the *forms* of missionary discourse, allowed for contestation within constraining terms of reference already set by the project of a civilising colonialism. In addition, the 'school' elite which had most strongly adopted Western terms of reference were, as Cobley (1986:99) argues, highly influential.

Again, it is Noni Jabavu who provides a direct insight into the traumatic transition of her forefathers. Jabavu's testimony here is the closest one can get to oral evidence handed down over several generations of striving by the people she describes as the *amagqoboka*. Narrating a visit to East Africa (1960:129-30), she writes:

> I was reminded of the accounts handed down to us young ones by the big people of mine and other families back in the Cape, about the religious zeal of their fathers and grandfathers to adapt themselves when the 'transition' first hit us in the South; how those earlier generations had made conscious and constant efforts to measure up to the new requirements, the higher standards of life; to stretch the intellect to try and meet the new ideas. We young people in the forties and fifties of this century listen and shudder to think how unbearable life must have been in such a hive of puritanism, of perpetual endeavour. We catch glimpses of the earnestness that must have accompanied it when, nowadays, our elders associate to fight 'Demon Alcohol' under the banners and badges of 'The International Order of True Templars' for example ... I asked myself: Where in this part of Africa were the equivalent of our Southern frenzied or earnest, 'pierced' people, *amagqoboka*, who, in our language, were pierced with something of the urge to triumph over the slough caused by the former way of African life being broken and made invalid in the present era.

In Noni Jabavu's language the metaphors of 'light' and 'dark' are gone. Two generations after her grandfather, John Tengo Jabavu, had tried to fight the missionaries in their own language and on their own terms, and one generation after her father, D.D.T. Jabavu, had addressed the question of 'various native problems' in a book called *The Black Problem* (1920), Noni in the third generation (and during the reign of H.F. Verwoerd) shows no sign of the old language. Instead, she carefully refers to overcoming the 'slough' not of 'barbarism', but of 'the former way of African life being broken and made invalid in the present era'. But as she suggests, there was a long period of living 'in a hive of puritanism, of perpetual endeavour'. In the next chapter I wish to dwell on her grandfather's time, when African public expression in English in his newspapers sought to find the justice promised by the appeal to 'civilisation' and loyalty to the British Crown.

# 4

## SUBVERSIVE SUBSERVIENCE

You have placed the School Kafir in mid-air,
between the heaven of civilization
and the hell of savageism;
and will you have him there?
– *Langham Dale,*
*quoted in Imvo Zabantsundu 24 November 1884*

It is not a question ... of being able to retrieve the lost
subaltern subject as a recovered authentic voice who can be
made to speak once more out of the imposed silence of
history, because that subject is only constituted as a subject
through the positions that have been permitted.
– *Robert Young,*
*White Mythologies ( 1990)*

Langham Dale's 'heaven of civilization' and 'hell of savageism' are characteristic colonial tropes in which African subjectivity was melodramatically
reconfigured in public forms of representation. As Superintendent-General of
Education in the Cape, Dale was, however, alert to the false simplicity of the
stark choice between 'heaven' and 'hell'. In his words quoted above, Dale was
implicitly acknowledging that the millenarian 'heaven' envisaged by early
missionaries would never be realised. Instead, the superintendent saw in the
demand for inexpensive labour and 'useful' education a middle path, which in
his view was a viable alternative to both the 'hell' of the barbarian wilderness

and the false Utopia of a civilised 'heaven'. Dale was arguing for industrial education so that there might be fewer 'educated idlers', who, he maintained, were 'a greater pest to society than the red-blanket Kafir' (*Imvo* 24 November 1884[1]). More interesting than the mere substance of Dale's comments is the fact that they were carried in the fourth issue of John Tengo Jabavu's weekly newspaper, *Imvo Zabantsundu*, with apparent editorial approval.

This is not insignificant. *Imvo* was the first South African newspaper to be owned and run by an African, and it was also the only such paper for a considerable period.[2] Switzer & Switzer (1979:4) write that *Imvo* became the most influential organ of black opinion in the Cape colony, while Walshe (1970:4) describes Jabavu as 'perhaps the most widely known mission-educated African in Southern Africa' until 1910. Odendaal (1983:174-75) argues that Jabavu became a national figure in the 1880s and 1890s, having an effect on elections (as in the return of J.C. Molteno in Tembuland in 1894), and generally influencing African opinion through *Imvo* (see St. Leger 1974:104; Saunders 1970). Jabavu also had explicit links with Lovedale, so that he is a leading example of a successfully mission-educated subject in the age of Victorian imperialism. His discourse, particularly as an independent newspaper editor, is a revealing source of insight into how African subjects in the Cape (and elsewhere) internalised and re-articulated the signs under whose influence they emerged into the colonial order.

Jabavu introduced Dale's opinions on the 'heaven of civilization and the hell of savageism' as 'luminous and instructive', and commended his readers to 'address themselves to this difficulty' (*Imvo* 24 November 1884). This example of response which is both independent of, and seemingly captive to, the vocabulary of colonial thinking on the 'African problem' seems to confirm Robert Young's statement that only the 'permitted positions' of colonial subjects are recoverable by modern scholars. In this case, the question arises whether the modulated voices of the elite subjects of missionary education, speaking in the highly formal register of public, journalistic English, did little more than repeat the educational discourse under which they had 'risen'. Or does the Victorian English of Jabavu and others in *Imvo* offer scope for a reading of subversive response which was only apparently subservient?

In considering responses of Africans to colonisation and missionary indoctrination, 'permitted positions' do indeed predominate. However, even within such positions, there are clear indications of agonistic response in which a 'reciprocal incitation and struggle' and a 'permanent provocation' (Foucault 1982:790) are inscribed in highly ambivalent public expression.

Clearly, present-day researchers of colonial history should be wary of trying to retrieve the lost subaltern subject as a recovered authentic voice, as Young advises, lest further representational impositions are committed. One can, however, characterise the voices which are discernible, seek to interpret their nuances of expression, and be wary of misrepresenting these as evidence of a unitary colonial subject or a general colonial 'consciousness'. Describing the work of Spivak, Young (1990:158-59) sketches the task of the critic as an obligation to 'ask who is represented, who is not', and to show what Young calls the 'dissimulation', in imperialist history, of the mechanics of the constitution of 'facts'. Further, in Young's view of Spivakian critique, the critic should 'utilize the methods of literary analysis to demonstrate the indeterminacy of the distinction between truth and fiction in such histories, as well as to construct counter-narratives'.

In the earlier chapters of this book, I have sought to pose questions about the concealments and fictions implicit in orthodox (usually white) representations of the generalised, putative African colonial subject. I have also sought to employ literary categories to question the supposedly factual nature of this (imperialist) discourse. But my task in this chapter is to go beyond a questioning of the 'dissimulation of imperialist history' to a consideration of selected public expression by African colonial subjects themselves, as expressed in journalism, and to consider whether or not the speech of these subjects can be seen as a mere confirmation of the missionary law of the African subject, or whether a more trangressive element of colonial *mimicry* can be discerned behind masks of conformity. In the course of the chapter, I shall examine examples of counter-narrative in *Imvo*, both in relation to Lovedale and to the wider colonial world. In the latter category, I place particular emphasis on the campaign by Jabavu and *Imvo* against the Parliamentary Registration Bill of 1887, and conclude with a consideration of Jabavu's position in relation to the South African War of 1899-1902.

# I

Notwithstanding Young's caveat about recovering 'authentic voices' and the dangers of presenting homogenised positions, the 'voices' examined in this chapter are those of a strategically important sector (the educated African elite) whose significance as leaders of black political organisations (see Odendaal 1984b) became evident in the outcome of elections for the Cape parliament under the limited franchise system. *Imvo* itself came to represent a political constituency with a distinct identity. The early pioneers of black journalism were among the first to contribute to public debate in English as independent interlocutors outside of a missionary institution. The kinds of utterance they made, therefore, and the way in which their beliefs were expressed, can be analysed as constructions of a public identity by this sector, unmediated by direct missionary patronage in the form of financial or administrative control.

However, the question might well be posed why a small weekly newspaper such as *Imvo*, with an uncertain readership (if an acknowledged sphere of influence),[3] should be conferred such importance in the colonial context. In my view, the independent African newspaper came to fulfil an important legitimating function in the realigned colonial order of the late nineteenth century. No longer could matters of the highest public concern for African people be settled by precolonial forms of authority in an independent locus of legitimation. By the 1880s power in the Cape Colony had shifted substantially to the colonial bureaucracy of governors, judges, magistrates, law enforcement officers and other delegated functionaries of government. Crucial matters such as land rights, and the arbitration of such rights, were dealt with in terms prescribed by the new order. In such a situation, the only manner in which political claims could be pressed (however imperfectly), was by petition in the English language, and the only independent public forum for such petition was the autonomous African newspaper, which in turn sought to mobilise African opinion and bring pressure to bear on both colonial and imperial authorities.

Jabavu himself alluded to the shift in the public loci of legitimation when he took a government minister to task for asserting that 'the native does not understand fighting on constitutional grounds' and that 'the ['native'] nation does not wish for representation' (*Imvo* 1 June 1887). Jabavu wrote that the minister was 'not aware that the natives' own form of government is the very quintessence of representation. For the chief's *Inkundla* (Great Place) used to be graced by *Induna* hailing from every corner of the chief's dominions, representing those from whom they came.'

Jabavu's use of the past tense ('used to be') suggested the partial demise of autochthonous forms of representation, and the unstated implication was that *Imvo* would seek to fill the breach. In rebutting the minister, *Imvo* was engaging in a public, discursive struggle for adequate representation. This was to become the mission of the newspaper, as I hope to demonstrate.

The scene for an independent African newspaper had already been set by James Stewart, who in 1880 had argued in an address to the Lovedale Literary

Society that the press was a precondition for the creation of a civil society among Africans ('The Educated Kaffir, An Apology'). However, Stewart asserted that in ten years of the Lovedale newspaper *Isigidimi Sama-Xosa*'s existence, nothing beyond a few exceptions had been written 'by native men of a kind to warrant the belief that they have ideas beyond the average; or if they have them, that they can put them into proper form and expression' ('native' *women* were presumably left out of Stewart's reckoning entirely). He went on to assert that there appeared to be little promise of rapid improvement in this regard:

> Before the educated portion of any people is qualified for public positions, there is generally a previous period of preparation, by the spread of intelligence and information; and ... one of the agencies for that purpose is the Newspaper. And so far as I am able to judge, that period of preparation has barely yet begun. And in so far as it has been begun, and is being carried on ... it is chiefly by white men; ... the educated native young men of this country with one or two rare exceptions, have not thrown themselves into the preliminary work of diffusing information, or of qualifying themselves for higher positions, or of preparing their less educated countrymen for exercising a right, and obtaining a privilege they may reasonably expect one day to enjoy. (SP BC 106 D28:11-12)

Stewart in this passage placed his listeners in an awkward position by advising the need for an African press so that the privileges of civil society could be obtained, but then reminding his African audience that they were not yet good enough to write for themselves. It is no wonder, therefore, that *Imvo* was received with such scorn by Lovedale when Jabavu and others began to put their own, decidedly above average ideas into very proper form and expression. *Imvo* set out to do precisely what Stewart had posed as a distant aim, within only five years of Stewart's speech: 'Diffusing information' and 'preparing their less educated countrymen for exercising a right' (presumably, full participation in civil society).

It is significant, therefore, that both *Imvo* and its later rival in the Cape, *Izwi Labantu*, made a point of proclaiming themselves to be organs of 'native opinion'. *Imvo* prominently proclaimed itself, under its masthead and its English title, 'Native Opinion', to be the 'Authorised Medium for the

Publication of Government Notices addressed to Natives throughout the Colony and the Territories'. Both *Imvo* and *Izwi* carried Xhosa and English columns, but used English for editorial comment on their front pages and for the discussion of issues likely to draw the attention of government or others whom the newspapers sought to convince of a particular case. The papers attempted to provide precisely the civil, textual forum for independent African opinion which had not existed before. They sought to be the new bearers of African aspirations in the literate 'civilisation' being constructed and thus to provide a more adequate representation of colonial African subjects. In the first issue of *Imvo*, Jabavu wrote:   ·

> A whole homily can very easily be written on the good that a journal, professing to be the medium of communication between the vast masses of the aboriginal population of this country and the ruling power which hails from Great Britain, could do ... Although the columns of the Colonial Press have ever been open to any Native to unbosom himself ... in addressing Europeans, our countrymen felt ... that they spoke or wrote 'out of courtesy' ... Students of the Native Question, then, may well rejoice at living to see a regular organ of native opinion set up. In that organ they will, no doubt, not only expect 'to see themselves as others see them', but also to see us as we see ourselves. (*Imvo* 3 November 1884)

Jabavu's tone of respectful deference to the 'Colonial Press' in the above excerpt is qualified by his firm belief in the need for an independent public forum for African expression. Such autonomy was precisely the significance of *Imvo*. But if *Imvo* (and later African newspapers) sought to be forums which could legitimate the voices and the claims of African people (by putting them in colonial form and expression), it was a corollary of this function that such legitimation drew its force from (apparent) conformity to the values and the linguistic/stylistic protocols of the English colonial world, symbolised by its figurehead, Queen Victoria. The public voices of 'native opinion' were therefore severely compromised by their necessary acquiescence to the new power formations and the new forms of 'civil' discourse. These voices were products of what Spivak (1985:131) calls the 'planned epistemic violence of the imperialist project'. The educated African had little option but to speak in the colonial language. Nine frontier wars had eliminated all possibility of effective armed resistance, while missionary education had imprinted its own language of civility on African pupils. The link between power and knowledge existed in an immediate sense for a newspaper editor such as Jabavu, since he was able to open a route for independent African opinion to the powers that be only by his knowledge of the appropriate forms of address and the proper register of public, 'civil' language.

What is of particular interest is the establishment of a teleology of ultimate justice and equality founded on the figure of the British Crown. This teleology was buttressed by what one may term, following Lyotard, a 'narrative of legitimation' (a master narrative governing the social bond),[4] in terms of which British constitutionality, validated by Christianity, would maintain and protect the rights of its subjects, regardless of colour or origin. As Michael Ashley (1982:54) argues, missionaries saw the British Empire as the divinely appointed instrument for the spread of 'civilisation'. Ashley adds that the bible, as 'supreme legitimating source for the Christian universe, was unequivocal about the fundamental equality of all men, derived from the account of the creation'. Missionaries therefore 'saw the extension of empire as leading to the extension of human rights. The vision was of a society where eventually all would be endowed with equal rights and privileges' (p.55).

In similar vein, David J. Bosch (1991:313) reminds scholars of missionary history that Protestant missions were imbued with strong millenarian elements, which he defines, citing James Moorhead, as 'the biblical vision of a golden age within history'. John L. Comaroff (1989:674) remarks that the nub of the 'civilizing colonialism' of mission in South Africa lay in replacing native economy and society with an imagined world of free, propertied and prosperous peasant families. Comaroff recalls David Livingstone's vision of 'the creation of a space, a "body of corporate nations" under *Pax Britannica*' in which British values might flourish (p.675). Describing different 'levels' of colonialism, Comaroff provides insight into the appeal of the missionary message for Africans. It was sharply set off against other 'levels' of colonialism: while the 'upper-class gentlemen of His Majesty's administration might govern by right of their worldly nobility and authority, and the lowly Boers might dominate by brute force', missionaries were 'emissaries of the Empire of God' whose task was to 'implant a reign of civility' and 'an imperial dominion of middle-class liberal virtue' (p.675).

If British imperialism, more particularly in the millenarian missionary guise, was divinely appointed and legitimated by the Bible, the symbolic copula was the figure of the Crown, in this case Queen Victoria. Thus one finds Jabavu invoking the Queen in references such as 'the fundamental principle in the British Constitution that all subjects of the Queen are equal in the eye of the law' (*Imvo* 4 May 1887), and giving expression to the master narrative of 'civilisation' in contentions such as the following about the Constitution Ordinance (see Davenport 1978:78), by which responsible government and the qualified franchise was granted to the Cape in 1853:

> [The framers of the Constitution] did not make a Constitution to suit the natives or Europeans but simply fixed a standard which was to apply to individuals irrespective of colour or nationality. We contend that in doing so they showed their wisdom and acted in the best English traditions. (*Imvo* 11 May 1887)

*Imvo* placed the 'native question' firmly within the cheering boundaries of this master narrative: 'The final settlement of the great native problem should rest on the broad and solid foundation of absolute justice for the good of the commonwealth' (*Imvo* 20 April 1887).

It remains one of the most trenchant ironies of the late colonial period in black South African politics that, against all odds, the belief was persistently proclaimed that British justice and ultimate constitutional fairness would prevail. As David Chanaiwa (1980:16) writes, 'African elites wholeheartedly accepted the famous maxim: Equal Rights for all Civilised Men South of the Zambesi'. This belief was given some support in actuality by the existence of the Cape franchise, which allowed the vote to all Africans who earned a minimum of £50 a year or occupied a site or structure together worth £25 a year. Sol T. Plaatje, editor of the *Koranta ea Becoana* and author of *Native Life in South Africa* (1917), was to describe the Cape franchise as 'the most liberal, logical, just, and humane' system of voting because it had recognised that, 'socially and politically, the Bantu people are in their teens'. Plaatje added that the Cape system had 'made a point to shape and help on [African] development by all possible means – education in arts and crafts, instruction in the use of political privileges, exercise of power, and self-government after the British representative system' (in Chanaiwa 1980:16).

Plaatje here captures the characteristic political ethos of the public, petitioning black voice in the late nineteenth century: acceptance of the infancy/teenager metaphor, respectful admission of tutelage, and acceptance of gradualism in the process of acquiring political rights under the 'British representative system'. The teleology implicit in this idealistic, comedic narrative foresaw an eventual point of arrival at 'adulthood' in the attainment of 'civilised' status and the concomitant full participation in constitutional government. As Chanaiwa (1980:16) puts it, 'To the African elites, the theory and, to some extent, the practice of Cape liberalism represented nonracialism, justice, democracy and common citizenship'. He points to the important fact that African faith in ultimate British justice was reinforced by the international forces of the nineteenth-century humanitarian movements, especially the Aborigines Protection Society and the Brotherhood Movement in England. 'Like the missionaries and Africans, the aboriginists believed in a universal "Empire of Man", in trusteeship, and in the progressive perfectibility of people,' Chanaiwa writes. 'They conceived the Africans, Indians, Maoris, and aborigines as integral parts of a universal imperial community which was to be patterned along British culture, institutions, values, and socio-economic classes.' In Ranger's (1983:238) description, following Willan, 'These men aspired to become secure denizens of the nineteenth-century British liberal universe – a universe of freedom and equality under the common law, of secure property rights and of entrepreneurial vigour'.

As suggested above, the professed belief in British values was deepened by the contrast between the Utopianism described above, and the perceived realities of Boer and settler aspirations. S.M. Molema (1920:359) articulated this contrast as follows:

> The history of the relation of Britain to the Bantu is the history of the British government over the subject races all over the world, a history which, whatever its faults and blemishes, is characterised by justice and respect for human rights. These facts are even more forcibly borne out in South Africa, where they stand out in shining relief against the diametrically opposed Boer system.

Plaatje, on the other hand, denounced the Natal 'Native Policy' as 'at once illiberal, unjust and inhumane, a policy entirely subversive of the British traditions and sense of fairplay, such as we see more or less adhered to in the Cape Province' (in Chanaiwa 1980:16). Chanaiwa relies on Albert Memmi's idea that certain groups are afflicted by a 'sociology of good intentions', and on Aimé Cesaire's notion that 'no one colonises innocently' in his scathing judgment of the African elite in South Africa in the late nineteenth century.

He finds that in their 'search for identity in the alien settler society', African elites adopted the humanitarianism of Victorian England and used it to guide and fortify their private and public lives. They acquired the 'pious optimism, utopianism, and universalism of missionaries, white liberals, and, especially, aboriginists' (p.31). However, considering the realities of racism, exploitation, and repression of their settler society, Chanaiwa writes, their humanism made them 'unduly naive, self-deceiving and even otherworldly' (p.21).

Chanaiwa's assumption that Jabavu and members of the elite in general were a deceived group alienated from the African masses (1980:34) is shared to some extent by Roux (1964), Ngcongco (1974), and Odendaal (1983).[5] In my view, however, Chanaiwa's assumption fails to recognise the possibility that Jabavu and *Imvo* were engaged in constructing counter-narratives in which the discourse of 'civilisation' was reappropriated and redeployed. This redeployment drew its legitimation from adherence to *apparently* conformist values and positions, which the critique of missionary-based African 'elitism' takes as *absolute* conformity. Such argument takes little account of the discursive complexity of, and of the possibility of slippage in, supposedly conformist positions. It also underrates the importance of figures such as Jabavu and Plaatje, who, as newspaper editors, provided a rare public 'route' of address to the official colonial world. It seems to me, therefore, that the paradox of seemingly captive but independent (and possibly oppositional) discourse such as that evident in *Imvo* requires some analysis. I wish to argue that the supposed discursive conformity of *Imvo* was a mask for subtle and subversive self-assertion within the constraints of the available language. In this regard, the concepts of ambivalence and mimicry are helpful.

# II

The postcolonial theorist Homi K. Bhabha discerns ambivalence at the heart of colonialist discourse. In his article, 'Sly Civility', Bhabha identifies, within what he calls 'the problematic of colonial governmentality' (1994:94), the difficulties of establishing a mode of governmental discourse 'that requires a colonial substitute for democratic "public discussion"' (p.95). He cites J.S. Mill testifying before the House of Lords in 1852: 'The whole government of India is carried out in writing' and 'All the orders given and all the acts of executive officers are reported in writing' (p.93). Citing Mill's claim that 'to govern one country under responsibility to the people of another … is despotism' (p.96), Bhabha introduces the notion of the deferred address of colonial discourse. He broadens the ambit of différance to include deferment not only in the realm of signification, but also between the geographical locations of enunciation and address. For him, the *supplementarity* of colonial governance implies a doubling of signifiers which creates a deep and enduring ambivalence (p.97). In the southern African context, the imperial ideal (in this case, the ideal of civility under the *Pax Britannica*) is deprived of its customary *civil* reference, resulting in a peculiarly colonial doubling each time signifiers such as 'freedom', 'civilisation', 'justice', 'equality' were enunciated – as they frequently were – in South Africa in the nineteenth century.

The Cape Colony under the system of (so-called) representative government instituted in 1853 was an example of what Bhabha sees as an intermediate body in the imperial chain of government. The 'colonial supplementarity' of the Cape's supposedly representative government is evident in the contradiction, at the most elementary level, of a *restricted* franchise, which would be further restricted as time passed (Davenport 1987:32). In other words, 'civil' society at the Cape was ruptured by the deferral of signs wrenched out of their temporal and geographical context. In this phantom of 'civil' society, ambivalence would reside in all the claims of an editor such as Jabavu to fairness, constitutionality and fair treatment.

The implication of this view is that the supposedly independent journalism of Jabavu and *Imvo* was founded upon just such a distortion of signs. If one takes Chanaiwa's view as correct, then the likes of Jabavu and Plaatje were indeed naïve, for they insisted piously on a singularity of meaning for terms such as 'justice' or 'equality' when these terms were in fact under erasure as a result of the space (or difference) between their enunciation as concepts and their address in the colonial context. However, distortions of such legitimating concepts would, in an alternative reading, be evident to a figure such as Jabavu because of his sense of the location of these concepts in a network of prior textual and verbal enunciation. One may then argue that Jabavu was not necessarily deceived, that he realised the ambivalent potential of the signs he used and sought to close the space of difference by insisting on what he imagined was their primary reference, with frequent repetition so as to embarrass his rulers and all others who derived their moral justification from adherence to the legitimating idea of 'civilisation'. Jabavu can then be seen as fulfilling the function of what Bhabha in another article has described as mimicry, in which 'the look of surveillance returns as the displacing gaze of the disciplined, where the observer becomes the observed' (1994:89). Mimicry, Bhabha says, is 'at once resemblance and menace' (p.86). The supposedly dependent colonial subject may, in this view of things, be seen to have seized upon the displacements of civil society, and on the 'agonistic uncertainty contained in the incompatibility of empire and nation' (p.96), by deploying a *consciously*, perhaps even a mockingly, ironic use of the legitimating signifiers of civilising colonialism. Such discourse *appears* on the surface to be conformist in the pious manner criticised by Chanaiwa and others. In effect, though, it forces into immediate awareness the ambivalence of signifiers such as 'justice' or 'equality' within their deferred, colonial application, without necessarily commenting explicitly on such doubleness (although the figures examined in this chapter certainly do offer explicit comment of such a nature). One had simply to look at the prevailing conditions, as Jabavu would consistently do, and respectfully continue to call upon the promise of British constitutionality. Even without the intention to deploy the authorising concepts of civility ironically, the quality of implicit accusation in such cases would be all the more forceful because the colonial rulers would be hoist with their own petard.

# III

To illustrate how menacing such mimicry appears to have been to Lovedale, I shall look at some examples of controversy between Lovedale and *Imvo*. What appears to have disturbed Lovedale's rulers unduly was that two of its own former African editors of *Isigidimi*, John Tengo Jabavu and Elijah Makiwane, used the independent forum of *Imvo* to express a critical intelligence which was not necessarily in awe of Lovedale's views.

The background to these controversies is Jabavu's 'defection' from Lovedale, where he edited *Isigidimi* between 1881 and 1884. It was during his editorship of *Isigidimi* that Jabavu passed the matriculation examinations of the University of the Cape of Good Hope, a rare achievement among educated Africans. He was only the second African to achieve this mark of distinction, the first being the Reverend Simon P. Sihlali (Ngcongco 1974:25). Jabavu's close association with Lovedale is evident in the fact that in addition to editing *Isigidimi*, he also taught classes in elementary Latin and Xhosa (Ngcongco 1974:24). But his interest in politics led him into conflict with James Stewart, principal of Lovedale. Ngcongco writes that Jabavu's interest in politics grew steadily into a powerful motivating force as he made diligent studies of the Cape Parliamentary debates. He became convinced of the value of the legal and constitutional process as a method of struggling for political rights instead of war or other forms of violent agitation. During the Legislative Council election of 1883, Jabavu began writing and travelling on political missions, especially to his home village of Healdtown, where he exposed the utterances in Parliament of certain members who depended a great deal on the votes of the African electors of the Eastern Cape. *Isigidimi* under Jabavu's editorship 'gained fresh life and vigor', as the editor sought an opportunity to represent what he considered to be the black person's point of view. According to John Knox Bokwe, this brought a sharp difference of opinion between Jabavu and James Stewart, leading to Jabavu's resignation (Ngcongco 1974:26-27).

Jabavu was thus an outstanding product of missionary education, but as the above account suggests, he became a menace to Stewart when his brilliance was translated into political expression. After breaking with Lovedale and Stewart, Jabavu set up *Imvo* with the backing of Cape politician James Rose Innes and two of Rose Innes's supporters, who agreed to enter into a joint guarantee for Jabavu at a local bank (Odendaal 1983:105). The question of the paper's relative independence surfaced almost immediately: The first issue, scheduled for 27 October 1884, was stopped by the promoters because it treated missionaries 'after a free-lance fashion'. Jabavu confronted the managerial board and asserted that he was 'not their tool' and must be free to conduct the paper in his own manner (Brock 1974:261). While Jabavu was thus not entirely independent in his editorship, he was able to assert editorial autonomy as a condition of his role, something that would never have been possible at Lovedale.

*Imvo*'s launch was greeted with silence at Lovedale, which 'neither express[ed] praise nor dispraise', in contrast to the many messages of good wishes received from colonial newspapers (Ngcongco 1974:42). The first open conflict followed upon *Imvo*'s publication in 1885 of the presidential address of the Reverend Elijah Makiwane in his capacity as newly elected head of the Native Educational Association. This address is of interest because it offers an example of discourse that can be considered on the basis of mimicry, and it suggests the possibility of a subversive 'subservience' to the dictates of missionary conformity.

After much formal introductory talk, Makiwane announced that he would address a 'delicate matter' on which 'so much has been said ... that I feel myself called upon thus early to draw your attention to it'. The matter was no less than the dispute, raised by Stewart, whether Africans could be regarded as the equal of Europeans. Makiwane recalled Stewart's challenge about great

European men and their achievements (cited in Chapter 3) and countered as follows:

> In other words, it is asserted or assumed that the rising generation forgets that the natives are an inferior race. To remind them of this, a reference has on various occasions been made to great names and great deeds. Reference has been made to such names as Shakespeare, Milton, Bacon, and others, and to railways, wire fences, and other public and private works which show the skill and energy of the English people. Then it has been asked if the Kafir can produce anything to equal these names and these works. It has been represented that no one could expect anything else in as much as the English have had 2000 years of civilisation while the native is as yet a barbarian, or, at least, only semi-civilised ... (*Imvo* 26 January 1885)

Few things had astonished him as much, Makiwane averred, as 'the labour, energy, learning and heat which have been expended on this point'. Then his argument took an apparent turn in favour of the antagonists of equality – Makiwane professed to agree with them:

> I suppose there are not many natives, if any, who do not readily acknowledge that the English are a great nation, that the English Nation is a greater nation than the Kafir. The possession of Christianity and civilization for so long could indeed not fail to make a difference. For that matter, I do not think you will find many natives who will dispute the statement that the English Nation is greater than any other European nation, when all things are considered. One may doubt if their pre-eminent position will always or will be long preserved, but I think there is no room for disputing the superiority in the past or the present. As a born subject of the Queen I do not only acknowledge this lofty position – a position the influence of which has been applied to noble objects. I say I do not only acknowledge it but rejoice and glory in it.

In this part of his speech, Makiwane appears to be dutifully reproducing orthodox sentiments of loyalty and subservience to the English as a master race. His register is formal, proper and respectful, and he appears to re-articulate a Manichean duality in terms of which nations are 'lesser' and 'greater' by racial-cultural determination.[6] However, in his subsequent comments, Makiwane seems to have made a subtle manoeuvre in which, while agreeing and paying due respect to conventional wisdom, he yet managed to disagree:

> What requires to be noted however after all this is stated is this. If the English took 2000 years to reach their present stage are we to understand that it is impossible for any other people to come up to it within a shorter time? Is it to be expected that those nations or tribes who enjoy the advantages which are given by the Missionaries and the Queen's government are to proceed at the same rate as the English, whose early advantages are not to be compared with our own? If a man takes 20 years to make a road are those who are to travel after it is made necessarily to take 20, or even 10 years? It may be absurd to expect that a nation can become civilized in the course of one generation; but is it reasonable to imply that 2000 years are necessary under all circumstances?

Makiwane here initiated slippage and play within the too-rigid language of scale and race by appealing to those very ideals which often served to justify and legitimate colonial endeavour, education and 'upliftment'. If the English had achieved such a level of refinement, then surely their excellent teaching abilities should be able to bring 'lesser' nations up to standard in less than the entire time it took the English to achieve such refinement? The argument was unassailable. More, it was a rhetorical strategy in which Makiwane sought to remove the erasure under which the hallowed signifier 'civilisation' had been placed. The promise of 'civilisation' and the *Pax Britannica* was the inaugural message of early missionaries, but its meaning would have been deferred in the colonial space. Makiwane comments precisely on the undue deferment of 'civilisation' and reminds his interlocutors of this doubling of meaning. Why should a value that had been developed over a long period not be transferable within a shorter period if its professed meaning implied just such a possibility of transmission in the first place, Makiwane asks by implication.

Makiwane went on to undermine further the argument of absolute superiority in a 'scale' of civilisation:

But further what the natives or, if you like, the rising generation do dispute is the assumption, that every European is necessarily above every native. Of the rising generation you will find very few who believe, that every European who is in William Kama's Location is necessarily above William Kama because he is a European; that every European in Fingoland is above such men as Feltman, Mazamisa and others ... or that Tiyo Soga was not equal to some Europeans. If those who refer natives to Milton and Bacon and other great names mean to suggest even remotely that every countryman of Milton and Bacon is to be considered as equal to and deserving of the same respect as these distinguished names, all I can say is that such persons are likely to require at least 2000 years of loud and constant preaching before they get a convert among the Kafirs ... What I am chiefly concerned about is a correct statement of what the natives really feel and say *because I believe it has been mis-apprehended and mis-represented.* (Emphasis added)

Whatever one may wish to say about Makiwane's class affiliation and his elite status, there is little doubt that he was working against what he considered to be a false representation of Africans. What is remarkable is just how severely Makiwane undermined the orthodox belief in racial superiority while remaining within the general ambit of the given missionary-colonial 'truth' that the English were a 'greater nation than the Kafir', as he had expressed it earlier in the speech. If every European could not be said to be superior to every African on the basis of race, and if every European could not be said to deserve the same respect as the likes of Milton and Bacon, then the entire basis for a *general* or absolute racial superiority such as Stewart insisted upon in his speech, 'The Experiment of Native Education', fell away. What Makiwane was saying, in effect, was that every European had to earn respect, just as every African should. Under the mask of mimicry, then, in which he appeared to reproduced orthodox sentiments, Makiwane exposed the degeneration of civil ideals into a distorted colonial stasis in which the two-thousand-year-development argument was likely to be used, repetitively and perhaps obsessively, to keep cheeky natives at bay indefinitely. How far from millenarian ideals of uncompromising equality!

In the second instalment of Makiwane's speech, published in *Imvo* on 2 February 1885, he offered a eulogy to Queen Victoria, in reference to the mission of Sir (General) Charles Warren, who was then in the country to proclaim Bechuanaland as a British protectorate in the name of the Queen (Potgieter 1975:327):

> I need not do more than merely to call attention to this matter, and to express in the name of this Association and of all our young people and all my countrymen our joy at the Queen's arrival, as we express it; to express the hope that the Queen will not leave the country again; that General Warren will find his work less difficult than many anticipate, that he will have a speedy and a *complete* success, against open and secret foes of that Great Gracious, and Noble Queen, who has been one of the greatest blessings of the present age, a Queen who is not only the Queen of England, but who in a sense may be said to be the Queen of Queens. Long may she live. Oh, Queen Victoria, thou shalt never know how many hearts even in this far off Africa thou hast cheered in their passage through 'the wilderness of this world'. Thou art not only a Queen, but a Mother. Prosper thou in all places; prosper thou in South Africa.

The sudden lyrical turn into biblical English at the end of the passage serves to emphasise the passionate feeling of loyalty to a Queen who represented imperial rule. This may appear to suggest lowly subservience, but I would argue that Makiwane was celebrating the idea of a queen in the guise of a 'mother', a queen of equality and civil rule in the philanthropic sense of the word. My view is borne out by the more explicit suggestions in this regard by John Tengo Jabavu when he campaigned against the Registration Bill of 1887 (below). Was it coincidental that such an invocation of the Queen and what she stood for appeared in a speech which also raised the questions of racial equality and African 'ungratefulness'? It seems Makiwane was implying that the African's gratitude was not unconditional but would be directed at those manifestations of imperial-colonial rule which were consonant with the discourse of civility *before* its deferral in the colonial space of address. Makiwane's adulatory tone of reverence for the *figure* of the Queen would have been potentially embarrassing to the *real* Queen's functionaries. Their actions may have fallen very far short of the constitutional ideals embodied in the 'Queen' as a signifier – ideals which had long since begun to degenerate in colonial South Africa.

In my view, then, there is a subtle yet serious discursive challenge in an address such as the above, a challenge which is masked by the mimicry of correct form, style and register. Makiwane's speech is indeed a case in which the look of surveillance returns as the 'displacing gaze' of the disciplined, and it produced an exceptionally ungracious reaction in Lovedale's *Isigidimi*, which, in the translation from Xhosa by *Imvo*, reads as follows:

> [The address] was the shooting of verbal cannon-balls and empty aspirations which have risen very high as soap bubbles blown up by boys with bone pipes, or with tubes which, when filled with air, fly into the atmosphere as little bright globes, and while you gaze at them apparently satisfied, they burst and vanish into thin air. (*Imvo* 9 February 1885)

In the same issue, Jabavu commented editorially in reply:

> We are very sorry the *Isigidimi* has chosen to deal with so able an address in this carping, captious and uncatholic spirit. The address is admitted, or all but admitted, as a brilliant and masterly defence of the work of missionaries among the natives against the assaults of enemies, disguised and undisguised of that work; it was aimed, it seems to us, moreover, at revivifying the hopes of some of the missionaries themselves, which had been shattered by the unbecoming behaviour of some of our young men (not the sufficiently educated, however,) who had been trained by them. It comes with a questionable grace from a missionary print to misrepresent the spirit, not to say the letter, of the address by describing it as the very embodiment of 'empty aspirations', which, whatever else it may have been, it was not.

Like Makiwane's, Jabavu's argument served to move the locus of legitimacy away from Lovedale, which had revealed itself to be mean and small-minded ('carping, captious and uncatholic'), to the independent African sense of a higher appreciation of the role of missionary work. The fact that *Isigidimi*'s criticism emanated from African editorship at Lovedale serves to emphasise that missionary discourse was now being contested even among Africans, and that one side seemed to be affirming its loyalty to the Lovedale institutional base while *Imvo* felt itself free to begin redefining terms according to its own view of things. In contesting *Isigidimi*'s criticism, however, *Imvo* seems to have been addressing Lovedale as a whole. In the above excerpt, Jabavu suggested, without saying so explicitly, that missionaries with flagging morale should attend to Makiwane's lessons about the true meaning and role of instruction, and about the truer sense of that ultimate legitimating cause, 'civilisation'.

Jabavu here fulfilled his inaugural aim of setting up a 'regular organ of native opinion' in which Africans would not only expect to 'see [ourselves] as others see [us], but also to see us as we see ourselves' (*Imvo* 3 November 1884). The strength of the above passage lies in its confident assertion of misrepresentation, and in its resultant function of serving a more accurate and a more professional sense of truth. This debate, in the early history of *Imvo*, serves to render questionable the notion that the African elite in the late nineteenth century were generally self-deceiving and naïve followers of an English-inspired Utopianism. On the contrary, figures such as Jabavu and Makiwane were using their erudition in a *contemporaneous* discursive struggle for adequate representation. The Native Educational Association (NEA), to whom Makiwane's remarks were addressed, was '[t]he first, most lasting and most widely representative of the early [political] associations' of Africans in the Eastern Cape (Odendaal 1983:54). The association 'soon developed from a kind of teachers' trade union dealing with exclusively educational matters into a general political movement' (p.57). Later the association began expressing dissatisfaction with pass laws and lobbying for blacks to sit on juries. In 1887 it raised the question of parliamentary representation for Africans in the newly annexed Transkeian districts, among other matters (pp.57-58). But Odendaal reads Makiwane's *tactical* 'admission' that the 'natives are an inferior race', without enquiring into the possibility of ambivalence, as evidence that Makiwane was 'still firmly in the old school of missionary thinking' (p.58).

The point is surely that the master narrative of 'civilisation' with its teleology of ultimate fairness and equal justice in a British constitutional system was used strategically, rhetorically, and tactically in the process of a very material and *political* struggle. In this struggle, *Imvo* served as a legitimating organ for African aspirations by contesting the grounds of truth and representation as these affected Africans. The discursive struggle for adequate representation was fundamental to the political struggle, since conceptions of the self and perceptions of African identity at large would have been at the core of decision making with regard to the 'native question'. And what better way to contest the grounds of truth and representation than by calling upon the very founding principles of the missionary-colonial enterprise: equality, freedom, and justice for all humankind in the eyes of God? The contemporaneous effectiveness of this discursive struggle is a separate question. The historical record suggests that African rights were eroded rather than boosted, but the moral high ground of political struggle on legitimate grounds – in the face of nefarious political actions on the ground – surely began here, in the 1880s.[7] This is a tradition that was carried forward by other editors such as Plaatje (*Koranta ea Becoana*) and A.K. Soga (*Izwi Labantu*). Even in 1993, President Nelson Mandela (as he was to become in 1994) still found occasion to resort to the teleology of an ultimate parliamentary democracy seated in Britain. Explaining his affinity with British values and institutions, President Mandela said in an interview: 'You must also remember that Britain is the home of parliamentary democracy and, as people fighting against a form of tyranny in this country, we look upon Britain to take an active interest to support us in our fight against apartheid' (in Carlin 1993:11).

Despite the dissension, in the nineteenth century, between different African editors, all of them relied on a similar teleology supporting a comedic narrative of conclusive justice and equality based on humanitarian British values. This reliance suggests not subservience or naïvety, but the subversive conformity of joining the representational struggle in the language of civility, even when the effects of power continued to be adverse. Plaatje was a founder-member of the ANC, and the ANC's *leitmotif*, one might argue, has always been the legitimate moral struggle. In the late twentieth century, descriptions of the minority white government as 'illegitimate' and the struggle for democracy as 'legitimate' almost came to represent accepted wisdom, even among members of the ruling white clique in the crucial years leading to May 1994, when majority government arrived for the first time. I suggest, therefore, that *Imvo* and early 'elite' African journalism has an importance that goes far beyond a museum display of old-style African subjection to colonial values. This journalism represents the beginnings of discursive struggle in South Africa against misrepresentation and the rigging of 'truth', and who would argue today, in the new language of the 'new' South Africa, that the discursive struggle was not influential in forcing sanctions and isolation on South Africa, leading to the *volte face* which saw a National Party president in 1990 adopt the language of mass-based democracy, equality and justice?

The issue of Makiwane's address was by no means an isolated example of a struggle between Lovedale and independent minded 'school' Africans for adequate representation. Another instructive example is the 'classics for natives' debate, which occurred in the columns of *Imvo* a few months after the Makiwane controversy. In this case, it was Jabavu who took exception to a statement by the *Christian Express*, which, reporting on results achieved by other educational establishments for Africans in the Cape, said the teaching of classics to Africans at Lovedale 'ha[d] been found to do no special good but to produce positive evil' (in *Imvo* 4 May 1885). Jabavu replied, in the same issue:

> We shall be extremely sorry to say anything which may appear to charge the Editor of the *Christian Express* with hostility and unfairness to Natives. With all due respect to the worthy and esteemed Principal of Lovedale Institution, we ask, what positive evil have classics produced to Natives trained at Lovedale? We desire information and light on this subject. The native lads are complaining loudly to their parents and guardians that they do not enjoy the advantages now in the Lovedale classes that the European lads enjoy. This difference has been made quite recently. They cannot understand why the difference is being made. Among students of the same class, who have reached the same standard in examinations by their teachers and Government Inspectors of Schools, a difference is made. The Europeans are given other subjects to study, but Natives are prohibited, even when they express a desire to study those subjects. These are classical studies. The parents know nothing of Latin and Greek, but would like to be informed as to why the difference is made. The *Express* has partially told us the reason for this. It does not arise from unwillingness to see natives enjoying the same advantages as the white race, but in the native mind classics produce positive evil!

Jabavu, always deferential to the protocols of respectable public address and compositional form, nevertheless seeks in such writing to draw attention to alarming slippages in signification, which were perhaps all the more disturbing because meaning in the Victorian era was taken to be reasonably stable. The urgent question, 'what positive evil have classics produced to Natives trained at Lovedale', is an attempt to stabilise the trajectory of 'civilisation' rhetoric which seemed to be veering wildly from its assumed *telos*. Suddenly Jabavu and other Africans were given to understand that Latin and Greek corrupted the minds of natives, but remained good for European pupils. How could such a deeply unsettling differentiation – a perfidious deferral of the once pure promise of civilised equality – suddenly be slipped in? Jabavu resorted to what firm ground he could muster. He challeneged Lovedale on facts. He wanted 'a list of African young men educated at Lovedale, who had a classical education while there, but who are now a disgrace to Lovedale and a failure', and a list of African scholars who 'have been educated at Lovedale and have never reached classical studies while there, who are now a credit to the Institution and a success in the country'. In both cases, Jabavu asserted, it would be possible to provide the opposite: Names of scholars who never read classics and who had become a disgrace and a failure, and of former pupils who did read classics and who were now a credit to the institution as well as a success outside it.

Jabavu concluded his editorial comment by charging that it was not fair to exclude the African pupil from subjects which 'are required and made compulsory by the Cape University', since this 'practically prevents him from competing in the Cape University examinations' (matriculation). Jabavu's final sentence implied that it was difficult to escape the conclusion that racial prejudice was evident: 'While we do not charge the Lovedale organ with prejudice against colour, we fail to see why the native student only is shut out from subjects required by the public examining bodies.'

In subsequent correspondence, Jabavu's earlier plea for factual verification, and similar calls by other correspondents, were alike ignored by the *Christian Express* and Lovedale spokesmen. This was clearly an argument in which facts had little purchase on the missionary institution's *desire* to configure Africans within stereotypical conceptions of relative human worth within a scale of values influenced by Social Darwinism. Earlier missionary discourse had to be adjusted so that the same language might express a new turn, a foreshortening in which reference was displaced, subject to the ambivalence of colonial doubling.

Evidence of such a process became palpable when the *Christian Express* itself entered the debate with a deeply condescending editorial entitled 'A Suggestion to the *Imvo Zabantsundu*', in which it claimed, 'We should be sorry to put the slightest obstacle in the way of any native acquiring any language living or dead, if he himself chooses to take the trouble of learning it, and paying the cost of teaching'. It continued:

But we may, in taking leave of this subject, be *allowed to make a single suggestion to the Imvo Zabantsundu*, which is the great champion of classical education for natives, and also of higher education, as it understands that question. It has the ear of that not very large portion of the native people who read. What should it tell them, if it really desires their welfare, if it loves them both wisely and well? *Tell them this – that the life and death question of the native people in this country now, is not classics or even politics – but industry*; that the foothold the natives will be able to maintain in this country depends almost entirely on the habit of steady conscientious work; and that it is of more consequence for them to understand this, than to be able to read all the lore of the ancients. (*Christian Express* 1 August 1885)

Jabavu could not leave matters here, since *The Christian Express* was proclaiming that all the great vistas of elevated life, both on earth and afterwards, had suddenly turned from the glorious promises of a golden age, and were now foreshortened into suspicions about the indolence of the native! Jabavu harnessed all his aplomb in his answer, in which he combined courtesy and challenge in the same register:

[The *Christian Express*'s editorial] is so good, and we look at it as a compliment to ourselves. It is not with the object of detracting from it that we propose to offer an observation or two on it, but rather to point out some errors into which the writer, unintentionally, to be sure, would seem to have fallen, so as, if possible, to improve it. To begin with, our mentor starts with the idea that this paper is 'the great champion of classical education for natives, and also of higher education'. It does not follow because we are thorough believers in the doctrine that, as a rule, the more a man is educated the better fitted he is for whatever post it may please God to call him, we are therefore 'champions of classical education for natives', and so forth. In connection with the educational controversy, in which some have been engaged in these columns, we have taken our stand against those who were understood to imply, if not to suggest that 'conscience has a colour and quality of work a hue' and

> who were for the equipping of the Native for the future in such
> a manner as to lead one to believe that the contrary were the
> fact. So minded then, we have merely claimed for our people 'a
> fair field and no favour' in the matter of classical or higher
> education. (*Imvo* 19 August 1885)

In this passage, Jabavu observes how the enunciation of an ideal in which one
seeks the greatest possible level of education, is taken as a newly deferred
meaning: that *Imvo* is a 'champion of classical education for natives', which
itself then points to yet another meaning: a yearning for bombastic or
'inappropriate' learning. Jabavu seems very consciously to want to undercut
this chain of deferral, by resorting to epigrammatic restatements of the original
ideal ('conscience has no colour' and 'a fair field and no favour'). Yet the
evidence suggests that no sooner had he uttered these anchoring statements
than they were again misheard, and that, in addition, he seemed to be aware
of such slippage in the marshes of meaning and reference.

In historical perspective, it appears that the principle of absolute equality
before God was being undercut by the labour needs of an expanding economy.
What Lovedale's educators in the high imperial era saw were not the
idealistic, comedic possibilities of equality in civil society, but the satirical,
cynical prospect of 'educated idlers' – buffoonish fops – trapped between the
'heaven of civilisation and the hell of savageism'. The deferred and
ambivalent address of colonial governance meant that educated Africans were
potentially trapped within the parameters of this crude conceptual calculus.
On the one hand, Africans had been taught the doctrine of free will at
Lovedale, while at the same time they had to endure the effects of
stereotypical metaphoric configurations – and their debased forms of
expression – consequent upon this displaced repetition of nineteenth-century
humanitarianism. The only way to begin escaping such crude representations
of the self was through the assertion of counter-narrative.

*Imvo*'s struggles for truthful representation were thus founded upon a sense
of ambivalence. There is a superbly telling indication of Jabavu's possible
awareness of this in the final words of his reply to the *Christian Express*'s
'suggestion' to *Imvo*, when he wrote:

> Our friend, it will be observed, winds up the valuable advice,
> for which we are grateful, with the significant statement that 'If
> [*Imvo Zabantsundu*] has any doubt of the soundness of these

views *because of the source whence they come*, let it make inquiry
at all true friends of the Native people, or for proof, abide the
teachings of experience.' We confess we cannot account for the
expression we have taken the liberty to italicise; for we have
been trained to give great deference to the opinions of the
Editor of the *Christian Express*, even when we had the
misfortune to differ from them. Of course, there is in this world,
what the sacred bard called the 'searchings of the heart', and it
is not for us to enter into that mystic field. With these prefatory
remarks, however, we have great pleasure in re-producing 'A
Suggestion to the *Imvo Zabantsundu*' ...

With this delicate act of intertextual interstition, Jabavu both reproduced the
*Christian Express*'s editorial in full, and placed discursive markers around it
which deconstructed its ostensible meaning. Jabavu recognised a crack in the
civil mask of the editor of the *Christian Express* in the remark that should the
soundness of his views be regarded as compromised by their source, then
confirmation should be sought elsewhere. Jabavu's enigmatic suggestion of
'searchings of the heart' implied that only the editor's *own* ambivalence could
have led to the thought that his Lovedale base should be capable of suspicion,
because its graduates had been taught to show great deference to the
institution, its personages and organs. If it were so convinced of the legitimacy
of its truth claims, why be perturbed by a deviant statement in the mouth of
one of its former pupils?

At the same time, however, Jabavu's phrase 'even when we had the
misfortune to differ', seems to contradict the assertion of willing conformity in
the earlier statement that 'we had been trained to give great deference to the
opinions of [Stewart]'. Jabavu seems here to have allowed his own civil facade
to drop by revealing an awareness of two levels of discourse: the public voice of
*apparent* conformity and obedience to orthodox Lovedale civility, and the
secondary awareness of ambivalence. By allowing this secondary awareness to
become apparent while ostensibly showing obeisance to proper form and the
highest standards of civility, Jabavu reproduced the *Christian Express*'s piece
under the counter-suggestion of its ambivalence. Here indeed is an example of
'sly civility' in which the look of surveillance rebounds as the gaze of the
observed. The 'suggestion to the *Imvo Zabantsundu*', thus reproduced in *Imvo*,
now read as a testimonial to the instability and vulnerability of missionary
representations.

In my view, then, *Imvo*'s struggle for adequate representation was no naïve hankering after the lost Utopian ideals of the brotherhood of man enshrined in early missionary teaching, but a carefully considered manipulation of the legitimating potential of the *enunciation* of those ideals within the distorted 'civil' context of the 1880s. This is not to suggest that someone like Jabavu did not believe in the ideals represented by nineteenth-century philanthropic humanism or that he was cynical. On the contrary, his only power was to use the comedic master narrative of 'civilisation', passionately, against those who had colonised in its name and who would now rewrite it as a satiric parody.

## IV

Jabavu's battles were not only with Lovedale and the missionary view of things. *Imvo* also contested the more general colonial authority and what he saw as its distortion of constitutional principles. Jabavu's strategy seems to have been to expose and emphasise the discrepancies between British constitutional principle and colonial fiat. In dealing with the colonial administration Jabavu was often compelled to muster the authority of legitimate cause: if he could not change the actual course of events, he could at least disrupt the *moral* authority of colonial governance.

In 1887 a Bill was proposed in the Cape Legislative Assembly which was to take the protest of the African voters of the Cape, led by Jabavu and *Imvo*, beyond the 'moribund [Cape] parliament' to 'the highest court of appeal open to any Queen's subject who has accepted his place among British citizens' – 'her Majesty's Government and the English people' (*Imvo* 20 July 1887). This was the Parliamentary Registration Bill, which proposed to strike off the roll Africans whose right to vote was based on communal rather than individual land tenure (see Roux 1964:58; Ngcongco 1974:69-76; *Imvo* 23 March 1887).

*Imvo*'s campaign against the Bill, which eventually led to approximately twenty thousand Africans losing the vote in the Cape Colony (Odendaal 1983:137), was remarkable because it forced an open confrontation between loyal Cape African subjects and their 'mother', the Queen, in the form of 'her' government. As Jabavu wrote in *Imvo*, 'If the natives are, under Her Majesty's Government, to be unjustly deprived of the rights of citizenship, let us have it deliberately from the lips of Her Majesty's Government' (10 August 1887). It was to be a bitter lesson for the Cape African of 'civilised' persuasion when, later in the same year, Her Majesty's government obliged.

For our purposes, this controversy demonstrates, paradoxically, both the captivity of *Imvo*'s discourse within the parameters of imperial loyalty and colonial civility, and *Imvo*'s ability to wield such discourse menacingly against its purveyors, both imperial and colonial. In terms of the notion that the address of colonial governance is deferred, *Imvo* can be seen here to be insisting, to the point of sending a delegation to the Queen's government, on the cancellation of that deferral. I hope to show that this insistence forced into the open, at least momentarily, a realisation that the millenarian promise of British civilisation as an ultimate recourse was a deception.

The crisis caused by the Bill was made acutely poignant by the fact that the year of its introduction was Queen Victoria's jubilee year. In his writings on the subject of the Jubilee, Jabavu played heavily on the emotional appeal of a mother and protector, and on 'the inestimable privilege of being subjects of the freest and most magnanimous monarch in the world'. Africans were 'grateful to their Mother, the Queen, for the beneficent and kind treatment they have received at the hands of her Majesty' (*Imvo* 25 May 1887). In an editorial, he wrote:

> Of the myriads of the peoples of the globe who claim allegiance to the British Queen, there are none, we venture to say, who had stronger cause of entering heartily into the festivities in celebration of her Majesty's Jubilee than the weaker and subject races in the British Empire, and more particularly the aboriginal inhabitants of the Queen's dominions in South Africa … as another motive to unfeigned rejoicing among the natives on this occasion, there has been the priceless privilege to be permitted to enjoy everything permitted to a British citizen – freedom, equal laws, and protection. (24 June 1887)

Jabavu was not quite as self-deceiving as the seemingly inaccurate profession of freedom in this passage implies. He went on to drive a wedge between the signifier 'freedom' and its colonial supplementarity:

> No doubt the stupendous machinery known as the British Constitution has sometimes worked in such a way as to make these terms appear as a mere mockery and a sham to natives: but with their growth in knowledge these erroneous notions are bound to disappear. Our people happily know well enough how to accommodate themselves to these circumstances, and

even the curtailed and curheaded rights that have been
revealed to them by agents of British rule in these parts are
sufficiently liberal for them to show that the government of the
Queen is kind and magnanimous to the weak, even if they
belong to an alien race. For these reasons, then, the rejoicings
of our countrymen over the Jubilee of the Queen have been
genuine, although the doings of those who in this country act
in the Queen's name have, on this Jubilee year, served the
purposes of a wet blanket to their enthusiasm. Yet we rejoice to
think that our people are now able to discriminate between the
local politician who is the troubler of the natives' peace of
mind, and the Sovereign whom they have learned to love and
appreciate because she can, in every sense of the expression,
'do no wrong'.

This passage, with its conceit of 'curheaded rights' being 'sufficiently liberal',
displays an extraordinary ambivalence which perhaps accounts for the
conceit. For Jabavu is clearly struggling to deal with the painful divergence
between the Queen who can do no wrong and the perceived wrongs being
done in her name. He strains to separate the Sovereign and the local
politician, perhaps realising that 'agents of British rule' are no more and no
less than the 'Queen', a titular figurehead who existed in practical politics only
through such agents. But whether or not Jabavu entertained such thoughts
privately, he would never publicly allow the distinction to dissolve. The
Queen as the legitimating signifier for empire was useful to Africans because
its promise of freedom, justice and citizenship created the terms for a counter-
discourse in the colonial milieu. It enabled Jabavu to say of the African in
relation to his British colonisers, 'It is not the sterling metal that irritates him,
it is the spurious coinage, than which no one is quicker than he at detecting'
(*Imvo* 13 April 1887). The 'curheaded rights' passage should also be read in
the context of the Registration Bill. Jabavu's appeals to a 'magnanimous and
kind' sovereign and to 'freedom, equal laws, and protection' were calculated to
reveal the cupidity of a Bill which, Jabavu wrote on another occasion, sought
to disarm Africans 'even of constitutional weapons' after the Africans
themselves had turned to 'Pen and Speech as the new and effective weapons'
(*Imvo* 8 June 1887).

The introduction of the Bill had struck such a deep chord because it was
perceived as a direct attack on the African franchise in the Cape which,

Jabavu reminded his readers, had been granted directly by the imperial government (therefore, the Queen) in the form of the Constitution Ordinance of 1853. Jabavu wrote:

> It serves the purposes of the Ministry to contend that their Bill does not affect the Constitution Ordinance in the slightest degree. For if they admitted that it did, then by her Majesty's Letters Patent, under which Representative Institutions were granted to this Colony, they would have to reserve the Bill for ratification and confirmation by her Majesty. And Ministers know that the 'free hand' has not been allowed the Colony to play ducks and drakes with the immutable rights of the weaker races. They know, moreover, that the chances are that if her Majesty is satisfied that the measure has solely been introduced … to get rid of the electorate of its opponents, the measure will indubitably be disallowed. (*Imvo* 29 June 1887)

Jabavu went on to quote from an official dispatch on the 1853 Constitution Ordinance, in which the Governor of the Cape, Sir George Cathcart, had been informed by the imperial government that the Cape Legislative Assembly's amendments to the franchise qualifications (which would have made the franchise more restrictive), had been disallowed. The dispatch said that it would be 'exceedingly undesirable' so to restrict the franchise and added:

> It is the earnest desire of her Majesty's Government that all her subjects at the Cape, without distinction of class or colour, should be united by one common bond of loyalty and a common interest, and we believe that the exercise of political rights enjoyed by all alike will prove one of the best methods of attaining this object. (Quoted in *Imvo* 29 June 1887)

These were the 'Queen's own words': In the same editorial, Jabavu interpreted this dispatch as the medium by which '*our* Queen gave us *our* present freedom' (emphasis added). The case therefore seemed clear. In the instance referred to in the imperial dispatch to Cathcart, a restriction of the franchise was opposed by the imperial government on the basis of lofty rhetoric about the 'exercise of political rights by all alike' without 'distinction of class or colour'. In the

present case, Jabavu was opposing a measure which would result in just such a
restriction, since the disqualification of communal land tenure as a basis for
voting rights affected Africans only. *Imvo* was thus able, in its counter-
discourse against the Bill, to call upon precisely the legitimacy claims used by
the British government in the dispatch quoted above. Frequent examples can
be found of references by Jabavu to 'the fundamental principle in the British
Constitution that all subjects of the Queen are equal in the eye of the law'
(*Imvo* 4 May 1887). The question was, would the Queen agree?

The Bill was passed in July 1887, and *Imvo* led a campaign to organise a
deputation to the Queen, since the 'government over the blue waters', which
had created the franchise, was 'the proper tribunal to decide about its
withdrawal'. This was the 'only constitutional way ... of seeking redress' (*Imvo*
3 August 1887). The following week Jabavu said that it was greatly to be
doubted that 'Her Majesty the Queen would not see fit to pause before
granting the Royal assent, in her Jubilee Year too, to that which is an Act of
injustice, of oppression, of wrong' (*Imvo* 10 August 1887). *Imvo* also made it
plain that, in terms of British constitutional law, the Act could be rescinded
by the imperial parliament within two years (17 August 1887). In addition,
*Imvo* published the text of a petition, entitled 'The Petition of the South
African Natives to the Queen' (10 August 1887), which contained the appeal
that 'to deprive any class of your Majesty's subjects of the franchise is opposed
to those principles of Government under which all parts of your Majesty's
extended empire have progressed during [your] long and beneficent reign'.

By 28 September of the same year *Imvo* was able to report that the then
imperial Secretary of State (Sir Henry Holland) had 'informed the Natives
that Her Majesty's Government are prepared to receive their representations;
and on the strength of this information Native delegates from Herschel,
Queen's Town, Glen Grey, Tembuland, King William's Town, East London,
Fort Peddie, Fort Beaufort, Seymour, Cradock, Grahamstown and Port
Elizabeth are shortly to assemble in this town [Kingwilliamstown] to confer
about the best way of having the Native case represented to the Imperial
Government'. But already the signs were inauspicious, for in the same
editorial, Jabavu was compelled to report that the imperial Secretary of State
had 'signified ... an inability to disallow the Act'. *Imvo* wrote that 'we cannot
... persuade ourselves to believe that Sir Henry Holland has made up his mind
to recommend the Queen's assent to the Act' because the same Sir Henry
Holland had undertaken in the House of Commons to consider a report on
the Registration Act 'side by side with the representations of the Native

people ... and then, and not until then, would the Secretary of State decide the question of withholding the Royal Assent or otherwise'. The taint of duplicity was now getting uncomfortably close to the Queen herself. Jabavu continued:

> If, in the face of these facts, the information is correct, that the matter has been decided against the Natives, and before they had even stated their case, which they have been invited and encouraged to do, then, no terms will be too strong to condemn the duplicity and perfidy of the Colonial Minister. But we are charitable enough as to disbelieve the report.

A month earlier, *Imvo* had said, 'If the Natives were, under Her Majesty's Government, to be unjustly deprived of the rights of citizenship, let us have it deliberately from the lips of Her Majesty's Government' (10 August 1887). Now such an eventuality could be denied only by a 'charitable' act of disbelief. In his use of the word 'charitable', Jabavu was turning the weight of imperial language (the exercise of rights 'by all alike') against itself. Only the possible 'duplicity and perfidy' of the Queen's own minister stood between the Africans of the Cape and imperial betrayal.

On 12 October Jabavu wrote in a letter to the *Cape Times*, 'If ... the natives are shut out of the pale of British citizenship – then the confidence of our people in British justice will be rudely shaken, and the vaunted government of the people by the people will be shunned by the natives as a delusion and a snare' (in *Imvo* 12 October 1887). The organisation of a deputation to England was in progress when this appeal was stopped in its tracks by the Colonial Minister's emphatic statement in a letter to the Native Committee planning the protest that they should not waste their efforts: It was impossible to disallow the Act because the subject was 'one of purely local character'. The Crown's legal advisers disagreed with the African interpretation of the Act, but even if their interpretation was found to be correct, the imperial government would not be able to interfere (*Imvo* 30 November 1887). In his editorial in the same issue, Jabavu lamented:

> Hitherto it has been the cherished hope and consolation of the Natives that if their grievances could but reach the ear of one whom they lovingly and reverently term their Mother, the Queen, they would receive a sympathetic and patient hearing,

with the result that even-handed justice would be done
without fear, favour or prejudice ... We only lament that
through the fickleness of the Secretary of State in this business,
the *prestige* of Her Majesty will be damaged in the eyes of the
South African Natives. Henceforth, seeing that they cannot
hope to secure an impartial hearing of their complaints even
when they had been promised an audience by the Queen's
Government, their condition will be one of despair. For the
sake of the British name in this vast Continent of vast
possibilities, it is very much to be deplored that the affairs of
the Queen are not confided to men who would disdain to
pander to the prejudices of the crowd, but tread in the paths of
exalted statesmanship, which bring credit to a nation and to
their frequenters an undying fame.

By this point, despair would appear to have been the only reaction consistent
with the situation. Jabavu, 'the acknowledged leader of African voters in the
Cape' (Roux 1964:76; Saunders 1970:45), and with him a great number of
mission-educated Africans, had gone full circle, from Western education and
the promise of 'civilisation', to the very door of the imperial government.
There, armed with all the eloquence of the best missionary education, they
were turned away. They had learned to use the discourse of civility and been
forced to turn it against its bearers when circumstances seemed to indicate
that the 'justice' of British constitutionality – for which they had forsaken war
and weapons – somehow admitted inequality in the name of equality. Seizing
upon this space of difference in the colonial context, they sought to eliminate
the incongruity by returning to the source of 'civilisation', but there they met
with 'duplicity and perfidy' in one who directly represented their 'mother', the
Queen.

# V

The growing complexity of politics in the Cape Colony towards the end of the
nineteenth century made Jabavu's position increasingly difficult.[8] I do not
wish to attempt an analysis of the merits of the historical issues concerned
here. What is of interest from the point of view of this study is the fact that the
discursive invocation of British values as a legitimating strategy in resisting
*colonial* pressures to weaken the position of Africans, was riven by partisanship

in the field of South African politics in the 1890s. In the 1880s Jabavu was able to support Cape liberalism in the form of 'friends of the natives' such as J.W. Sauer, John X. Merriman and James Rose Innes. In these politicians Jabavu found the actual equivalent in Cape politics for ideals of British constitutionality. But this arrangement did not last. One result of the Jameson Raid of 1895 was that the liberal independents led by Rose Innes, Merriman and Sauer broke up. In the run-up to the election of 1898, Jabavu first supported Rose Innes, but then switched support to Merriman and Sauer, who were working closely with the Afrikaner Bond.

In the past, *Imvo* had been wary of the Bond. It was the Bond, and any other unconstitutional influence, against the Queen. But in 1898, after Jan Hofmeyr of the Bond had made a speech in which he professed that he was not an enemy of the African's political liberties, Jabavu gave his full support to the coalition between the Bond and Jabavu's 'friends of the natives'.

This stand cost Jabavu the support of many of his African followers. At the outbreak of the South African War of 1899-1902, *Imvo* surprised many readers by adopting a critical attitude towards Milner, Rhodes and members of what he termed the 'war party'. Meanwhile, *Izwi Labantu* had been set up in 1898 as a rival to *Imvo*. *Izwi* was backed by capital provided by Rhodes (Nasson 1991:35-36). This meant that African public figures in Cape newspapers which were independent of missionary influence began, for the first time, to argue amongst themselves for the moral right to the legitimation represented by the British Crown. Despite Jabavu's support for the Bond, one finds him saying, in an editorial of 1898, that Hofmeyr's 'native policy' is benevolent, in contrast to Rhodes's policy of 'equal rights for white men only', and that 'Mr Hofmeyr's is the *true British principle*' (*Imvo* 31 March 1898; emphasis added). *Izwi*, on the other hand, now vociferously proclaimed loyalty to 'the imperial factor' and could hardly contain its joy when *Imvo* was closed down under martial law in 1901. It cited *Imvo*'s 'pro-Boer policy', and wrote that 'Nemesis dogs the footsteps of those who violate the laws of truth'. It concluded: 'The first principle to justify the existence of any paper white or black, is loyalty to the Imperial factor' (*Izwi Labantu* 27 August 1901).

This rivalry demonstrates the insecurity of the African elite in the Cape, whose loyalty to the British Crown was based on the unreliable expectation of fair dealing in the *local* body politic. During the war an atmosphere of 'Boerophobia' prevailed (Nasson 1991:32), in which Boers were seen as treacherous villains, while the expectation was encouraged by imperial propaganda that the war was at least partly being fought to establish African

rights, similar to those in the Cape, in the rest of South Africa (Warwick
1983:111; Odendaal 1984a:30). Cape Africans feared that if the Boers
triumphed, Cape liberalism, 'already being undermined from within, would be
toppled from outside' (Nasson 1991:32). Jabavu was a lone dissenting voice.
Already considerably chastened by the Registration Act experience, he stated
that 'Natives in the Transvaal have no vote; nor is the war being waged,
intended to give them the vote' (*Imvo* 20 December 1899). Nasson writes that
in the end, it was Jabavu's sceptical attitude to imperial intentions which was
proved correct. The 1902 Peace Treaty pushed the issue of African
enfranchisement into the background, saying 'the question of granting the
franchise to Natives will not be decided until after the introduction of self-
government' (in Nasson 1991:39). Nasson concludes: 'It was this
discriminatory basis to the unification of settler South Africa which ensured
that the Cape petty-bourgeois [African] strata would emerge from the
reconstruction years somewhat chastened. They were to enter Union with the
threat of probable curbs upon their most prized "civilised" right, the franchise,
hanging over them' (p.39).

The question of the African's position had become subordinate to rivalry
between Boer and Briton. In this rivalry, jingoism and blind partisanship was
the order of the day. There was no place for the subtlety of Jabavu's considered
stance on the war, in which he denounced the 'sabre-rattling of the war party'
on the grounds of 'unfairness', while at the same time carefully emphasising
that as a subject of the Queen, he wished for the triumph of British arms
(Ngcongco 1970:7;11). Jabavu was repudiated by his own sponsors, R.W. Rose
Innes and James W. Weir, who withdrew their financial support of *Imvo* in
1899, and who said to Jabavu in a letter published in the *Cape Mercury*, 'It is
not a question of politics, or Government, or any government. It is a wider,
deeper and more important question – one of loyalty and fealty to the British
Crown and Queen, to whom you and your people owe so much' (22 December
1899, in Ngcongco 1970:12). This reaction by *Imvo*'s sponsors was caused by
an editorial which, in Jabavu's words, sought only to 'show what
complications war might bring about, whereas if a settlement without it had
been arrived at these might have been avoided'. In the same editorial, Jabavu
averred, 'a wish was expressed that there were but one Power in South Africa,
and that the British' (*Imvo* 9 January 1900). But this affirmation of loyalty was
disregarded, as was his article earlier, entitled 'Conscience in Journalism', in
which he argued that the 'Protean type which can be all things to all men ...
can without any qualms of conscience trim its sails to the popular breeze and

merrily glide along', which is no doubt what Jabavu felt A.K. Soga, editor of *Izwi Labantu*, was doing.

One of Jabavu's supporters in this crisis, a correspondent who styled himself 'A New Subscriber', wrote trenchantly that Jabavu had 'not conformed to the revised interpretation of the word "loyalty", i.e. abject surrender to Messrs Rhodes and Co., surrender of opinion and conscience' (*Imvo* 15 January 1900).

The new definition of loyalty, according to this reading – 'abject surrender' to the motives of imperial strategists on the ground – had never formed part of Jabavu's 'mimicry' strategy. He had always relied on the discrepancy between the imagined ideal of constitutionality in Britain and its colonial shadow, but now the crisis of war in South Africa in the name of the Queen had closed this space of difference. The Queen was at large in the country, waging war, and had to be supported at all costs. So, in a sense, Jabavu became a victim of his own strategy, for now *he* was being called to account for disloyalty to the ultimate cause of the British Crown. The possibility that this cause might have been corrupted was not allowed in the heat of the moment. As in the crisis engendered by the Registration Act, the removal of the gap between the colonial and the imperial manifestations of the Queen's rule proved to be a great disillusionment. The vaunted teleology of the Queen's rule – the firm expectation of a mother's compassion and justice – collapsed entirely.

Jabavu's desertion by his former financial supporters and the bitter opposition against him by *Izwi Labantu* – in both cases, in the name of loyalty to the Crown – suggest how unstable the correlation between African interests and the promise of British constitutionality was. Here, suddenly, the transcendental value of things British (the 'imperial factor') was transformed into jingoistic loyalty for doubtful acts of imperialism, while the later settlement of South African affairs in the South Africa Act of 1909 would reconcile white interests at the expense of Africans.

It was the colour bar in the Act of Union which once again drew together the rival African factions reflected by *Imvo* and *Izwi Labantu* (Odendaal 1983:258-60). A delegation including Jabavu went in vain to London to persuade the English authorities to disallow the preservation of racial prejudice in the constitution of a nascent South African union. But the interests of Africans had been subordinated to conciliation between white South Africans of different persuasion. After this, there would be one last appeal to the higher constitutional authority of Britain in the face of local oppression: the desperate appeal for redress in the face of the Natives' Land

Act of 1913, in which the basis was established for unequal relations with regard to land. In Keegan's description (1982:205), the Land Act allowed the state to 'lay down the conditions and delimit the battleground for the struggle between landlords and tenants'. In the appeal against the Act, another missionary-educated figure, Sol T. Plaatje, would play the most prominent role. However, Plaatje's tireless efforts, culminating in an extended stay in England and the publication of his book on the matter, *Native Life in South Africa* (1917), came to nothing in the short term (see Willan 1984).

It is clear, then, that the African progeny of missionary education in the age of high imperialism were able to internalise the language of civility and use it, in a kind of mimic counter-text, against the inconsistencies of its purveyors in the colonial context. But it is equally clear that their responses were constrained by the limits of this 'civil' discourse. The strategy identified in this chapter in which African public expression ostensibly showed respect for imperial values, but in fact confronted the colonial world with the supplementary incongruities of those values in the deferred South African context, depended on a stable presence of 'civilisation'. But there was no undoing the ambivalences of colonial identity. Thus the paradox that when Africans adopted missionary discourse and used it to fight for the equality implicit in the promise of 'civilisation', 'civilisation' itself proved to be the most ambivalent signifier of all.

# 5

## MISSIONARY HEROES AND THE MIRACULOUS CONVERSION OF AFRICA

### A Story in Books

Who will penetrate through Africa?

It is a goodly thing to see
    What heaven hath done for this delicious land!
    What fruits of fragrance blush on every tree!
    What goodly prospects o'er the hills expand!

Martyrs, all things for Christ's sake resigning,
Lead on the march of death serenely brave.
          – From J.J. Ellis
    *Life Story of David Livingstone (undated)*

The European missionary incursion into southern Africa in the eighteenth and nineteenth centuries occurred not only within various day-to-day narratives of legitimation, but also in the context of a developing canon of book-length accounts of missionary travels and adventures. These accounts, which began to proliferate at a steady rate in the nineteenth century, provided a British home readership with stories of the heroically expanding evangelical spirit, while consolidating an increasingly influential written corpus in which certain representations of southern Africa were being objectified. 'Accounts of missionary "labors and scenes" had by the late nineteenth century become an established European literary genre,' write the Comaroffs (1991:172). This was 'a literature of the imperial frontier, a colonizing discourse that titillated the

Western imagination with glimpses of radical otherness – over which it simultaneously extended intellectual control'. It was within this general corpus that a sub-genre arose, namely the 'rise' of the putative, generalised African subject from supposed degradation to salvation. In this chapter, I wish to look at this sub-genre as well as more general narratives in which missionary labour in southern Africa was celebrated in literary form. My discussion covers both the northern and the eastern frontiers, and should not be mistaken for an empirical account. My aim is to examine two important missionary book-narratives, Robert Moffat's *Missionary Labours and Scenes in Southern Africa* (1842), and David Livingstone's *Missionary Travels and Researches in South Africa* (1857), as outstanding examples of writing which helped to establish a strong legitimating context for missionary work in general, both in Britain and South Africa. I then move on to examine a sub-genre of this more general type of work, the rise of the African missionary subject in book-length narratives – in this case, the examples are taken from the Eastern Cape. My account deals with John A. Chalmers's biography of Tiyo Soga, *Tiyo Soga: A Page of South African Mission Work* (1877), as well as examples of Soga's own writing, recorded in Chalmers's work and in Williams (1983). Finally, I deal very briefly with Ntsikana as an example of narrative transformation in the account of his life by John Knox Bokwe, *Ntsikana: The Story of an African Convert* (1914). The focus of my discussion is therefore on formal properties of these narratives and not primarily on the history they embody. I have consequently allowed myself the flexibility of discussing them in order of publication rather than in terms of the exact geographical and chronological history to which their content relates. Evidence suggests that the works of Moffat and Livingstone were generally influential, exemplifying many of the standard textual strategies resorted to by missionaries when reconstituting the land and people of southern Africa. Separately or collectively, they appear to have set the tone for other, less conspicuously grand works such as those I examine later in the chapter.

# I

Robert Moffat's *Missionary Labours and Scenes in Southern Africa* (1842) emerged from the first wave of missionary activity which followed the early advances of Dr Johannes van der Kemp and the Reverend James Read snr. (Mostert 1992:454). Moffat's work is notable, since he was to become, in Mostert's description, 'one of the country's most celebrated missionaries' (p.454); only David Livingstone, Mostert writes, 'would stand higher in the pantheon of nineteenth-century African missionaries in Britain' (p.553). Moffat's book is formally structured in terms of the conventions of romance, despite his claim to being a mere recorder of facts. He establishes a mood appropriate to the individualistic, romantic quest when he introduces his story in language such as the following:

> Philosophy must eventually confess her impotence; the pride of Science be humbled; and the fact be universally acknowledged, that the Gospel of Christ is the only instrument which can civilize and save all kindred nations of the earth. This has been verified by the labours of Missionaries in South Africa, and we have only to publish it through the length and breadth of that great Continent, in order to elevate and cheer its degraded and sorrowing inhabitants, and introduce them to the fellowship of civilized Nations. (1842:ii)

In Moffat's text, the mission to achieve African salvation is granted the highest stature, more important than the strong claim of scientific enquiry and philosophical reflection. His reading of southern African people as 'degraded and sorrowing' owes much to the apprehension of the African world as *lacking* the spirit of industrious self-upliftment which was so strong in the early part of the nineteenth century in Britain as the Industrial Revolution transformed the human landscape (Mostert 1992:283-86). Moffat would continue to read the cultural manifestations of otherness, which he had no way of understanding, in terms of difference and lack. He was therefore engaging in a classic act of 'erasure', in which subjects are both constituted (textually objectified) and effaced (given meaning in terms of a misrecognition, and a transcoding, of difference) as they are reconfigured in language (see Spivak 1988b:11).

In order to do this, Moffat set the scene with a gesture which erased heterogeneity on a wider scale than the 'sorrowing' African continent alone. The missionary project had to be seen as universally legitimate so that its local encounters with otherness could be conceptually integrated in a readily understandable manner. Moffat's act of global erasure in the name of Christianity reads as follows:

> [The book] will further show that, amid circumstantial differences there is a radical identity in the operations of

human depravity, in Asia, in Polynesia, and in Africa; and that while the Gospel is the only, it is also the uniform remedy for the distress of a world convulsed by sin, and writhing with anguish. It will present striking examples of the complete subjugation of some of the fiercest spirits that ever trod the burning sands of Africa, or shed the blood of her sable offspring. (1842:v)

It remains remarkable to what extent observers such as Moffat, in their transcultural readings of otherness, recoded the diverse realities of Africans (and other non-Western people) into the cramping confines of a tragic literary stereotype. Africans were then necessarily 'convulsed by sin' and 'writhing with anguish' because they did not lead conventional Protestant lives. The demands of Moffat's salvation narrative were, however, self-serving: others were written into a discursively constituted/erased subjectivity so that the missionary protagonist could present *himself* as an unquestionable hero of civilisation. In Moffat's case, this heroism was a curious mix of self-aggrandisement and exotic fictionalising on the one hand, and self-abnegation, supported by postures of humility, on the other. One of Moffat's early rhetorical moves in his book, in almost identical style to many traveller-writers (see Paterson 1790:vii-viii), was to argue that his own status was that of an unassuming, humble soul who did no more than record what he witnessed on behalf of God:

> The Writer has indulged but slightly in philosophical disquisition, as he deemed it his province principally to supply facts. He leaves it with men of leisure and reflecting habits to analyze, compare, and deduce from those facts such doctrines as they supply ... He feels confident that lettered men will look into the pages of an African Evangelist for things far more substantial and important than the graces of composition – an accomplishment which the Author much admires, but to which he makes no pretension. He makes his present appearance before the British public less in the capacity of an Author than of a Witness, who most earnestly desires to establish and to enforce the claims of perishing, and helpless, and all but friendless millions, for whom he has hitherto lived and laboured – whom he ardently loves, and with whom – all

black, barbarous, and benighted as they are – he hopes to live,
labour, and die! (pp.v-vi)

This passage displays a conventional rhetorical manoeuvre by which travel
writers sought to escape the charge of literary embellishment and self-interest.
By appealing to the status of an impartial 'witness', and by removing himself
from the domain of speculation, Moffat sought the legitimacy of truth beyond
discursivity. He implied that others, with more leisure – those who did not
work as hard as Moffat in the arduous mission fields – were freer than him to
indulge in analysis, comparison and deduction. This may have appealed to the
work ethic of the middle classes where the evangelical spirit was strong, but
while presenting himself in the chaste role of 'Witness', Moffat also concocted
an eminently *literary* form: the romantic-heroic quest. In this quest, he would
be the protagonist, among 'perishing, helpless, friendless millions', whom he
loved despite their 'black and barbarous' status, and wished to save, even if this
meant to 'live, labour, and die!' for them. The triumphal conclusion to this
passage is neatly in keeping with the formal characteristics of a romantic
hero's delivery (after a descent into a dangerous secular underworld) in
Northrop Frye's theory of the romance-archetype as 'secular scripture' (Frye
1976). There is, in Moffat's book, also evidence of the narrative imperatives of
comedy in the formal sense of resolution and reconciliation of conflicting
parties and values.

Frye (1976) notes in his discussion of romance archetypes that the themes
of romance and comedy often converge. Comic narratives present themes of
*social* resolution in which pragmatic common sense or goodwill prevail. Such
social resolution is a strong trope in most missionary narratives, but in Moffat's
case the *individual* heroism of the missionary is emphasised in a way that tends
strongly towards the romance form, in which a 'higher state of individual
identity' is achieved (p.149). The comedic emphasis on *social* resolution in
Moffat's text is therefore less prominent than the romantic tendency to depict
the ascending and descending fortunes of the missionary as an individual hero.
Romance, Frye writes (1976:53), frequently reveals a mental landscape in
which heroes and villains 'exist primarily to symbolize a contrast between two
worlds, one above the level of ordinary experience, the other below it'. The
upper world is idyllic, while the lower world, associated with exciting
adventures involving separation, loneliness, humiliation and pain, is a
'demonic or night world'. In romance, the 'narrative movement keeps rising
into wish fulfilment or sinking into anxiety or nightmare' (p.53).

Moffat's text clearly utilises the vertical movements of ascent and descent (Frye 1976:129) typical of romance narratives. His claim to be providing 'things far more substantial and important than the graces of composition' is, in view of the formal properties of his narrative, itself an act of literary subtlety and cannot be taken at face value. It is instructive to note the view of Moffat expressed by the early missionary James Read snr. (see Saunders 1977), whom Moffat repudiated after the scandal of Read's adultery with a Khoikhoi woman in Bethelsdorp (Mostert 1992:439-41).[1] Read, a missionary in the early mould who believed in equality between African and European, and who was reportedly loved and revered by the Khoikhoi, had this to say about the self-appointed romantic hero Moffat: '[He] will ... do all the mischief he can. He will be setting up himself and trying to cast others down ... with all his malignity ... with all that pompous ambition, with an authoritarian tone and tone of superiority ... An ambitious, arbitrary, self-important, narrow-minded man is the most detestable of all men' (in Mostert 1992:553).

In Moffat's own literary presentation of himself, however, he is a humble but daring missionary who transforms the difficulties of living in a barely-domesticated southern Africa into pleasing narrative form. This form incorporates the ubiquitous Manichean conceptual prefiguration of reality ('... sunk into the lowest depths of ignorance, superstition, disorganization, and debasement' (1842:2)) and relies upon the customary polarities of a nineteenth-century linguistic constitution of mission. Written into a narrative in the romantic style, these dichotomies are re-cast as the ascending or descending fortunes of the missionary:

> It has been refreshing to recount the mercies of the God whom he serves, which have been abundantly vouchsafed to him and his household in distant climes, and amid savage men ... Of time, however, he has often been reminded that, as much is gone, little remains; while even that little trembles in the balance of an awful uncertainty. Of those who began at the same period with himself the career of missionary toil, the greater number have sunk into the grave. (pp.vi-vii)

It is striking that Moffat *figures* himself as a divine emissary, facing his antagonists, 'savage men', whom he must win over to God, and among whom he must survive to tell the tale. In the above passage the comedic imperative to reconcile Africans to a social good in line with the will of God is markedly subdued in favour of the emphasis on personal danger within a story of descent into a dangerous underworld. The 'awful uncertainty' of success in the secular version of Hades is marked by extreme personal danger (the heroic-romantic quest) and, for those who cannot survive the perils of the journey, death.

Moffat's rambling and overwritten narrative is held together precisely by the structural coherence of the romantically conceived quest/journey. It is in the familiarity of such a form that Moffat's otherwise uncomprehending home readers could digest culturally unfamiliar African phenomena. British readers would have recognised the (entertaining) literary form of a quest, and within this known convention of storytelling southern Africa could be domesticated by textual, representational means. Moffat's need to sustain the conventions of adventure is apparent early in his book. The excitement of the journey and the danger of the quest figure strongly, and yarns about wild animals – along with their natural companions in the missionary view, wild barbarians – met Moffat's requirements perfectly. A good example is Moffat's retelling of the story in which the pioneer missionary Johannes van der Kemp survives the dangers of an untamed southern Africa:

> Vanderkemp, who was a native of Holland, seemed, from his experience, natural firmness of character, and distinguished talents, prepared for the Herculean task, at once to force his way into the headquarters of the enemy, and raise the standard of the cross amidst a dense population of barbarians [in this case, the Xhosa], the most powerful, warlike, and independent of all the tribes within or without the boundaries of the Cape Colony ... The party arrived at Graaff Reinet [from Cape Town] on June 29, after having, with their attendants and cattle, experienced many narrow escapes from lions, panthers, and other wild beasts, as well as from Bushmen and Hottentots, of character still more ferocious. (p.23)

Later accounts of missionary history, such as that of Shepherd (1940:11-12), would take a severe view of Van der Kemp for marrying a slave girl of seventeen and dispensing with 'civilised' dress, but for the purposes of Moffat's story Van der Kemp had to be firm in character to face his 'Herculean' confrontation with 'barbarians'.[2] As for the 'ferocity' of 'Bushmen' (San) and 'Hottentots' (Khoikhoi), more recent accounts suggest that these hunter-pastoralists were the mildest of people until they became the objects of European derision and were hunted down, killed in large numbers and reduced to the status of despised vagrants (Mostert 1992:22-39; Elphick 1977:217-39; Comaroff & Comaroff 1991:96). Nevertheless, Moffat's narrative required Van der Kemp to be cast in the role of the intrepid adventurer on a mission to survive the barbarian secular underworld – fraught with physical dangers from demonic denizens such as 'panthers' and Bushmen – and to rescue the barbarians for salvation. Travellers in the Cape in the eighteenth and nineteenth centuries did indeed appear to have met with wild animals, including elephant and lion (Mostert 1992:599-601), but Moffat's exotic coupling of 'panthers'[3] and human denizens 'of character still more ferocious' suggests his need to create an imaginatively resonant setting of danger for his story.

Missionary literature reveals other figurative variations of the environment in which evangelical work is typically described. A prominent example is the view of an African 'wilderness' (Comaroff & Comaroff 1991:172-78; Bosch 1991:300) in which seeds of industry and salvation are 'planted'. For the purposes of romance narratives, however, this wilderness was enhanced by the presence of sinister adversaries to make it a worthy challenge for a literary hero. Moffat quotes the description of another missionary writer, the Reverend Stephen Kay (1833), whose striking imagery is perfectly suitable for an evocation of risk and extremity: 'The mission stations in Kaffraria literally constitute folds, surrounded by evil spirits, as well as by beasts of prey; and all that rally round our standard are like so many sheep gathered together out of the wilderness' (in Moffat 1842:31).

In his own summing up of Van der Kemp's work in the Cape, Moffat summoned the idea of a thankless wilderness in a crescendo of adulatory praise for the work of God's emissaries in these 'dark folds':

> [Van der Kemp] came from a university to stoop to teach the alphabet to the poor naked Hottentot and Kaffir – from the society of nobles, to associate with beings of the lowest grade in the scale of humanity – from stately mansions, to the filthy hovel of the greasy African – from the army, to instruct the fierce savage the tactics of a heavenly warfare under the banner of the Prince of Peace – from the study of physic, to become the guide to the balm in Gilead, and the physician there – and, finally, from a life of earthly honour and ease, to be exposed to

the perils of waters, of robbers, of his own countrymen, of the heathen, in the city, in the wilderness. (pp.30-31)

Moffat's rhetorically striking antitheses in this passage rely on the conception of a sacrificial journey by the missionary from a state of ease (civil life) to the dangers and hardships of missionary work. Although Reformed theology certainly prescribed suffering as a necessary element of service to a Christian God,[4] the professed self-sacrifice, hardship and humility in the above passage are belied by the tacit literary *emplotment* of the material as exhilarating adventure. Moffat's self-congratulatory *celebration* of missionary hardship, evident in his use of romance conventions, should be read as qualifying the tradition of earthly sacrifice, which he was also calling upon in his description.

It is very probable that missionaries did suffer great physical hardship in the extremes of African weather conditions. Moffat's own account of his travels with an Oorlam Khoikhoi chief, Jager Afrikaner, in search of more hospitable land, suggests physical hardships of a severe degree. But it is the literary transformation of such hardship into narratives reinforcing what Grove (1989:180) calls 'an evangelical environmental moral economy' which is of more interest here. Before describing his own adventures as a missionary in the north-western Cape ('Transorangia' in the early nineteenth century), Moffat (1842:65-66) stated his desire to 'sketch the character of the country, and the circumstances connected with the early efforts of these men of God, to sow the seeds of the everlasting Gospel in a most ungenial soil'. In his sketch, Moffat envisioned the land as barren, heavily imbued with the consequence of sin, and peopled by immoral barbarians, in contrast to the implied ideal of a paradisaical, fenced garden of Protestant industry and virtuous cultivation. As Jean Comaroff (1985:138) has noted, 'agrarian metaphors came to pervade the evangelists' vision of a Christianised Africa'. The Comaroffs (1991:175) argue that the act of telling itself transformed the landscape in works such as Moffat's: 'The eye searched in vain for recognizable margins and limits. In this void it was the very act of narration that imposed an order of space and time, making the metaphorical leap from these formless wastes to known cultural referents.' Such 'known cultural referents' were based on the idea of discovering a new Eden in the African wastelands based on 'the mythic rural domain as a model of the British past' which was to become 'a model for the African future' (p.75). Before Eden could be established, however, Moffat would narrate the land from the viewpoint of a rigorous moral economy which equated drought with retribution:

As an inhabited country, it is scarcely possible to conceive of
one more destitute and miserable; and it is impossible to
traverse its extensive plains, its rugged, undulating surface, and
to descend to the beds of its waterless rivers, without viewing it
as emphatically a 'land of droughts,' bearing the heavy curse of

> 'Man's first disobedience, and the fruit
> Of that forbidden tree, whose mortal taste
> Brought death into the world, and all our woe.'

(p.66)

For Moffat, therefore, the land itself carried the heavy curse of sin. Moffat
'read' the land and rewrote it into a narrative in which he was the central,
determining protagonist/narrator. The land provided a setting, within an
archetypal romance narrative, for heroic endeavour in a secular version of the
underworld. Not only was the land blighted by sin, but the hero himself
suffered severe doubt. Typical of the protagonist in a romance-quest, Moffat as
prototype missionary-hero in a perilous land resolved his doubts by recourse to
the superior art of his own culture:

I was young, had entered into a new and responsible situation,
and one surrounded with difficulties of no ordinary character.
Already I began to discover some indications of an
approaching storm, which might try my faith. The future
looked dark and portentous in reference to the mission ... Here
I was, left alone with a people suspicious in the extreme;
jealous of their rights, which they had obtained at the point of
the sword ... I had no friend and brother with whom I could
participate in the communion of saints, none to whom I could
look for counsel or advice. A barren and miserable country; a
small salary ... No grain, and consequently no bread, and no
prospect of getting any, from the want of water to cultivate the
ground; and destitute of the means of sending to the colony.
These circumstances led to great searchings of the heart, to see
if I had hitherto aimed at doing and suffering the will of Him in
whose service I was embarked. Satisfied that I had not run
unsent, and having in the intricate, and sometimes obscure
course I had come, heard the still small voice saying, 'This is

the way, walk ye in it,' I was wont to pour out my soul among the granite rocks surrounding this station, now in sorrow, and then in joy; and more than once I took my violin ... and reclining upon one of the huge masses, have, in the stillness of the evening, played and sung the well known hymn, a favourite of my mother's,

> 'Awake, my soul, in joyful lays,
> To sing the great Redeemer's praise,' &c.

(pp.105-108)

Reading against the grain, one imagines an overdressed, sunstruck missionary in the 1820s among people who could only have seen Moffat as a curious, marginal spectacle. Perhaps they did not realise the consequences of his strange colloquys with himself or his equally incomprehensible habit of playing a fiddle in an African semi-desert. But these strange habits were part of a narrative in which *they* would be given very specific roles to play. By the time Moffat had returned to London in the late 1830s to compose his book and transform his Transorangia forays into a story, very similar stories were being enacted in more contexts, by an increasing number of missionary protagonists, and they were being reinforced by the consolidation of a colonial order in southern Africa. Moffat's otherwise mediocre fusion of biography and romance would, therefore, resonate in a context of Victorian expansion and growing self-confidence. Moffat was not the only person to 'read' the country and rewrite it into a quest in which the missionary was a hero of a supposedly benign Christian dispensation. This act of reading was widespread: among a home readership in Britain, and feeding back from Britain into southern Africa, where ever more evangelists would perform similar acts of reading and rewriting. The colonial script was diverse and contradictory – hence the battle between missionaries, local authorities at the Cape and settlers – but their contests concerned how best to inscribe the project of Westernisation, not the project itself. Moffat's book served as an important self-consolidating (and self-legitimating) proto-text in which 'race relations' were given a definite narrative configuration. The roles of missionary and convert, and the identities of each, were embodied in the powerful new medium of the book, which was perhaps the single most transformative change encountered by people who had emerged from oral cultures. As suggested in Chapter 3, the changes related to literacy were central to major structural changes in power relations in the emerging colonial society.

As suggested, Moffat's depiction of himself as an emblematic individual besieged by doubt and fear, and surrounded by physical and spiritual barrenness, is belied by the context in which his 'anti-conquest' story was told. In Pratt's formulation (1992:7), 'anti-conquest' refers to the 'strategies of representation whereby European bourgeois subjects seek to secure their innocence in the same moment as they assert European hegemony'. The writer of anti-conquest is described by Pratt as the 'seeing-man': 'He whose imperial eyes look out passively and possess' (p.7). Pratt's category refers more specifically in her work to writers of travelogues such as John Barrow who 'secure their innocence' by indulging in no more than the writing of 'natural history'. In Pratt's argument, such writers in fact 'provided means for narrating inland travel and exploration aimed not at the discovery of trade routes, but at territorial surveillance, appropriation of resources, and administrative control'; travel writing 'code[s] the imperial frontier' in particular ways (p.39). Moffat's possessing eyes, transcoding their observations into missionary-romance narrative, also served the dual purpose of representing innocent exploration (Moffat as hero-victim in the desert is the farthest thing from a conqueror) which was yet integral to imperialistic modes of cognition and narrativisation. More to the point, 'anti-conquest' narratives such as Moffat's helped to regulate perceptions of social order and legitimate the conquest of physical resources under the banner of 'civilisation'.

In Moffat's book, the roles assigned to the underworld antagonists of the missionary-hero are conspicuously formulaic. The Oorlam chief Jager Afrikaner, whom Moffat earlier described as a 'notable robber' and the 'terror of the country' (p.72), undergoes what is presented as a swift and miraculous conversion. Peril and privation are swiftly succeeded by Divine success. Titus, another member of the Afrikaner family, similarly changes swiftly from being a 'terror' and a 'fearful example of ungodliness' to a 'steady and unwavering friend' who 'at last entered the house of God' (p.110). But Moffat did not stop here. If his descriptions reduced the African subjects in his story to sentimental caricatures, he also unwittingly depicted himself in terms of the flimsiest melodrama. Like so many African adventurers on celluloid who were to follow Moffat in the twentieth century, he develops a 'bilious fever' which induces the customary delirium (p.113). Now his erstwhile antagonists, the former heathens, sit before his couch, 'gazing on me with eyes full of sympathy and tenderness'. The chief asks Moffat, 'with a big tear standing in his eye, if I were to die, how they were to bury me'. But Moffat recovers, as a romance hero must, and he is 'speedily restored' to his post (p.113).

This set piece of romantic narration is concluded by the contrasting motifs of drought and rain, with all the binary associations of sin and blessing, crisis and resolution. In all this, it is the agency of the missionary as hero which makes possible the salvation of a world he also created by his act of narration:

> The drought was excessive; the people were distressed at the idea of being compelled to leave the station in search of grass. Special prayer meetings were held to implore the blessing of rain. Prayer was soon answered, and the heavens, which had been as brass, were covered with clouds, and thunders rolled, and rain fell like a torrent. The display of Divine condescension produced a powerful effect on the minds of the people, and many were the eyes that wept tears of gratitude ... [Kobus, a convert] asked [his wife, an unbeliever] how she could be afraid of a God so kind, and who could send down the rain of his grace, with equal abundance, on dry and parched souls; and, falling on his knees, he adored God for the blessings of salvation. (pp.114-15)

In 'anti-conquest', Pratt (1992:60) writes, the world 'presents itself' to visitors. Similarly, Divine Grace in the form of rain is a powerful manifestation which is incontrovertible and beyond the control of earthly individuals. In this way, Moffat inscribed a very ordinary rainstorm in the north-western Cape with the import of Divine resolution, just as he melodramatically reconfigured his own presence there as a Christian romance quest. Moffat went further, however: he implicitly suggested a parallel between his own position and that of St Paul, one of the great protagonists of Christian heroism. After an account of a dire journey with Jager Afrikaner and his people in search of better land, in the course of which yarns about lion and other wild animals reinforce the implicit heroism of an otherwise unremarkable story, Moffat made the following comment:

> In my experience, I often found it not only profitable but animating, to read the sufferings of the messengers of the cross in past ages; *to which ours of the present bear no comparison*; and especially to the great Apostle of the Gentiles, and his

coadjutors, who became 'all things to all men, as the ministers
of God, in much patience, in afflictions, in necessities, in
distresses, in stripes, in imprisonments, in tumults, in labours,
in watchings, in fastings,' 2 Cor. vi 4,5. (p.143, emphasis
added).

Moffat's immediate denial of any 'comparison' between his own story and that
of St Paul, suggests that he at least depended on such a comparison being
formed by his readers. His disclaimer, too, sounds merely rhetorical in the
presence of the evocative comparison he establishes. Modern works of history,
which relate the story of missionary labour on the northern frontier with a
much greater awareness of conflicting perceptions, and without Christian
partisanship, tend to undermine the idea of Moffat's singular, apostle-like
status (see Comaroff & Comaroff 1991; Du Bruyn 1980:127-76; Legassick
1969). Du Bruyn recalls Moffat's view of himself as a Christian warrior 'on a
warfare which requires all prayer and supplication, to keep his armour bright
... to wrestle and struggle, and toil, in pulling down the strongholds of Satan'
(Moffat 1842:255). However, Du Bruyn's analysis suggests how contingent
Moffat's 'success' was on his practical usefulness to the Tswana among whom
his main work was done. Various external factors, mainly the upheaval caused
by the Mfecane, as well as raids by groups such as the so-called 'Bergenaars',
and the need for guns and liaison with other parties with whom the
missionaries had contact, rendered Moffat useful to the Tswana, although at
one point he was deserted by many of the people among whom he was living
because they realised he could not protect them against attackers (Du Bruyn
1980:167; 171). Du Bruyn describes Moffat as 'one of the most unsuccessful
missionaries to work among the Tlhaping [a clan of Tswana-speaking people]'
(p.171). Although Moffat did become influential and established a famous
mission station at Kuruman, it appears to have been on the basis of diverse and
contradictory factors far removed from the linear causality of the heroic quest
which, in Moffat's book, culminates in the triumphal statement, near the end
of his narrative, that 'the moral wilderness was now about to bloom' (p.496).
The individual agency of the missionary seems to have been far outweighed by
the large-scale social upheaval characteristic of the period. According to Du
Bruyn (1980:171), Moffat's station eventually became a site of protection for
outcasts of different origins. Contra his narrative of individualistic success on
behalf of Christ, Moffat's mission seems to have gained importance because of
external factors, in whose context the station acquired a significance to people

primarily for reasons of political expedience. Even Moffat's sympathetic biographer, Cecil Northcott (1961), reports that the Tlhaping, among whom Moffat had worked for many years, failed to move with him when he established a station at Kuruman. Instead, he was left to 'build a following from variegated groups of Bechuana' (Northcott 1961:111).

## II

The story of Robert and Mary Moffat is particularly striking also because, despite the evident discontinuities at many points between professional historical accounts on the one hand, and Moffat's own narrative (as well as the many derivatives of Moffat's story in the popular sub-literature about him), the Moffats created a mythology about themselves which seems to have served partly as a denial of unwelcome reality. In their story, one begins to perceive a surprising new aspect of missionary discourse: its function as a source of sustaining, legitimating and validating self-delusion for missionaries in circumstances of extreme adversity which would otherwise be too much to bear. Failure and futility in the scorching heat of the northern Cape became narrativised as heroic endurance and unfailing perseverance once recoded into romance forms. It seems that this recoding was no mere act of calculated embellishment, but an imperative borne of the need to survive. The missionaries therefore constructed their *own* identities within the very constraining limits of narrowly defined role models: they were always to be crusading, virtuous standard bearers of Protestant industriousness and practical godliness in a semi-desert where their efforts were frequently met with derision (Northcott 1961:76;117). They were always to be the antithesis of the 'heathen' African. However, just as African missionary subjects at Lovedale existed in an agonistic relation to the identities prescribed for them by the metanarrative of civilisation, so one detects in the narratives of the Moffats some revealing indications of what they most sought to silence and deny: their own Africanisation.

Mary Moffat betrayed such inevitable Africanisation in private letters in which she nervously explained her own adoption of certain domestic habits which usually fell under the category of the 'obscene' or 'heathen' in the official missionary view. In one letter, she explained her liking for Bechuana milk. Her description of how the milk was made betrays a repressed awareness of her own possible irregularity:

They get a goat-skin and scrape the hair clean off, *so that you could not tell that it had been hairy.* Then they turn the outer side in, sew it up into a bag with a narrow neck like a bottle. At the bottom they have a very small peg stuck in, a thick peg at the top which closes the mouth of the sack. Into this sack of goat's skin they pour their milk as it comes from the cow … It is hung in a pretty warm place … The milk … comes to the table wet, but not swashy. This when served up looks like a dish of light curds. The milk here being very rich it has quite a yellow appearance. It is rather sour, and with a little sugar and new milk it is quite delightful. I did not fancy it at first, but probably it was on account of its being brought in their dirty vessels. *I have got over that now* and eat it with relish. (In Northcott 1961:82-83; emphasis added)

Mary Moffat's squeamishness is evident in the delicacy of her descriptions, which counterbalance her distaste (goat-skin which was once *hairy*, the *yellow* appearance and the *sour* taste of the milk, *dirty* vessels) with mitigating factors (hair removed, looks like a dish of light curds, the addition of sugar and new milk). What she was struggling to camouflage in the above passage is no less than cultural 'conversion' in the wrong direction. Her embarrassment is plainly evident, even in the safety of a private letter. In the same letter, she confessed to what would widely have been regarded in official missionary positions as a 'descent' into heathen domestic practice: the use of cow dung on her floors. This was a practice originating from the very heart of cattle-rearing African cultures, given the benign associations of cow dung, but one which would normally have been regarded as anathema along with round dwellings, red clay and other 'filthy obscenities' of supposedly degraded living.[5] In the safety of her private correspondence about the use of cow dung, however, Mary Moffat provided a glimpse of what must have been an even larger but repressed dimension of the ironic Africanisation of the Moffats in the heathen wilderness:

We smear all our rooms with cow dung once a week at least. At first when I saw Sister Helm do it I thought to myself, 'But I'll do without that dirty trick, or I will try hard.' However I had not been here long but was glad to have it done, and I have hardly patience to wait till Saturday. It lays the dust better than anything, kills the fleas which would otherwise breed abundantly, *and is a fine clear green*. It is mixed with water, and laid on as thinly as possible. *I now look upon my floor smeared with cow-dung with as much complacency as I used to do upon our best rooms when well scoured*. (Northcott 1961:83; emphasis added)

Moffat's stated ambivalence about cow dung floors ('dirty trick') is magically overcome by recasting the green of putrefaction into a green of aesthetic beauty ('a fine clear green'), although her eagerness to emphasise this transformation, aided by the hurried addition of water dilution and minimal application ('laid on as thinly as possible'), betray self-consciousness and ambivalence. Such 'Africanisation' would have been partial and shot through with contradiction, just as the Westernisation of Africans was never quite as complete as missionaries would have liked (one should note, however, that the pressure to Westernise was far stronger). Robert Moffat dressed himself in veld-going, home-made leather trousers and jacket (Northcott 1961:116). At one point in his travels, Moffat relinquished his trousers to an African to use as a master design for general duplication (Northcott 1961:119), suggesting the two-way trade in cultural influence and interdependence (see Comaroff & Comaroff 1991:171).

Such is the suggestion of an uneven influence and counter-influence in missionary texts when read against the grain. Moments of absurdity and futility are sometimes evident despite the delusionary imperative of the quest narrative. A moment of comical vulnerability is discernible in Northcott's account when Moffat deliberately enters a linguistic wilderness by spending eight weeks alone in the veld in order to learn Sechuana:

> [Moffat] halted his wagon on the open veld at Tswaing ... some ninety miles northwest of Vryburg, and there started his eight weeks of listening, talking, and writing; while the flies pestered him, drank the very ink from his pen, and the 'genteel beggars' swarmed around, demanding tobacco and beads. From the wagon he made 'crooked speeches' and got riotously laughed at, and grew disheartened at the few words he really knew in Sechuana and the many hundreds that circulated amongst the chattering people and eluded him. (p.117)

The image of Moffat in this account is far removed from the heroic quester in conditions of dire adversity. On the contrary, his position is plainly absurd. But in Moffat's own narrative and in some of the popular recirculations of his story, this period is refashioned as a prelude of suffering in the wilderness before the onset of a breakthrough to the heart of the heathen (for example Deane, *Robert Moffat the Missionary Hero of Kuruman*, no date:79-83; Anon., *Rivers of Water in a Dry Place*, 1892:113-19). Viewed dispassionately, however, Moffat is almost touchingly ludicrous, his 'crooked speeches' hinting at a reciprocal learning process and a kind of enforced humility otherwise lacking in the official missionary attitude.

Moffat's sojourn in the wilderness of linguistic incomprehension is reported to have occurred in 1827. Eleven years later, he set off triumphantly to Britain, carrying with him his own translation of the New Testament in Sechuana. He remained in Britain for a period of almost four years (1839-43), during which he met another great missionary hero, David Livingstone, who would later become Moffat's son-in-law and transcend him in fame as a missionary-explorer. Whatever Moffat did or did not achieve in South Africa, during his stay in Britain his African experiences were irresistibly transformed into the tropes of heroic enterprise which his audience implicitly demanded. Northcott (1961:169) observes that 'Moffat now stepped into the glow of Britain's evangelical life as a master-man, an authentic pioneer from beyond the bounds of civilization, and therefore a symbol of the whole enterprise of missions, then moving into the jubilee period of its beginnings'. Despite his claim to being no more than a mortal witness, Moffat made speeches in which he relished the opportunity to transform his ambiguous experiences in the northern Cape into melodrama. 'I admit I have suffered in Africa,' he declares, 'I have hungered in Africa; I have experienced extreme thirst in Africa; I have been in perils … among savage beasts; in peril among men more savage than beasts' (in Northcott 1961:169). Moffat's reception in Britain was triumphant:

> Wherever he went Moffat represented exciting prospects of new adventures, the mystery of the unknown, and an association with danger and personal bravery. He stood in the pulpits and on the platforms of mid-nineteenth century Britain as the symbol of the unattainable for many thousands of hearers whose restricted lives were lifted into realms of wonder by his presence and speeches. For the factory-bound workers of

the industrial north who crowded to hear him in their chapels, he was a prince of Christian pioneers, a field-marshal in the army of the Lord, doing battle on their behalf against the forces of darkness in Africa ... (p.172)

The force of such delusion, based on literary archetypes which are demonstrably discontinuous with the analyses of events by modern professional historians, had sustained and would continue to motivate Moffat in his missionary work in southern Africa. This should not be surprising in view of the large public consensus in Britain of which Moffat was a part and which in a sense left him with little choice but to interpret his experiences as he did. Moffat's famous *Missionary Labours and Scenes in Southern Africa* was written and published during his stay in Britain between 1839 and 1843, providing him with a 'fresh wave of fame' and selling 'in thousands' (Northcott 1961:170). This fame has endured to the present day as Moffat's story has been bowdlerised, condensed, rewritten and further fictionalised in popular books, often written for child readership.

I have examined a sample collection of these works. They range in date from accounts in the *Cape Monthly Magazine* in 1870 to an ecumenical booklet published in Johannesburg in 1983 entitled *Roll On, Wagon Wheels*, written by Hugh F. Frame and first published in 1944. The 1983 republication, to commemorate the centenary of Moffat's death, indicates how pervasive and enduring literary tropes about the civilised and the savage are, and that they remain in currency even in the supposedly postmodern era of refined scepticism about master narratives in general. Frame's highly condensed story (21 pages) draws on the fact that Moffat was apprenticed as a gardener at the age of fourteen and that he was inured to virtuous toil at an early age. It portrays the 'natives' as naïve brutes who speak a curious pidgin-English and who are swiftly subsumed into the logic of the conversion narrative. Moffat's work among the Bechuana achieves success in the same measure as his gardens at Kuruman begin to yield abundant crops and his printing press rolls off Christian literature. Other popular publications, notably *Rivers of Water in a Dry Place* (1892), draw strongly on the convergence of physical characteristics (Moffat being a gardener, his struggles in an arid environment) and their irresistible metaphoric parallels (the benediction of God's water in the African desert-wilderness, and so on).

In the more professional accounts, it is notable that Moffat's life is structured on a series of travels: from Britain to South Africa, the Cape to

Transorangia, Jager Afrikaner's village to other regions in search of a better area for habitation, back to the Cape to show Afrikaner off, to the Bechuana to set up a mission, and later further north to Mzilikazi and onwards in search of ever new missionary pastures. The northward thrust was taken further by David Livingstone, who also seized on the potential to recode physical journeys as heroic pilgrimages of the soul. In this regard, the Comaroffs (1991:173) observe that such stylized narratives of overland travels 'reveal an important dimension of the evangelical enterprise: a pervasive belief in the author's passage itself as emblematic and hence as worthy of record'. The missionary journey was 'an odyssey of sacred and imaginative incorporation, bringing the "regions beyond" under European gaze', and re-enacting, in spirit at least, *The Pilgrim's Progress*. Through it, 'the ideal of Christian transcendence became a model for imperial conquest. From the vantage of their oxwagons, the missionaries constructed a pristine vista, extending the horizons of their European audience – and, with them, the conceptual frontiers of empire'.

A dispassionate view of Moffat's life story as journey indicates a rich complexity of political, moral and philosophical factors which would confound any single narrative trope, but in the sub-literature on Moffat this inviting correspondence between the journey in reality and the journey in romantic reconception is exploited fully. Some journeys are selected for their narrative potential, while others are conflated to serve the needs of the particular story line. The convergence between environmental reality and metaphor in Moffat's experience is amply demonstrated in Northcott's account of how Moffat developed the Kuruman station. Moffat had become aware of the Kuruman 'fountain' in the area of his Bechuana mission, his gardener's eye cherishing the value of such an oasis in the desert. Here was both metaphorical and physical relief after long years of largely unsuccessful attempts to convert the Bechuana (Northcott 1961:69-110; Du Bruyn 1980:127-76). Northcott writes:

> The miracle of everlasting water in a dry land drove Moffat to the new site. It was close to the 'Eye of Kuruman', the fountain which still gushes out its five million gallons a day from a dolomite cave … the gardener's eye of Robert planned a series of conduits and canals to irrigate the sandy soil. This, 'one of the finest fountains in South Africa', was too good to be missed, a conviction that Robert pursued all during these

troubled years on the veld. Here by the waters of Kuruman he felt he could practise his working philosophy of 'Bible and plough' and dig himself into the soil of Africa as well as save the souls of the Bechuana. Here he could offer some evidence of the 'superior civilization' he was fond of talking about, and go a long way to convince the feckless Batlhaping that the way of the *moochan* (the white man) was worth following. But it was all dependent on water ... (p.110)

In Northcott's account, Moffat struggled for nearly ten years to make Kuruman a secure place and 'to provide it with the symbols of civilization from a white cloth on the table to grapes ripening in the garden' (p.111). While his success in imposing his own physical-metaphorical oasis of civilisation upon the environment is remarkable, he failed to draw his intended subjects into the mission in large numbers. This suggests that missionary work had to draw on the self-created fictions of its textual teleology as much as on the fortuitous circumstance of water. According to Northcott, circumstances ultimately played against Moffat's desire to convert Africans *en masse*: Moffat succeeded in providing Kuruman with the symbols of civilisation, as the steady train of visitors for the next forty years acknowledged, but he was not able to foresee that the tide of southern African life would sweep past his beloved Kuruman, veering to the east rather than to the west. The Batlhaping failed to rally in strength to the new station, leaving Moffat to build a following from scattered groups of Bechuana people (Northcott 1961:111).

In Moffat's own narrative, however, there is only the linear notion of 'progress of civilization' (see for example Moffat 1842:558). At the new station 'the moral wilderness was now about to blossom ... The simple Gospel now melted their flinty hearts' (p.496). Even admission of failure had a rightful and necessary place in the missionary's appointed text: in Northcott's account, Moffat drew strength from the metaphors of barrenness (of soil and soul), since 'seedtime and harvest were within the divine ordering and were not to be presumed or anticipated' (p.78). Moffat's text, both in its printed book form and in the daily textualisation of his physically embedded metaphorical life, gradually accrued weight and authority, and it could assume a life of its own, regardless of discontinuities outside its perimeters. In the geographical and cultural 'contact zone' (Pratt 1992:6) of Moffat's frontier, missionary discourse was less of an imposition on Africans – who seem to have largely ignored it – than a form of self-defence, in narrative appropriation, against a world which remained intractable outside the structures of narrative, and outside the neatly demarcated boundaries of the Kuruman mission. In the words of Cornwallis Harris (1841:37), author of *Wild Sports of Southern Africa*, Kuruman was 'a lovely spot in the waste by which it is completely environed' and a 'speck of civilization, seeming as though it had been accidentally dropped into the very heart of the wide wilderness'. So too was its transcendental narrative of conversion, embedded in the moral values of 'bible and plough', a speck of isolated, sustaining self-deception in a sparsely populated semi-desert landscape. Apart from providing an important site of acculturation for those who chose to use it, Moffat's success was political, as an agent of modernisation on the frontier, and as a broker in firearms, but never as a romantically conceived hero of Christian miracles, which is what he seems to have most desired to be.

# III

David Livingstone, whose career in Africa was inspired partly by Moffat and whose marriage to Moffat's daughter drew him even closer to the Kuruman zealot, recognised the minuteness of influence possible for a missionary in the thankless northern Cape mission fields. Livingstone and Moffat together would later be recognised as the 'acknowledged monarchs' of a group of influential missionaries around whom the mid-nineteenth-century missionary movement built its propaganda (Northcott 1961:171), but Livingstone, though inspired by Moffat, was to follow a very different course. After eleven years as a missionary in areas further north of Kuruman, he could claim exactly one convert, a chief named Setshele, whose alliance with Christianity appears to have been influenced by the political and military threat of the Boers (Northcott 1973:32) and who later fell from grace (Boucher 1985:21). Livingstone expressed impatience with the repetitious labour and small progress involved in the 'perpetual tutelage' of mission work in areas already encountered by missionaries (Boucher 1985:21,45; Northcott 1973:28; Jeal 1973:42). He was not a man for humble labour. He would become famous as the missionary-explorer, geographer and naturalist who wrote his own famous missionary-book, *Missionary Travels and Researches in South Africa* (1857), a huge volume of almost seven hundred pages which was a 'resounding success', although it was thought that the 'pictures did it' (Boucher 1985:55) rather than the impact of Livingstone's dispassionate and detailed observations on dung-beetles, ants, the tsetse fly and countless other minutiae of the veld.

Livingstone's impact was nevertheless to elevate the grand tradition of book-published missionary heroism to the greatest height of consensual Western self-delusion: the appropriating fantasy of 'discovering' Africa and the large-scale conversion of Africans to Christianity by what was often expressed as 'opening up' the continent to the influence of 'commerce and Christianity', which was Livingstone's alternative to Moffat's maxim of 'Bible and plough' (Northcott 1961:147). Livingstone did ultimately 'open' Africa for Western influence. His 'discoveries' may have been contestable and wrong – as with his celebrated misapprehension that he had discovered the source of the Nile – but he does appear to have 'discovered' in a different sense. Livingstone generated an interest in the outright colonisation of large areas of Africa by presenting, in a singularly powerful way because of his fame and reputation, a narrative of benign imperial influence. He arrived in Africa at a time when the humanitarian anti-slavery campaign had achieved most of its successes, but he also formed part of a greater context of explorers who sought to discover Africa in a gentlemanly fashion and bring it under the civilising influence of commerce.

Livingstone's forerunners included Mungo Park, who had found that the Niger flowed westwards into the Atlantic and sought to discover Timbuktu (Pratt 1992:71), as well as Hugh Clapperton, who had trudged across the Sahara (Northcott 1973:16). Like Livingstone, both these men were Scots who died in Africa after writing famous travel stories. Park and Clapperton were part of a broader scientific-humanitarian movement in Britain. Park had travelled in the employ of the Association for Promoting the Discovery of the Interior Parts of Africa, or the Africa Association (established in 1788). Another famous organisation, the Society for the Abolition of the Slave Trade, was formed shortly afterwards. The famous humanitarian member of parliament, William Wilberforce, was affiliated to both organisations. Remarking on the Africa Association's declared aim of 'enlarging the fund of human knowledge' by exploring Africa, Pratt (1992:70) writes that the image of human knowledge as a 'fund' suggests the predominantly commercial aims of the association. Its members were 'economic expansionists interested in "legitimate commerce" ... and not the slave trade' (p.70). In Northcott's description (1973:17), Africa represented 'teeming millions who might become their regular customers'. Livingstone himself embodied the complementary ideals enlarging scientific knowledge, spreading Christianity and promoting commerce. Early on in *Missionary Travels*, Livingstone wrote:

My observations on this subject [free trade] make me extremely
desirous to promote the preparation of the raw materials of
European manufactures in Africa, for by that means we may
not only put a stop to the slave trade, but introduce the negro
family into the body of corporate nations ... Success in this, in
both Eastern and Western Africa, would lead, in the course of
time, to a much larger diffusion of the blessings of civilization
than efforts exclusively spiritual and educational confined to
any one small tribe. (p.28)

It is clear from this passage that Livingstone's missionary idealism was of a
more ambitious brand than Moffat's. Livingstone was to entertain visions of a
'larger diffusion of the blessings of civilization' throughout his life, and die in
pursuit of them. He became emblematic of the crusading missionary quest-
hero in the nether regions of Africa, and he was one of the most important
forerunners of the late-Victorian notion of Britain's 'manifest destiny' to be a
'great civilizing power' (Jeal 1973:382; see Bosch 1991:298). He therefore
embodied the ideals of expansionism in Christianity, science and commerce.
Such expansionism found its physical and metaphorical equivalent in
travelling, exploring and 'penetrating' Africa. Northcott (1973:16) writes that
Livingstone is 'the most significant figure in the century of European
penetration of Africa which stretches from James Bruce's Ethiopian journey in
1768 to his own death in 1873'. Northcott adds that it was a century
dominated by the mystery of the great rivers, the Nile, Niger, Congo and
Zambesi which fascinated a remarkable group of independent travellers: 'It
was to these great rivers that Livingstone would continue travelling in search
of an elusive "highway" into an Africa that would be civilised by the agency of
humanitarian missionaries and traders, and thereby saved from slavery'
(Northcott 1973:335-36; Jeal 1973:93). The 'highway' of water was
Livingstone's alternative to Moffat's allegory of the fountain in the desert.
Both men were physically and metaphorically driven by the appeal of water.
The fact that Livingstone's greatest failures were related to physical
limitations and errors regarding the rivers he was so obsessed with (Jeal
1973:354-69) did not detract from the influence exerted by textual versions of
the missionary-explorer's quest. Livingstone achieved considerable fame
during his lifetime. After his death, Henry Morton Stanley, who had gone to
find Livingstone in present-day Tanzania, further consolidated the
Livingstone legend in his famous book, *How I Found Livingstone* (1872). The

narrative of benign imperialism in the second half of the nineteenth century – specifically expressed as 'manifest destiny' by Joseph Chamberlain in 1894 after the annexation of Uganda – found a major persona in the figure of Livingstone as a questing humanitarian hero (exploring, fighting slavery, and defending Christian values).

Livingstone's own approach, apart from what was made of him, was that of the gentlemanly scientist and medical doctor observing and recording within the classifying paradigms of naturalist enquiry.[6] This was in contrast to his transformation, in the more popular textual renditions of his person and his travels, into a gloriously daring hero in an imperial narrative (see for example, C. Silvester Horne, *David Livingstone* (1929), W.G. Blaikie, *David Livingstone: Missionary and Explorer*, no date, and J.J. Ellis, *Life Story of David Livingstone*, no date).

For my purposes here, it is important to consider the nature of Livingstone's 'discovery' narrative, its contribution to a missionary-imperial text for Africa, and its mode of expression. This grand narrative, whose consolidation was assisted by the many recirculations of Livingstone's story, was later encountered by Africans in the colonial systems consequent and dependent upon the thesis of benevolent imperialism. It would also have a direct impact on the Eastern Cape and Lovedale via James Stewart. As a young man, Stewart idolised the figure of Livingstone, but learned to loathe him in person after escorting Mrs Livingstone to meet her husband at the Zambesi mouth in 1862. Stewart nevertheless set up the Livingstonia mission on Lake Nyasa in honour of his earlier hero (Boucher 1985:160; Shepherd 1940:188) and himself contributed to the missionary imperialism of the late Victorian era which gathered strength after Livingstone's death (see Bosch 1991:295).

My concern is not with the factual complexities of Livingstone's travels. A reading of professional modern biographies such as those by Jeal and Northcott suggests that Livingstone's experiences may have been greatly at variance with his legend and that he was an extremely unpleasant character. He did not succeed as a missionary. His campaigns of exploration appear to have been fraught with interpersonal conflict, illness, death and failure, and his scientific observations seem very questionable by modern standards (Siddle 1973). He made vast geographical blunders and died under the illusion that he had discovered the source of the Nile when he had in fact encountered the beginnings of the Congo River. But these inconsistencies were as nothing against the strong current of the discourse into which Livingstone was taken up.

This discourse of benevolent imperialism was premised partly on the elevation of book-published missionary heroism to the magnificent delusions of 'discovery'. Earlier missionaries in the Cape Colony had entered land already inhabited by Europeans, and Moffat helped to inaugurate the missionary-explorer type in southern Africa in a public way, but Livingstone became the apotheosis of the 'discovering', questing missionary in south-central Africa. In retrospect, he certainly 'discovered' this area of Africa for British colonisation by the pressure his stories, life and death brought to bear on Victorian Britain to pursue the ideal of 'commerce and Christianity' and to counter the Arab slave trade. It is also important to bear in mind that he was no mere explorer, but someone who saw himself as an instrument of divine providence (Jeal 1973:293). Livingstone's travel narratives, shaped by the motif of the journey, created a narrative persona who combined Christian dogma with the confident assumption of knowledge proper to a Renaissance man imbued with a sense of the necessary and providential expansion of Western Christian humanism. His science was the positivism of what Siddle (1973:87) calls the 'mid-Victorian field scientist'.

Indeed, if Pratt (1992:39) is correct in typifying 'science and sentiment' in travel literature as the two 'eternally clashing and complementary languages of bourgeois subjectivity' which code the imperial frontier, then Moffat and Livingstone's interlinked reputations are not accidental. In Moffat's writing, the sentimental narrative of romantic quest is employed to classify the relations between what Pratt calls 'Euroimperialism' and African people. In Livingstone's written work, the mid-Victorian field scientist 'whose work clearly reflected the uneasy relationship between science and religion' (Siddle 1973:87) brings to prominence the appropriating gaze of the humanitarian naturalist. Livingstone assumes as axiomatic Moffat's dramatisation of missionary heroism – see, for example, his stated conviction to devote his life to the 'alleviation of human misery' (p.5) – but his writing deliberately underplays individual glory while maintaining the empirically impersonal rhetorical posture appropriate to the observing scientist. Livingstone's narration of an encounter with a lion in which he was almost killed, for example, fails to capitalise on the sensational value of the account, but this value is seized upon by the publisher's dramatic illustration of the same incident in which a prostrate hero lies helpless under the weight of a giant, snarling lion's paw, his gun just beyond an outstretched arm, while one of Livingstone's companions readies himself to shoot the lion (p.11).

If the sentimental romance-version of the missionary's quest brings to prominence the individual hero's battle with evil and unreason, the scientific account emphasises a mastery over nature that relies on a wider certainty of Western technological and cultural supremacy than individual (if providential) agency. For example, Livingstone debunks the sensational notion of a lion's fearfulness with an appeal to precisely the Westerner's superior *general* ability to deal with nature:

> We hear of the 'majestic roar of the king of the beasts'. It is, indeed, well calculated to inspire fear if you hear it in combination with the tremendously loud thunder of that country, on a night so pitchy dark that every flash of the intensely vivid lightning leaves you with the impression of stone-blindness, while the rain pours down so fast that your fire goes out, leaving you without the protection of even a tree, or the chance of your gun going off. But when you are in a comfortable house or wagon, the case is very different, and you hear the roar of the lion without any awe or alarm. (p.141)

As this passage implies, the difference between victim and master in Africa is the difference between Africa in the raw and the beneficent Western technological intrusions of gun, wagon and house (Livingstone does not choose to consider African forms of shelter and protection). And it is within the superior protection of the culturally specific four-sided dwelling, protected by the gun, that the field-scientist enjoys the repose for 'writing up' the world he observes. It is here that one perceives the absurd delusion of 'discovery', as though natural phenomena came into full and proper existence only once the imperial Western eye fell upon them and transformed them into a European narrative of discovering the unknown. Africa was regarded as devoid of history. In the view of missionaries and explorers, the European's transforming energies 'would at long last historicize the African landscape' (Ranger 1987:159). In this way, the Victoria Falls came into existence for the Western world when Livingstone 'discovered', in 1855, what had been known to Africans for a long time as *Mosioatunya* (the smoke that thunders). In a different sense, though, the land was textually created as it was 'discovered', and once the implications of its inclusion in the cataloguing and classifying Western narrative were felt, the land so inscribed would never be quite the same again. Physical colonisation followed textual incorporation. Livingstone's *Missionary Travels* has an appendix of four pages of latitudes and longitudes of positions in the story, a map based on the travels, a geological map and a vast mass of descriptive detail. It is as though Livingstone was aware that nothing really existed until he brought it into textual form within scientific co-ordinates. His act of witness was an act of appropriation by Western knowledge. Here is a random example:

> A remarkable peculiarity in the forests in this country is the absence of thorns; there are but two exceptions – one a tree bearing a species of *nux vomica*, and a small shrub very like the plant of the sarsaparilla, bearing in addition to its hooked thorns bunches of yellow berries. (p.345)

Livingstone's text is dense with just such dispassionate, semi-scientific observation and description. The Victorian field-scientist was committed to the expansion of natural history. In Pratt's analysis, there is a mutual engagement between natural history and European economic and political expansionism. She writes:

> Natural history asserted an urban, lettered, male authority over the whole of the planet; it elaborated a rationalizing, extractive, dissociative understanding which overlaid functional, experiential relations among people, plants and animals. In these respects, it figures a certain kind of global hegemony, notably one based on possession of land and resources rather than control over routes. At the same time, in and of itself, the system of nature as a descriptive paradigm was an utterly benign and abstract appropriation of the planet. (1992:38)

Livingstone does not feature in Pratt's argument, but, as we have observed, he was one of the most important precursors of the Victorian era of grand and beneficent imperialism (see Schapera 1974:v-ix). He campaigned against slavery and his massive accumulation of written observation ostensibly served the interests of science. However, his 'benign appropriation of the planet' was soon to lead to a far more political kind of control in the form of new British colonies. Jeal (1973:370-84) argues that the colonisation of Nyasaland (Malawi), the Congo (Zaire), Uganda, Kenya and Nigeria can be directly related to the influence of Livingstone (see Oliver & Atmore

1972:66). The textual fantasies of discovery therefore fulfilled their own logic of possession.

Livingstone exemplifies the fusion of positivist empiricism and dogmatic Christianity which is often evident in missionary writings of the nineteenth century and which delivered an indisputable 'natural truth'. Siddle (1973:89) observes that as an amateur field scientist, Livingstone 'demonstrated his skill as a diagnostician with an acutely developed eye for physical detail', while as a Victorian missionary he 'showed his religious aptitude for selecting elements from the broad environmental picture to illustrate or augment the grand design (of commerce and Christianity) to which he became emotionally committed'. In most of Livingstone's writing on southern Africa, Siddle observes, 'Rivers become potential highways of commerce as well as interesting manifestations of a complex drainage system; plants are increasingly identified for their potential utility rather than their botanical interest; geological formations are viewed for their economic minerals; elephants are seen as the bearers of ivory and soils are only mentioned for their fertility' (pp.91-92). Further, Livingstone's 'benign' scientific observation minimised the importance of people as individuals and groups in favour of a conception of masses in a grand design. Siddle asserts that 'Livingstone's whole treatment of the man-land relationship was extremely myopic' (p.95) and 'There are very few observations in which attention is drawn to relationships between settlement, population density and agricultural practice' (p.93).

In Livingstone's influential representations of southern and central Africa therefore (see Lloyd *et al.*, 1978, for an idea of the vast literature by and about him), the missionary is combined with the Victorian scientist to produce a signifying taxonomy in which relations between autochthonous people, and their own relations with the environment, are overlaid by what Pratt suggests is a 'rationalizing, extractive, dissociative understanding', and in which the land is seen as a resource for the spread of commerce and Christianity, and not as a source of sustenance for its autochthonous people.

It remains briefly to consider what was made of Livingstone. Few people in Victorian history have been written about in the kind of volume devoted to the *figure* of Livingstone, which, if Jeal's discerning biography is to be believed, bears little relation to the evidence about Livingstone's personality. In the bibliography of Lloyd *et al.* (1978) there are no fewer than 764 items by and on the famous explorer. This includes 26 different versions of *Missionary Travels* (among them abridgements and translations), 10 major bibliographies and 179 other 'Lives and Studies of Livingstone'. As Jeal (1973:351) explains,

Livingstone was in fact a discredited and near-forgotten figure during his final African expedition of 1866-73, which followed the disaster of his government sponsored Zambesi mission of 1858-64 in which his wife and several missionaries died, including a High Church bishop (Northcott 1973:84-85). It was only when journalist Henry Morton Stanley seized the initiative of 'finding' a 'lost' Livingstone – no European had spoken to him in person for five years – and delivered a great story to the Western world, that the myth of Livingstone began to develop.

Livingstone's transformation into legendary status in the Victorian mind appears to have been a textual process in which particular tropes of his experiences served a strong public need. As with Moffat, Livingstone himself was only partially involved in this process. His story was appropriated by the publishers of his *Missionary Travels* who immediately illustrated his travels in images of high adventure (even as his own narrative sought to avoid the romantic in favour of the scientific). An enormous sub-literature about Livingstone began to develop, which was to continue into the late twentieth century. As a prototype-missionary, his textual influence was widespread. We know that Lovedale's James Stewart subscribed to the legend of Livingstone by his act of explicit veneration in founding the Livingstonia Mission, despite his aversion to Livingstone the person. Livingstone represented an important narrative potential for the British conception of its own imperial destiny. This potential is perhaps related to a central contradiction in the Victorian imperial project in general (embodied also in Livingstone's own views): the explicit coding of capitalist expansionism as spiritual upliftment. Such expansionism was part of a broader Western need to subsume Africa and the identity of its peoples into a classificatory taxonomy which would render it known and controllable.

If Moffat subordinated African subjectivity to the demands of a self-serving adventure story, draped in pious missionary sentiment, and Livingstone represented Africa as a passive resource, how would an individual African subject, ostensibly trained to a point of Christian perfection, apprehend his/her own self textually within such a context?

# IV

In 1857, the year in which Livingstone's *Missionary Travels* was published, Tiyo Soga returned to the Cape from Scotland where he had trained at the university of Glasgow and been ordained as a Presbyterian minister (Saayman

1991:58-64). It was within the constraints of developing textual currents such as described above, which were defining the destiny of Africa and individual African subjects in forums of public representation, that a model 'converted' subject such as Tiyo Soga was compelled to delineate his own role. After Soga's death in 1871 he was textually incorporated into a sub-genre of the more general tradition of book-published missionary heroism as an emblematic 'rise' of the 'model Kafir' (Chalmers 1877:488). Soga was Lovedale's own, proudly proclaimed emblem of heroic spiritual elevation, and his story was given book form in John A. Chalmers's biography, *Tiyo Soga: A Page of South African Mission Work* (1877). This work appears to have been largely plagiarised in the Reverend H.T. Cousins's *From Kafir Kraal to Pulpit: The Story of Tiyo Soga* (1899). These biographies are standard book versions of the missionary-colonial signifying imperatives, in which the African's 'rise' was given a stereotypical narrative shape by European writers. However, the same narrative was rendered agonistically by Tiyo Soga himself, as I shall argue in due course.

Chalmers's biography rings with the moral certainties of Victorian missionary imperialism which systematically sought to efface difference in the name of Christian civilisation. His narrative did this by transcoding details about Soga's life into recognisable formal patterns of descent and ascent drawn from the romance archetype. Chalmers depicted Soga's origins as typically depraved in an introductory chapter entitled 'The Polygamist's Village'. According to his account, the village is a site of degradation and barbarism. The polygamist is Tiyo's father, 'Old Soga', who was a senior counsellor of the Xhosa chief Ngqika. In Chalmers's interpretation, all useful activity in the village is sullied by the want of industriousness and civilised vigour. Craftsmen 'leisurely and indolently' ply their trades, while 'the patriarch of the village and his associates lounge and bask in the sun, alternately smoking and sleeping'. Women draw water, hew wood, prepare the food, and young boys tend calves and goats (p.2). Chalmers prefers not to view this sketch as pastoral or idyllic. It is a scene of 'dull monotony … varied by the visit of some chief on a begging expedition, a marriage festival … the *intonjane* dance – obscene in all its aspects …' (p.3). The village is a place of 'nocturnal revelries' where men dance to the 'most barbarous and obscene songs of an enraptured audience', and a place of superstition (p.3). But the link with civilisation and its benefits is found when 'Old Soga', Tiyo Soga's father, uses a plough to cultivate ground after being advised to do so by a European. The use of Western agricultural techniques becomes a 'silent emblem' of a 'still greater power which was secretly at work, and is destined yet to revolutionize the moral wastes of Southern Africa' (p.7).

It is Tiyo Soga who, in Chalmers's story, was destined to personify the transition from moral waste to redemption, but in so doing he also had to shed all outward trappings of Xhosa culture. This was the unstated *sine qua non* of the 'model Kafir', and as such Soga was to carry the Nguni people into modernity as a textual signifier of missionary success. He is therefore a narrative persona of considerable significance. Chalmers was able to present his biography, in a largely unproblematic manner, as a story of ascent (the 'rise' of the 'model Kafir') in the convenient form of a linear account which saw the external details of Soga's life as consistent with the needs of such a storyline. Soga did go to Lovedale as a boy. He was taken to Scotland on two different occasions to be educated. He did come home as the first ordained African minister and he did serve his life out as a missionary. But this narrative concealed and repressed everything prior to its own inauguration. Soga's own writing, however, provides evidence of contradiction and agonistic response,[7] even while he apparently reproduces an orthodox text of missionary sentiment.

In Chalmers's biography, then, Soga is born into the secular underworld of his father's polygamist's village, and he undergoes a 'baptism into heathenism' at birth – a rite of animal slaughter described in lurid detail (pp.11-12) which is meant to suggest the state of degradation the young hero has still to overcome. 'Amid such superstition and sensuality, barbarism and ignorance, there can be no intellectual growth, or purity of life,' Chalmers writes (p.12). Immediately following this evocation of an underworld, the second chapter proffers, as a stark alternative, a site of worldly salvation in the Tyumie mission station, described as a centre of 'light and knowledge' (p.13). But for the existence of such places, Chalmers narrates, 'the heathen world would never know that there is a higher life than that of eating, drinking and making merry' (p.13). Tyumie is also a 'city of refuge' from the injustice, violence and cruelties of 'witch doctors' (p.15). The hero of the mission station is the Reverend John Brownlee,[8] who is described as the antithesis of Moffat and Livingstone with their tales of sensational adventure:

> A true man in every sense was Mr. Brownlee. He was not eloquent in speech; but his life spoke volumes. He made no noise in the world. He had no egotism, no desire for fame, and never catered for the applause of men. He wrote no sensational tales of hair-breadth escapes, gave no romantic pictures of the

bright side of missionary work, and filled no columns of
missionary journals with thrilling incidents. (pp.14-15)

In this oblique reference to his own style of writing, almost certainly a reference
to the famous missionary narratives of Moffat and Livingstone, among others,
Chalmers gave notice that he would resist romanticising his material (in similar
style to Moffat). Like Moffat, his style may be described as anti-romance, or the
romance of what is supposedly real. However, implicit in the structure of his
story are the tell-tale levels typical of Frye's 'secular scripture', even though the
narrative becomes prosaic once the victory over heathenism is confirmed. In
Chalmers's story there is a fusion of two modes of emplotment: romance and
biography. The narrative creates the idea of an incredible elevation from the
dark netherworld of heathenism to the 'centre of light', but this quest is muted
because Soga is not allowed his own heroic agency. He is *led* out of darkness by
one of Brownlee's successors, the Reverend William Chalmers, who takes Soga
to Lovedale and initiates his wonderful transformation into a 'model Kafir'.
From this point on, his course is set by the greater narrative of conversion, in
which Soga himself has a limited role. The story then assumes the apparent
form of empirical biography, although the underlying romantic idea of heroic
ascent continues to provide a conceptual framework for the narration. Tiyo
must 'either advance or sink never to rise again' (p.31). His is a terribly linear,
earnest, and upward path of Protestant virtue and selfless service to Christianity.

    When the War of the Axe[9] interrupted Soga's schooling at Lovedale, the
Reverend William Govan resolved to take him to Scotland. Chalmers
interpreted this as 'a great venture thus to test the capacity of the Kafir mind'
(p.39). Soga became a prototype subject of conversion for the Xhosa in
general. He carried an awful burden, since he was to be tested on behalf of his
people for mental, moral and physical resilience against the standard of the
British gentleman. For the purposes of the British missionaries' desire for as
complete a cultural conversion as possible (Gray 1990b:143), it was important
to demonstrate that an African could become a close copy of a white
gentleman. In Chalmers's narrative, Soga takes the first step in this direction
by 'renounc[ing] all faith in the superstitious beliefs of his forefathers,
sever[ing] the links which bound him to heathenism, and receiv[ing] the seal
of adoption into the family of Christ by being publicly baptized ...' (p.46). It
was during Soga's second visit to Scotland a few years later – again after
another frontier war had disrupted orderly work in the Eastern Cape – that he
was assimilated into Scottish university life (at the University of Glasgow).

Soga was '[d]iligent ... but not distinguished' (p.72). Chalmers quotes one of Soga's former university fellows as saying that 'God's grace had made my African brother a Christian, a scholar, and a gentleman ... He was never bashful or awkward, but had the natural ease and manners of a born gentleman' (p.79). And after Soga's return to South Africa as a missionary in 1857, his transformation was such that the *Port Elizabeth Telegraph* could comment, 'In this person may be seen the transcendant operation and effects of Christianity, civilization, and science trampling under foot every opposing prejudice and difficulty ...' (in Chalmers 1877:133). Soga was by now a textually objectified figure: he featured in verbal as well as written stories about the miraculous possibilities of conversion, but his own writing suggests just how difficult it was for him to live in the space between this public, textually constituted persona, and his more ambivalent, private sense of self.

Soga returned to South Africa in the year of the Cattle Killing, the greatest disaster the Xhosa had ever known. This was an event of great complexity, and the culmination of extreme social distress among the Xhosa following violent frontier wars, great loss of land, and the stripping away of autonomous authority in the first half of the century (see Mostert 1992; Peires 1989). To a writer such as Chalmers, however, a crudely reductionistic conclusion was available: 'Tiyo Soga landed at Algoa Bay on the 2nd of July, 1857, and found that those to whom he had come to preach the Gospel were a dispersed nation, utterly destroyed by their own folly' (p.129). Soga is then styled by Chalmers as a saviour of his own race who returns to a savage wasteland of famine so extreme that in one instance, a father is reported by Chalmers to have decapitated his own child and begun to roast one of the child's arms to eat; the father is supposedly killed by an axe blow administered by his wife (p.144). Soga, along with another missionary, sets up a station at Emgwali, which Chalmers describes as follows:

> Now, in what was the very centre of this tribe [the Ngqika], two missionaries had erected the symbol of peace, which was becoming the rallying cry of men and women who had fled to the colony for help. The false prophet had taught the people to believe a lie, and their destruction was the result. Truth followed and asserted its power. The barbarians, humbled by famine and self-condemned, returned and acknowledged that the Gospel was the only truth, and the preachers of it their best and most faithful friends. (p.163)

Soga is now turned into a character in Chalmers's romantically troped story about Christian knights among unredeemed barbarians in Kaffirland. He fulfils a formal, although limited, narrative role as a standard bearer of Christianity in the midst of heathenism. The chapter headings liken the course of Soga's life to horticultural and organic metaphors of growth which suggest orderly, if uneven, progress towards a single outcome ('Getting into Harness', 'Bearing Precious Seed', 'Dark Shadows', 'Glimpses of Sunshine', 'Sunset'). But it is rewarding to read the one odd chapter in this sequence, 'Dark Shadows', in which Chalmers purports to present deeply private confessions of doubt, supposedly written by Soga in his private journal. In Chalmers's account, these doubts are resolved, much in the way of a conventional crisis of faith, and a glorious unity with God is eventually achieved when Soga later dies of tuberculosis.

In the chapter entitled 'Dark Shadows', Chalmers presents material which he says come from Soga's private journal. A perusal of the journal, however, shows that this is not the case. Donavan Williams (1983:11) speculates, in his biography of Soga, that Chalmers may have had access to material which has since been lost. David Attwell (1994), however, prefers the conclusion that Chalmers assembled most of the confessional 'journal entries' himself, based on the private journal and on letters. Attwell advances convincing reasons for this deduction.[10] When we read about Soga's supposed trials of faith, then, we encounter a dense sediment of textual traces. One the one hand, it does seem the case that Soga was given to morbidity, as Williams (1978:86-87) notes in his biography, which is far more reliable than Chalmers's – Williams describes Soga as possessing a 'tendency towards melancholia'. Further, Williams quotes a letter, which stands free of accusations of editorial meddling, in which Soga makes confessions of doubt which sound very similar to Chalmers's apparently embellished accounts (Williams 1978:86). There are, in addition, two journal entries in Xhosa in which Soga expresses severe doubt about his vocation (Williams 1978:22, 35). On the other hand, speculation about the *motive* for Chalmers's embellishments, if such they are, are best framed within his own narrative exigencies in writing Soga's biography. A standard account of Ignatian doubt, followed by a resurgence of faith, would arguably have strengthened his notion of a 'Model Kafir', since such crises of confidence were a textually recognisable, and fairly standard, motif in narratives of Christian belief. Attwell (1994:16) resorts to a similar argument: 'Chalmers wanted to show that the Protestant spirit could be found alive and well in an African. Soga's crises of faith could be read into a narrative of heroic, self-chastening individualism which provided ample justification for the missionary enterprise.' At the same time, however, the potential of the confessional passages to disrupt Chalmers's story of a fully 'converted' African Christian means that they would have read as a threatening supplement to Chalmers's text unless swiftly recuperated into the more recognisable motif of sporadic Christian doubt. In view of this, it seems unlikely that Chalmers would have invented the passages entirely: it seems more probable that he would have assembled and rewritten various shreds of Soga's writing drawn from elsewhere, and set about using them in a recuperative manner, while also satisfying his, albeit corrupted, documentary sense of record as a biographer. Chalmers thus conspicuously renarrativises Soga's doubts into resurgent faith, but it is significant that this move is effected in Chalmers's narrative voice, and not that ascribed to Soga.

The textual 'Soga' of these passages, then, shows signs that he is struggling to maintain his faith. Chalmers interprets this as a general Christian crisis. Soga was 'harassed by some of the bitterest trials, and by some of the darkest dispensations of providence' (Chalmers 1877:271). At one point, the (probably) embellished text purporting to be Soga's journal reads:

> *5th January.–* I have to complain of one grand defect in my character-irresolution. I cannot tell how many times I have resolved and re-resolved to be under God a better man than I know myself to be. All my resolutions in this respect have miserably come to naught. I have in reference to my state before God, to complain of the following things:-Although I know myself to be a great deceiver, although I know the consequence of this awful sin, although I know that I have a most responsible burden, in having taken unadvisedly upon myself the work of the ministry, although I know that all that I have hitherto been doing in the ministry has been in hypocrisy, and insincerity, I have to lament my *deadness* and hardness of heart in reference to these sins. When I attempt to peruse the word of God, it has no effect upon my mind. I remain unmoved. I have no sufficient sensibility to and perception of my sins. This I feel as if it were a barrier to my obtaining any true penitence regarding them. O God, by Thy spirit move me, and Thou shalt have the entire Glory. (p.272)

This passage, whether taken as Soga's 'authentic' voice or as a contaminated residue of his textual remains, suggests the most extraordinary agony of one who professes a certain kind of discourse – and is in some senses its vehicle – but who is not able to meet it with an individual, personal conviction of truth. In the letter quoted by Williams, which is verifiably written by Soga, the 'Model Kafir' writes as follows: 'I have sometimes great regrets that I ever went to Scotland and entered the ministry ... I wish sometimes I could go to some dark spot of earth – live and reside there alone' (in Williams 1978:86). In this regard, it is instructive to remember the poststructuralist idea that in regarding subjectivity via discourse, one does not encounter full 'consciousness', but what Spivak calls a 'subject-effect' (Spivak 1988b:12). 'That which *seems to operate as a subject* may be part of an immense discontinuous network ("text" in the general sense) of strands that may be termed politics, ideology, economics, history, sexuality, language, and so on.' Each of these strands, if they are isolated, can also be seen as woven of many strands. 'Different knottings and configurations of these strands,' Spivak adds, 'determined by heterogeneous determinations which are themselves dependent on myriad circumstances, produce the effect of an operating subject' (pp.12-13; emphasis added).

When Tiyo Soga is represented as expressing in one and the same passage of writing his 'deadness and hardness of heart' to the Gospel, *and* his desire to be moved by the 'spirit' of God, or when he expresses a desire to hide on 'some dark spot of earth', the 'subject-effect' created – *not* a 'sovereign and determining subject' (Spivak 1988b:13) – suggests conflict between different 'strands' of the discursive text which constitute a *seeming* subjectivity. It appears that Soga's subjectivity was most strongly influenced by the pervasive textual strand of missionary Christianity, but the purported passage from his journal, even in interpellated form, and the evidence of his letter and the Xhosa sections of his journal, suggest that his religion was just such a strand and no more, and that even in one so comprehensively 'converted' as he, no sovereign or fully 'present' Christian consciousness was possible. In these terms, Christian converts could never be what the missionaries wished to believe they were – re-made people, thoroughly in possession of a consciousness imbued with eternal grace. Indeed, in Spivak's argument, all human subjectivity is many stranded and not reducible to any one of its discernible 'effects'. It is therefore the very conspicuousness of Chalmers's attempt to recuperate the significance of Soga's doubts, which ironically emphasises the supplementarity of Soga's subjectivity, undermining Chalmers's avowals of Christian consciousness.

The textual persona of Soga in Chalmers's account continued to express severe doubt for a period covering almost a year and a half. Soga supposedly wrote of 'the most unaccountable hardness and unbelief in my heart' (Chalmers 1877:273); he feared he had been 'living the life of a mere formalist' (p.274) and that he was in 'a wretched state of darkness' in which 'prayer is an unprofitable burden'; he was 'inclined to objectionable light-heartedness' (p.275); he is alleged to have felt 'religious duties a burden … preaching and exhorting a burden … reading God's word a burden … prayer a burden' and he did all these things 'mechanically' (p.276); he was sure 'the prominent blemishes of my character have been indifference, indolence, unbelief, and faithlessness' (p.277); the concluding words attributed to Soga in this part of Chalmers's narrative asserted that it was 'impossible to conceive of anything more awful than the state of the human heart – *my* heart – when it can so much resist and oppose what God has done and said' (p.278).

At this point, Chalmers chooses to neutralise the potential force of these confessional declarations of ambivalence. He resumes the narrative in his 'own' voice – itself supplemented and conditioned by a tradition of Christian mysticism – by concluding that Soga's 'trials sent his thoughts inwards, and drew him closer to the Divine fountain for strength' (p.278). No such idea is uttered in the words ascribed to Soga. For the rest of the narrative, Chalmers concentrates on the outer features of Soga's life: His deteriorating health; his move to a new mission station deeper in 'Kaffraria', at Tutura; and finally, his death ('sunset'). His life is summed up in a final triumphal statement whose triangular reduction to a point of only three words visually illustrates the narrative closure of Chalmers's account (p.488):

> He was a Friend of God; a Lover of His Son; inspired by His
> Spirit; a Disciple of His Holy Word; an Ardent Patriot;
> a Large-hearted Philanthropist; a Dutiful Son; an
> Affectionate Brother; a Tender Husband; a
> Loving Father; a Faithful Friend; a Learned
> Scholar; an Eloquent Orator; and in
> Manners a Gentleman; a Devoted
> Missionary who spent himself
> in his Master's service;
>
> A Model Kafir.

# V

Despite this passionate asseveration of perfect conformity, there is evidence that the 'Model Kafir' Tiyo Soga was both less, and more, than the sovereign Christian subject represented by Chalmers. The variability of Soga's own discourse is shown by a comparison of two pieces written in different languages for entirely different audiences: One, a contribution in Xhosa to the first issue, in 1862, of *Indaba*, a Xhosa-English newspaper issued by Lovedale, and the other a lecture in English which he delivered to the YMCA in Cape Town in 1866. In the *Indaba* article, translated into English by J.J.R. Jolobe, Soga ostensibly speaks as a Xhosa and not as a missionary. 'We Xhosas are a race which enjoys conversation', he writes (Williams 1983:151), and proceeds to extol Xhosa cultural practices – the very practices which he also associates with 'degraded, despised dark races' (Williams 1983:192; see below).

Because Soga was writing in Xhosa for a largely African audience, one can reasonably speculate that his sense of rhetorical address was less constrained by the perceived need to produce orthodox missionary language than in his public utterances in English, and that he felt able to drop the habitual posture of judgemental censure about traditional Xhosa culture. In contrast to Chalmers's scene of indolence and 'dull monotony', Soga portrayed the Xhosa as vibrant conversationists:

> When a man who has things to relate comes to a home a meal is cooked in a tall pot because the people want him to eat to his satisfaction so that the happiness which is the result of a good meal will open his heart and the sore parts will heal. As soon as that happens there will be a stream of news flowing out of the mouth. The listener will continually assent. So will the narrator be encouraged. Silence will at times reign all ears listening. The damsel will constantly replenish the fire in the fireplace. When the news retailer finishes there will be a general hum, expressing agreement, rejoicing and acceptability of the visitor.
>
> That is the essential nature of the Xhosa people. You too, Mr. Editor, will confirm this opinion the day you visit our homes in the rural areas. Once our people realise you are a man of words and a conversationalist the tribesmen will surround you. Stiff pumpkin and pit-corn porridge (umqa wesangcozi), a

pumpkin and maize dish (umxhaxha), a mixture of sour milk
and broken bread (umvubo) will be placed before you to eat to
your fill. So I anticipate great happiness from the publication of
the newspaper. (In Williams 1983:151)

This passage is extraordinary because it not only suggests that Soga harboured
sentiments of Xhosa loyalty quite contrary to what was expected of a
missionary in 'Xhosaland', but also in view of its *textual* celebration of *oral*
culture. The picture of the 'damsel' replenishing the fire while the speaker
enthralls his audience suggests nostalgic longing for the joys of oral culture and
is quite contrary to the imputation of Soga's own biographer that 'there is
nothing in life at such a village either to stimulate or ennoble' (Chalmers
1877:12). At the same time, one should note the paradox that Soga was *writing*
this in the pages of a newspaper published by Lovedale, the very institution
which had already begun to play such an important role in eroding oral culture.

It is also paradoxical that Soga introduced the idea of *nation*, in his
sentence, 'One advantage we shall reap with the coming of this journal is that
we will be confident that the people will now get the truth about the affairs of
the nation' (Williams 1983:151). Soga's writing therefore presents the
contradiction of seeming to celebrate a pristine oral culture in an orthodox
missionary publication whose existence denies such a state of innocence.
Further, the idea that 'truth' about the 'nation' should be privileged in such a
publication is deeply problematic, since it suggests that the kind of truth found
in *Indaba* has a superior status to just the oral form of dissemination recalled so
nostalgically by Soga. He continues:

As people who are always hungry for news often we find
ourselves dupes of deceivers under the guise of relating genuine
facts. We are fed with half-truths by travellers who pass near our
areas. We are unreliable people Mr. Editor, to speak
confidentially, because we like to exaggerate. We have a sense
of humour and we can talk until light shines as if it was day-
time. When you examine the report you are surprised to
discover that there was not even a grain of truth in what was
being said. We should be careful of what is reported from our
areas at first. We must at times accept it with reservations.
Today with your newspaper you are initiating an enterprise for
banning falsehood. So we are pleased and grateful. (pp.151-52)

Soga was relying on a distinction between 'deceivers' and 'genuine facts' and between 'truth' and 'falsehood' which, significantly, depended on a central institution of truth-bearing such as the newspaper, but his argument entirely begged the question of the interest – which presumably underlies all 'falsehood' – of the newspaper and its missionary supporters. The mere existence of facts in a written form in a newspaper, according to Soga, gave them the higher status of 'truth'. One is irresistibly led to speculate on the invisible assumption behind this argument – that 'truth' was better served by Christians and missionaries.

Nevertheless, since the advent of literacy had become an inevitable condition at the time of Soga's article, it should not be so surprising that he should have called for a new, written repository of oral culture. His affiliation in the passage below remains with the idea of Xhosa culture and history as worthwhile in its own right:

> What are the corn-pits, the cattle kraals, the boxes and the bags. What are the skin shirts' pockets, and the banks for the stories and fables, the legends, customs and history of the Xhosa people and Fingo people? This is a challenge, for I envisage in this newspaper a beautiful vessel for preserving the stories, fables, legends, customs, anecdotes and history of the tribes. (p.152)

Soga's unstated implication was that the newspaper should 'preserve' the various oral forms of culture within the context of an ascendant new order of the *written* form.[11] His position therefore seems to have combined a reverence for Xhosa culture and history which would have been alien to the typical missionary attitude, with an implicit endorsement of the power and correctness of the new Western order of literacy of which he had become an agent. This paradoxical position allowed Soga to call for an entire recasting of Xhosa history and culture in literate modes:

> All is well today. Our veterans of the Xhosa and Embo people must disgorge all they know. Everything must be imparted to the *nation as a whole*. Fables must be retold; what was history or legend should be recounted ... Whatever was seen heard or done under the requirements of custom should be brought to light and *placed on the national table to be sifted for preservation*.

Were there not *several tribes* before? What is the record of their
history and customs good or bad? Had we no chiefs in days
gone by? Where are the anecdotes of their periods? Were these
things buried with them in their graves? Is there no one to
unearth these things from the graves? Were there no national
poets in the days of yore? Whose praises did they sing? Is there
no one to emulate this eloquence? In the olden days did not
some people bewitch others? What were the names of the men
of magic? Is it not rumoured that some were tortured severely
and cruelly? Are there no people who have an idea of matters
of this nature which happened under the cloak of custom? Are
there no battles which were fought and who were the heroes?
What feathers were worn by the royal regiments ... We should
revive and bring to the light all this great wealth of
information. Let us bring to life our ancestors; Ngconde, Togu,
Tshiwo, Phalo, Rharhabe, Mlawu, Ngqika and Ndlambe. Let
us resurrect our ancestral fore-bears who bequeathed to us a
rich heritage. All anecdotes connected with the life of the
nation should be brought to this big corn-pit our national
newspaper *Iindaba* ... (pp.152-53; emphasis added)

Both Williams (1983:1), and, following him, Saayman (1991:63), make the
claim that Soga was the first black South African who, in Williams' words,
formulated 'a philosophy of Black consciousness'. Williams grounds his
argument mainly on a journal entry and a letter to the *King William's Town
Gazette and Kaffrarian Banner* (Williams 1983:5-6) in which Soga contradicted
the charge of Chalmers (later to become his biographer) that the Xhosa were
doomed to extinction unless they could overcome their 'indolence'. In his
spirited reply to Chalmers, Soga argued that though 'sunk' in the 'barbarism of
ages' (Williams 1983:181), the Xhosa were progressing in civilisation at a
steady rate. To conclude from this, however, that Soga was propounding
'Black consciousness' in the modern sense seems to me to be forcing the point,
especially in view of Soga's explicit missionary bias and his belief in the origin
of Africans as 'sons of Ham' (see Soga's journal entry, 25 April 1865, in
Williams 1983:38-40). From the long passage quoted above, it seems far more
plausible to suggest that Soga was an important figure in the interpenetrations
of orality and literacy, and in the shift from independence to colonial
interdependence, but that his 'consciousness' was ambivalently stranded.

The explicit adoption of the idea of 'nation' – a word Soga uses in English as well, in the journal entry referred to above – seems to have been a significant linking concept in the marriage implicitly proposed by him between a literate cultural order and traditional, pre-literate culture. Soga writes of 'the nation as a whole' as opposed to the 'several tribes' of the past. As Bosch (1991:298-99) argues, the concept of 'nation' is a product of Renaissance humanism (in whose traditions Soga was steeped in his Scottish university education), and its use is a marker of Soga's contradictory impulse to protect pre-literate, pre-'national' culture by *museumising* it in a written form. This written form would never be neutral: it was affiliated to the orthodoxy of a colonising British nationalism, embodied by the Lovedale institution.

Soga's recommendation that 'everything must be imparted to the nation as a whole' barely conceals the centralising, censoring function of the 'nation as a whole' – to be represented by a missionary newspaper – as a site of 'sifting' on a 'national table for preservation'. The very suggestion that the anecdotes of the 'tribes before' and of the periods of the 'chiefs in days gone by' should have been buried with them in their graves, implicitly denies the remaining efficacy of oral dissemination. The only significant existence of such anecdotes now, in the new era of the colonially sponsored Xhosa 'vernacular' newspaper, Soga implies, is in written form, presented for 'sifting' by the new custodian of the 'nation', the regulating missionary institution and its agents, both black and white.

In view of the direct links between African nationalism of the nineteenth and twentieth centuries and missionary institutions, particularly Lovedale (see conclusion to Chapter 2), Tiyo Soga's role as a transitional figure who helped to inaugurate African 'nationalism' as a hybrid of African pride – 'Africa-consciousness' as Saayman calls it (1991:63) – and missionary-led notions of black 'advancement', is of considerable importance. He was indeed a 'progenitor of Black nationalism', as Williams (1983:7) claims, but perhaps in a far more ambiguous and agonistic manner than Williams allows for.

That Soga's discourse was deeply ambivalent is suggested by the juxtaposition of the article in Xhosa discussed above, and a lecture written and delivered in English to the YMCA in 1866. The lecture was written in the scholarly idiom of the day and dealt with academic questions of theology. On the whole it is not of direct relevance to my argument, but there is one startling digression in which Soga says:

> But about the theory of development: I was going to say that I
> trust that when the next great wave comes which is to lift the
> world to a higher eminence of goodness than it has now
> reached, I trust that within its mighty sweep it will embrace my
> poor countrymen of Kaffraria. For I cannot comprehend how,
> according the law of natural progress, they with other
> degraded, despised dark races of this vast continent should
> have been left so far behind in civilization and Christian
> enlightenment. I am not sure about the impartiality of progress;
> and I hope that when its next tidal wave comes, it will correct
> its manifest irregularities. (Williams 1983:192)

Soga's reference to his 'poor countrymen of Kaffraria' as 'degraded and
despised', viewed in relation to his letter to *Indaba* in which he addressed his
'countrymen' with far greater circumspection, suggests how constrained he was
to use the predictable language of 'degraded, despised dark races' when his
audience seemed to demand it. Soga's expression of this kind of sentiment also
leads one to speculate that the 'sifting' on the 'national table' would tend
towards the universalising ideal of (Western) 'natural progress'. Such progress
would relegate Xhosa culture to the museum-house of print, and assert African
rights and 'nationhood' in terms of British values of 'civilisation', as John
Tengo Jabavu was later to do. Like Jabavu, however, Soga would advocate
such values in terms of their founding claims, and not in their deferred,
colonial sense (for an example of such advocacy, see Soga's letter referred to
earlier, 'What is the Destiny of the Kaffir Race', in the *King William's Town
Gazette and Kaffrarian Banner*, 11 May 1865, in Williams 1983:178-82). Soga
is therefore a figure who exhibits agonistic response to textual incorporation
by the narratives of a civilising colonialism. In Foucault's sense of this term,
Soga exhibits the 'permanent provocation' of one who is drawn into power
relationships as a voluntary subject, but who shows 'recalcitrance of will' in his
own 'free' adoption of the values governing such relationships. His own
writings, in which loyalty to pre-colonial Xhosa culture and missionary
conformity are ambivalently inscribed, reflect a paradoxical shuttling in his
own recourse to available forms of textual apprehension, whereas his more
private textual residue suggests a tortured space of difference between textual
entrapment and private otherness.[12]

# VI

The other major narrative of the African's rise to Christian civilisation in the Eastern Cape was built on the persona of Ntsikana. Tiyo Soga's own 'rise' was directly linked to the tradition of Ntsikana and to Ntsikana's adoption of Christianity as a Xhosa prophet in his own right (Hodgson 1985:340-47). What is of interest here is how the Ntsikana tradition was employed in literate missionary sources to bolster a Xhosa nationalism which was Christian in character. As Hodgson (1985:334) argues, 'Ntsikana came to symbolize evolutionary change which went hand in hand with the development of a non-violent Xhosa nationalism.'

In the account by a leading African minister of a later generation than Tiyo Soga, the Reverend John Knox Bokwe (1914:1), Ntsikana's story was introduced as the 'progress made by the Gospel of Jesus Christ in Africa'. Ntsikana is the 'first Christian convert among the Kafirs' (p.1), and his story, writes Bokwe, 'forms a connecting link between that period of utter darkness, such as I have described, and the now dawning epoch of civilisation' (p.4). In Bokwe's short book, which draws together oral and written sources, Ntsikana's 'rise' is emblematic – it represents the rise of Xhosa Christian nationalism, and it functions as a myth of creation, or re-creation, in which African people generally are Christianised in a civilised world. The story combines missionary influences upon Ntsikana (pp.5-7) with the suggestion of an unmediated visionary experience:

> Ntsikana one morning went, as usual, to the kraal. The sun's rays were just peeping over the eastern horizon, and, as he was standing at the kraal gate, his eyes fixed with satisfied admiration on his favourite ox, he thought he observed a ray, brighter than ordinary, striking the side of his beast. As he watched the animal, Ntsikana's face betrayed excited feelings. He enquired of a lad standing near by: 'Do you observe the thing that I now see?' The lad, turning his eyes in the direction indicated, replied: 'No, I see nothing there.' Ntsikana, recovering from the trance, uplifted himself from the ground ... and said to the troubled boy: 'You are right; the sight was not to be seen by your eyes.' (p.8)

Bokwe went on to interpret this event, which was widespread in many versions of the Ntsikana story, as follows:

What can this mean? Is it possible the rays of that morning's
sun were to play an important part in the life of this heathen
man? Is it possible that on the outside appearance of that ox,
standing all unconscious of the charmed gazer's eye, there was
figured a totally different picture of a heavenly object? Can the
story of the Apostle of the Gentiles be repeating itself, though
on a lesser scale? 'Suddenly there shined round about him a
light from heaven. And he trembling, and astonished, said.
"Lord, what wilt thou have me to do?" And the men that
journeyed with him stood speechless, hearing a voice, but
seeing no man!' (Acts ix:3,6,7). We shall see! (p.8)

In the narrated event of Ntsikana's vision, and in Bokwe's interpretation, it is
striking that the central feature of traditional Xhosa culture and economy, the
ox, is also the vehicle of a vision from the Christian God. Bokwe's embroidery
of the event, to make it a repetition of a biblical vision, therefore seems to
imply that Christianity is universal and will permeate any culture. However,
Bokwe's story presents the important rite of transition from heathenism to
Christianity on the same day as that during which Ntsikana is unable to join a
traditional dance at a neighbouring village. A 'gale' rises around his feet when
he tries to dance (p.11). He suddenly remembers his vision of the morning and
orders his people to come home. At a small river he throws aside his blanket,
plunges himself into the water, and washes off the red ochre on his body
(p.12). And so begins Ntsikana's ministry, which, in Bokwe's account, subtly
combines autochthonous tradition with a rejection of the 'heathenism'
implicit in the coding of red ochre.

The narrative of Ntsikana is important because, as Hodgson argues
(1985:337), 'Ntsikana opened the way for the assimilation of the new on the
Xhosa's own terms and for maintaining a sense of belonging with a shared set
of symbols'. However, Bokwe's account suggests how the culturally-specific
transition from a pre-colonial to a colonial order is universalised as a mystical
experience in which 'utter darkness' is counterpoised with the 'now dawning
epoch of civilisation'. Ntsikana's narrative, in Bokwe's 1914 version, thus
became a national creation myth for Africans of Christian persuasion which
devalued and obscured the past while glorifying a particular colonial version of
Christian identity as universal.[13]

The textually consolidated 'rise' of the African in missionary books, we have seen, occurred within the context of particular narrative configurations of the nineteenth-century missionary project in southern Africa. These narratives, all premised on a Manichean prefiguration of people and phenomena, ranged from the sentimental romantic quest in which the individual missionary hero, such as Moffat, survived doubt, difficulty and physical ordeals, but emerged triumphant as the standard bearer of God's coming influence, to the earnest figure of the field scientist, discoverer and missionary-explorer whose travels appropriated vast areas for inclusion in an imperial text of benign British influence. In the Eastern Cape, the 'model Kafir' was a textual emblem and his 'rise', within the parameters of a missionary narrative whose heroes were British and triumphant, required the complete rejection of traditional culture. In the 'model Kafir's' own textuality, however, the missionary text was rendered ambivalently. Like the suppressed evidence of a counter-text of Africanisation in the Moffats, and the internal inconsistencies of Livingstone's grand 'highway' for commerce and Christianity, Tiyo Soga's rendering of the missionary narrative suggests the difficulty of maintaining so exclusive and so totalising a narrative expression of a world which resisted incorporation by its variety and heterogeneity. It was only in the fully orthodox rewriting of Ntsikana's story by an African minister who was himself produced by Lovedale, the Reverend John Knox Bokwe, that the missionary text of a universal God was unambivalently superimposed upon the preceding culture in a textual gesture of natural continuity which obscured a past of difference in the name of the one text of Christianity.

# 6

## AFTERWORD

This book has explored the discursive operations of a civilising colonialism in nineteenth-century South Africa, founded in English as a site of orthodoxy and as a medium for momentous representational struggle. It has sought, in addition, to indicate the nature of textual response to the 'civilised' order by Africans who were taught by missionaries to revere Western values in the nineteenth century, particularly in the later Victorian period. In the original conception of this study, the struggle to institute a civilised cultural order based on English was meant to be only the first part of an investigation into the ontology of 'English' as a disciplinary condition – one whose relations to power, and whose colonial history, were perceived to be deliberately disguised or obscured. It has proved impossible to compass more than the very beginnings of such a larger study, largely because one cannot selectively discuss literary issues without also revealing the full political and historical context of such matters. That, indeed, was the point of embarking on the project in the first place. It proved to be more than a matter of sketching text against a *background* of context. Rather, the background had to move into the foreground, be recognised *as* the foreground. This meant that 'English' had to be lifted out of its neat and politically clean confines as merely the language in which texts of literary merit were written. English in this sense had to be seen as the whole assemblage of discursive machinery by which it was sought, with uneven results but to profound ultimate effect, to cordon off the very souls of 'barbarous' people, and to *rewrite* their subjectivity.

This apprehension of a discursive operation in which subjectivity was negotiated in terms of textual inscription and prescription is more than a mere metaphor for some other, less finely understood unit of analysis. It is based on

188

the perception of a process in which the cultural domain of language was an integral site of colonisation. As I argue in Chapter 2, the assiduous construction of a new order of literacy in the nineteenth century, and its intimate relation to the ascendancy of European power, meant that 'English' became a complex of things: the place where 'civilisation' was cultivated, where the socio-cultural capital for intersubjective converse in the new order could be gained, or, in less portentous terms, where the tools of writing and numeracy were learnt so that jobs could become available in the growing economy of capital and class. But these new necessities did not come without a cost. The 'English' of economic empowerment, or of social mobility and political influence within the revised hierarchies of power, also carried in its very substance new narratives of personhood, of the proper presentation of the body, of the best moral choices, of the most suitable organisation of the land and the dwellings thereon, of a new cosmological scheme, of the very clothes one should wear, the thoughts one may think and the manner in which work – and rest – should be performed. In the wider sense, then, 'English' encoded such narratives: they were set in train in every sermon, classroom talk, literary society lecture, field foray, and in the steady, incessant textual production of an era wholly devoted to the act of writing as its principal means of knowledge dissemination. The apprehension of self and subjectivity was therefore mediated at every turn by language and the selections, hierarchies, values and exclusions characteristic, in the narrower sense, of 'narrative', and in the broader sense, of 'discourse'.

Such an understanding of struggles to refashion people and their cultures by an aggressive humanism which nevertheless relentlessly presented itself as benign and God-ordained, tends to knock over disciplinary beacons. It means that one must 'read' history with a new sensitivity to the potential of both fact and value, process and event, in the traces of signification and discourse which make up the so-called 'archive'. History, to appropriate a popular cliché, becomes an 'open book', to be read and reread in terms not only of its yield for the present, but also for its sense of a contemporaneous *narrative* constitution: its ways of telling itself to itself, and the means by which those who were constrained to adopt its dominant conventions of telling and describing, nevertheless tried to tell things differently, indeed, tried to tell *themselves* otherwise. However unsatisfactorily I have treated history from an historian's point of view in this book, I hope this point will survive.

The larger omission, however, relates to the unfinished potential of the project as originally conceived. This potential relates to the perception that the origins of what is today studied and canonised in South Africa as English in an exalted literary sense, and the institutional as well as discursive forms which underpin such studies, are themselves integrally related to the civilising mission. One scholar who has also looked into the origins of English studies in South Africa, Christo Doherty, discovered that university-level education in English literature came to the country because a standard qualification was needed for the civil service (Doherty 1990:81-82). How far removed is this not from the Leavisite notion of a 'great tradition', and the Arnoldian sense of high culture, which so many colonial teachers of literature saw as their lodestars! Not only was the grand history of English 'literature' brought into service as a means of qualifying people for the colonial civil service – which was, after all, deeply imbued with racial supremacy – but African subjects of missionary tutelage were offered the conceptual tools of what was to become 'black writing in English' within a context of outright cultural supremacy. These tools were the literate means of making meaning, and the cultural codes, as well as the generic forms, associated with a strangely deferred Enlightenment. How often have literary scholars not tried to 'account', make apologies for, or simply condemn the anachronistic use of Romantic, Augustan, Shakespearian or other idioms by early African writers whose subject matter seems not to fit the form? The focus of such discussions have seldom been the very *dislocations* by which such hybrid forms have come into existence, but the 'problem' of seeing such literature as 'good' within a paternalistic ranking system. In other words, the perceived inadequacies of such writing have tended to be regarded as a separate issue from the processes by which the writing emerged into its 'colonised' forms in the first place. My project has been to insist that this prior history of subject construction, of representational struggle in English as discourse and not merely as literary product, be integrated with a larger history of the emergence and influence of English in South Africa. The matter can be framed as the difference between asking, on the one hand, what Africans *wrote* in English, and, on the other, how they were *written into* English.

What my study has achieved, I hope, is to establish that the larger text of English in colonial South Africa not only buttressed, but extended the work of a haphazard yet ultimately murderous imperialism in the country. One should not forget that the 'Grey Plan' to educate and civilise Africans in the Eastern Cape (see Chapter 3), which harnessed institutions such as Lovedale to execute its pacification-by-education strategies, found its most fertile ground in the devastation of the Cattle Killing in the mid-1850s (see Mostert 1992).

If one accepts, even partially, the arguments of Crais (1992a), Mostert (1992), Keegan (1991), and, following them, Legassick (1993), then the emphasis in the *making* of the colonial order in South Africa has shifted, in historiographic terms, from Dutch-Afrikaans and the Great Trek to the English settlers in the first half of the nineteenth century, together with the British-ruled Cape state (Legassick 1993:332 *et seq*). English as a mode of seeing, telling, describing, capturing and teaching in this context sought to prescribe and narrativise the identity of people it perceived as barbarous, and as such it was integral to establishing the cultural firmament of the colonial order. From this flowed 'black literature', since the new cultural imperialists set the tone, prescribed the forms, and sought to induce captive states of consciousness in their colonial subjects. From this began the long struggle to reappropriate such forms and to turn them against their colonial interests. This much I have tried to establish.

The unfinished work relates to more detailed and explicit extensions of such arguments; to the development of African nationalism as a narrative of emergence from just such beginnings; and to the question of how institutional forms of English teaching, including university teaching, continued to be a central facet of the colonising process. In what ways were the early departments of English a direct extension of the Lovedale mission to introduce Africans to the fruits of English letters and civilisation, for example? Can the work of R.H.W. Shepherd, famous twentieth-century principal of Lovedale who bequeathed us titles such as *Literature for the South African Bantu* (1936) and *Bantu Literature and Life* (1955), be seen as logically continued by Guy Butler? Butler identified the advent of black 'literature' in Sol T. Plaatje's *Mhudi*, but his project of incorporation was less interested in the emergence of Plaatje himself and others like him within a broader context (De Kock 1992b; see Morphet 1994). There are many such questions which beg to be answered by fresh labours of cultural-historical archaeology. Most pertinently, the continuities and discontinuities need to be investigated between colonial English, and the supposedly more sublime English of university teaching as it developed in the twentieth century. In this century, South Africans of English persuasion have enjoyed the perception of themselves as purveyors of a liberal cosmopolitanism. This was particularly true of English in the apartheid era, until the Marxists came along and blew apart the cosy assumption that English interests were liberal and humanitarian, in contrast to the precepts of those nasty Afrikaner nationalists. Yet if you listen to debates today, in the post-apartheid age, within organisations such as the English Academy of Southern

Africa, for example, that benign history, and that convenient liberal opposition to apartheid, is still called upon as though the Marxist debate about English capital's deep collusion with apartheid never occurred. 'English' in its institutional forms often still wishes to present itself as innocent of a coercive colonial history for which it should bear any responsibility whatsoever. Equally, it often still wishes to consolidate itself as a dominant culture, although this desire has been recoded within an apparently multicultural ethos. English is a long way from learning to be humble, from toppling the pyramid which has English at the apex and 'other' langauges and cultures underneath. It is a very long way from unlearning its naturalised hegemony and submitting itself, for example, to regular tuition in Zulu, or Sotho, or Xhosa, and having its concord errors underlined, its spelling errors ringed in red. It needs to learn the taste of failure, and the pathos of struggle in an unfamiliar cultural environment.

Until quite recently, South African universities simply have not wanted to fix their conception of English within any colonial history at all. As a result, postcolonial studies have come to the country very belatedly. The developmental line of 'English' has traditionally run from Chaucer to the twentieth century, and did not even bypass southern Africa until the likes of Stephen Gray, Tim Couzens, Isabel Hofmeyr, Kelwyn Sole and others in South Africa began campaigning for the recognition of 'local' writing in the 1970s. It is still hard to credit such deliberate cultural blindness. And it is still a curious irony that universities in the larger Western world often teach more southern African writing, with better resources, more interest, and greater determination, than South African universities are frequently able to muster.

It was the desire to understand such powerful processes of cultural repression, and such conspicuous moves to obscure the involvement of one's own discipline in its colonial past, that originally motivated this study. But many of the important questions have of necessity remained unanswered. The history was much bigger and wider than I could have anticipated. I only hope that this story will not be abandoned. It lies open for many scholars to pursue. It will remain a history that should trouble us for as long as we profess to talk about a past in cultural or historical terms, and about a future which arises from that past.

In more general terms, the allegory of 'civilisation' and 'barbarians' must continue to be regarded critically as the ongoing attempts by different interest groups to consolidate the material base of power with the legitimacy of truth-value. In present times, particularly, when public debate seems to generate volume rather than depth, it would be salutary indeed if there were a more critical discernment of the history of discursive struggle in South Africa. That way, some of the acute ironies of whites handing over power to blacks on 'civilised' conditions might become more apparent, just as the irony of 'civilising barbarians' in the nineteenth century might be better appreciated.

# NOTES

CHAPTER 1. DISCIPLINARY INTERSECTIONS

1. Strictly speaking, it would be more accurate to refer to 'southern Africa' (a geographical entity) when discussing the making of what would only later become 'South Africa' (a political entity). However, using 'southern Africa' implies a more extensive range than I have compassed in this book. I have therefore chosen to use 'South Africa' as a term of reference for the geographical area that would only later become known as such. This is especially necessary in view of the fact that my archival sources refer largely to the Eastern Cape and that I regard the Eastern Cape as a pre-eminent centre of colonial education in the nineteenth century, whose influence became pronounced in African nationalism in South Africa as a whole (see Williams 1970). It is also true, however, that political leaders drawn from the Lovedale-Fort Hare tradition were to become influential in the wider region of southern Africa and beyond (see Chapter 3).

2. The term 'inscribe' suggests the analogies of 'text' and 'narrative' to describe the nature and functions of orthodox missionary discourse. On the notion of 'text' as a model of reality, see Paul Ricoeur, 'The Model of the Text: Meaningful Action Considered as a Text' (1971) and Richard Harvey Brown, *Society as Text* (1987). The idea is also strongly evident in the work of anthropologist Clifford Geertz (Geertz 1983; Biersack 1989; Dening 1980:86). An extreme Derridean position would hold that 'there is nothing outside the text', but I wish to avoid the implicit politics of such a position, which inevitably tends towards confinement within the idea of play, reduces human agency, and leads to passivity. My idea of text as an analogue for the colonising imperative and its ramifications draws partly on the ascertainable (non-metaphoric) *literary* basis of missionary and other forms of colonialism, according to which the terms of autochthonous culture were rejected and new terms for a 'civilised' culture were written into a strongly literary education in English, which became the basis for a new, colonial version of knowledge. 'Text' and 'narrative', which suggest selective constitution, are therefore used as analogues for the hierarchical, ordering function of a civilising

colonialism, in which some modes of expression, interpretation and signification were privileged above others. The linguistic basis of such a civilising mission (English was often the principal medium for encoding the new orthodoxies) means that the text-analogue is more than a fanciful literary idea. However, as I argue in the main text, material practices also encode a signifying dimension in which social relations are represented.

3. The term 'discourse' is used frequently in this book, although I am aware that in other contexts it is often employed rather loosely. It is not possible to eliminate or change the term, firstly because it does have a particular meaning which no other word adequately captures, and secondly because the term has become contextually embedded in scholarly literature in the literary field and, to a lesser degree, the historical and other fields. I have sought to use the term discriminately, in two very definite senses. The first sense of the word is its regular usage to denote a particular set of conceptions about a subject ('the discourse of postcolonialism', or 'missionary discourse'). In a study dealing with orders and types of signification, such as this one, this usage is understandably common. The second sense of the word is a special one, in which I characterise 'English' as a 'master discourse' of colonial orthodoxy (see Chapter 2). This sense of the word relies on a Foucauldian understanding of the relationship between knowledge and power. One critic describes this sense of 'discourse' as 'the name for that language by which dominant groups within society constitute the field of "truth" through the imposition of specific knowledges, disciplines, and values' (Slemon 1987:6). I see missionary discourse as a principal constituent of this larger site of 'English' as a master discourse in the colonial world of South Africa in the nineteenth century.

4. In the case of South Africa, where British imperialism came to a definite political end at the time of Union in 1910, and again in 1961 when the country shed its symbolic ties with Britain, there is not a clear-cut case for claiming general 'postcolonial' status. The intervening history has, to some extent, both obscured and perpetuated the colonial past. Attwell (1993a:6) therefore talks of 'colonial postcolonialism' in his discussion of J.M. Coetzee's fiction. Before the 1994 transition to majority rule, Carusi (1991b:96) wrote that for a large part of the white population, the label was not an issue at all, whereas for the black majority it could be regarded as pre-emptive to think of 'postcolonial' history until apartheid was vanquished in all its forms. Afrikaners who fought in the South African War of 1899-1902 believed they were fighting against British imperialism and the consequent forms of colonialism (see Du Preez 1993). From the point of view of the Afrikaner right wing, which has articulated the history of Afrikaner resistance against British imperialism in South Africa most persistently, colonialism was an evil which was eradicated a long time ago. For black South Africans, the long reign of apartheid in the twentieth century has tended to overshadow the importance of colonialism in the nineteenth century as a

determining factor in the make-up of what was to become a racially divided nation. By its excesses apartheid has made colonial (missionary) education look even desirable. There is thus the irony that missionary education is viewed nostalgically by its subjects or the descendants of its subjects in relation to apartheid (see Jabavu 1963; Kuzwayo 1985; Ntantala 1992). Describing his admiration for British values, President Nelson Mandela has expressed this sentiment: 'Britain exercised a tremendous influence on our generation, at least. Because it was British liberals, missionaries, who started education in this country – education for Africans – at a time when the South African government took no responsibility whatsoever' (in Carlin 1993:11). Mandela's view elides the history of missionary colonialism as a bearer of epistemic violence. The South African Communist Party, on the other hand, has long proposed a theory of 'internal colonialism' or 'colonialism of a special type' which combines 'the worst features of both imperialism and colonialism in a single national frontier' and in which 'Non-white South Africa' is a colony of 'White South Africa' (Kistner 1989:35). Theories of postcoloniality in present-day South Africa would have to rely on a similar argument about continuing forms of neo-colonialism, and emphasise the surviving importance of colonial forms of knowledge and culture in the present. Writing in this vein, J.M. Coetzee (1988a:11) argues in the introduction to his collection of essays, *White Writing*, that after 1948 white South Africans graduated 'from being the dubious colonial children of a far-off motherland' to 'uneasy possession of their own, less and less transigent internal colony'. 'Postcolonial' in this book denotes both a temporal relation (modern South Africa, no longer a colony, was constituted within a colonial past), and a causal nexus (the colonial past deserves study because it established the foundation for surviving forms of subjectivity, self-apprehension, and othering; 'postcolonial' theoretical approaches are designed specifically to identify and relativise colonial forms of knowledge and aesthetics, which might otherwise remain obscure constituents of a poorly understood modern 'reality'). The idea of the 'postcolonial' in South African literary-cultural debate nevertheless continues to provoke acrimonious response and righteous condemnation, since it is linked (often by Marxian scholars) with 'irresponsible' tendencies towards 'textual radicalism' in a tradition derived from what is seen as imported metropolitan post-isms. On this debate, see Attwell (1993b), Sole (1994) and De Kock (1995).

5. See, for example, Clifton C. Crais, *The Making of the Colonial Order: White Supremacy and Black Resistance in the Eastern Cape, 1770-1865* (1992a), and his 'Representation and the Politics of Identity in South Africa: An Eastern Cape Example' (1992b); A. Ashforth, *The Politics of Official Discourse in Twentieth-Century South Africa* (1990); Jean and John Comaroff, *Of Revelation and Revolution: Christianity, Colonialism and Consciousness in South Africa* (1991), and *Ethnography and the Historical Imagination* (1992); Isabel Hofmeyr, '*We Spend Our*

*Lives as a Tale That is Told': Oral Historical Narrative in a South African Chiefdom* (1993); David Attwell, 'The Transculturation of English: The Exemplary Case of the Reverend Tiyo Soga, African Nationalist' (1994).

6. See Michael Chapman's essay, 'The Liberated Zone: The Possibilities of Imaginative Expression in a State of Emergency' (1988).

7. A conspicuous exception is the work of Hofmeyr, who writes both as an historian and a literary scholar. She has commented as follows on the tendency of literary scholars to confine themselves to strictly literary parameters: 'Interdisciplinary debate is best fostered by example but, in the end, radical literary scholarship in South Africa had little as example to offer. It generally remains narrow, textual, and rooted in the canon of local literature. I find it instructive, for example, that in the recent collection of essays edited by Trump [1990], most are focused on written texts and most of these on texts that clearly belong to the informal canon of South African literature' (1990:63).

8. See for example M.H. Abrams, who in his *A Glossary of Literary Terms* (1981:110), relates 'postmodernism' to 'recent developments in linguistic and literary theory, [in which] there is an effort to subvert the foundations of language itself, so as to show that its seeming meaningfulness dissipates … into a play of unresolvable indeterminacies'. This is a clear reference to poststructuralism.

9. Jefferson (1986:113) provides the following explanation: 'Logocentrism is the term [Derrida] uses to describe all forms of thought which base themselves on some external point of reference, such as the notion of truth. Western philosophy, with Plato as an exemplary first instance, has generally acted upon the supposition that language is subservient to some idea, intention or referent that lies outside it. This idea is at odds with the Saussurean principle that it is language which is primary, and that far from preceding language, meaning is an effect produced by language.' Abrams (1993:226) writes: 'By logos, or **presence**, Derrida signifies what he alternatively calls an 'ultimate referent' – a self-certifying absolute, ground, or foundation, outside the play of language itself, that is directly present to our awareness and suffices to 'center' (that is, to anchor and organise) the structure of the linguistic system in such a way as to fix the bounds, coherence, and determinate meanings of any spoken or written utterance within that system.'

10. See Ashcroft *et al.* (1989); Slemon & Tiffin (1990); Adam & Tiffin (1991); Williams and Chrisman (1993) for a sense of this scope and range.

11. Manicheism is described as follows in the *Collins Dictionary of Philosophy* (1990:180): 'Manicheism, n., a religion named after its Persian founder, Mani (*c.* 215-276). There are two opposed principles, Light (goodness) and Darkness (evil). Man's soul is good, his body evil. Salvation consists in freeing oneself from the evil material elements in one's nature.' The *OED* adds that 'Manichean' relates to a 'religious system (3rd-5th c.) that represented Satan as coeternal with

God', and that from this the philosophical meaning of 'dualist' is derived. The use of the term 'Manichean' with reference to the discourse of missionaries or other colonial figures should not, however, be read as implying that such people were themselves 'Manicheans', but as a reference to the dualism inherent in their speech or writing.

12. The word 'agonism' is borrowed from Foucault to describe the paradoxical position of apparently free agents who are constrained by larger power structures, but who nevertheless interpret the regulatory practices of such structures creatively or antagonistically. See Chapter 2 for further discussion.

13. I have deliberately left out Afrikaans as a language of colonisation, not because I wish to ignore that it played such a role, but because I believe an exclusive focus on English orthodoxy is required to bring into relief the important role English played as the language of governance and of formal colonial education, particularly in the Cape Colony. Further, mission-educated Africans in the late nineteenth century displayed a very strong loyalty to the figure of the British Crown and the English tradition of democracy and humanitarianism as the source of 'civilised' values, in contradistinction to Afrikaans as the language of a hostile counter-nationalism. See, for example, *Imvo Zabantsundu*, 18 January 1888, in which editor John Tengo Jabavu writes as follows in the context of the Registration Bill of 1887, which sought to disenfranchise thousands of black voters in the Cape on a technicality: 'In every division in the country where the Native vote exists Bondsmen, or Dutchmen, are busy placing what obstacles they can in the way of the Natives, to what our people believe to be their rights. Among these rights we may mention the common privilege of the Franchise, to which every British subject, who thinks he possesses certain qualifications, is entitled.' See also *Imvo*, 20 April 1887, 18 May 1887, 6 April 1888, and 31 March 1898. (See discussion of the Registration Bill in Chapter 4.)

14. For further discussion of this idea, see De Kock (1992b).

15. Frequently in scholarly dispute about the implications for historiography of what is perceived as postmodernism, the debate tends to place a hard version of postmodernism (seen as an irresponsible severance of discourse from reality) against a supposedly corrective view. The corrective view abhors what it perceives as the disinclination, in postmodernism, to observe the ethical responsibility of conveying a responsible understanding of the past. See, for example, the articles in the journal *History and Theory* by Ankersmit (1989) and Zagorin (1990). I find this polarisation unhelpful. In my sense of a postcolonial imperative to renarrativise the past, the point is not to sever the connection with reality, but to *reconfigure* it in a manner which more fully embraces the implications of textuality and representational self-reflexivity. For a more extensive discussion, see De Kock (1995).

16. For a fuller argument about the agency of critics acrossintercultural divides, and

the role of postcolonial criticism in either assisting or obstructing such endeavours, see De Kock (1993b).

## CHAPTER 2. THE MAKING OF COLONIAL ORTHODOXY

1. Switzer (1983:5) writes that Citashe's poem is thought to have been translated into English by A.C. Jordan. The poem, published in Xhosa as a letter to *Isigidimi Sama-Xosa* on 1 June 1882, is attributed by Odendaal (1983:48) to Isaac Wauchope. Odendaal writes that Citashe more frequently used the surname Wauchope and is remembered as Isaac Wauchope. Hoho is a site in the Amatole mountains in the Eastern Cape where, according to Xhosa tradition, Rharhabe paramount Sandile was killed in the ninth frontier war in 1878 (see Gérard 1971:41).

2. One of the earliest manifestations of this, typically acrimonious, kind of debate was the exchange between M.C. O'Dowd (1970), Jean Marquard (1971), and M.B. Gardiner (1971) in the pages of the literary journal *Contrast*. O'Dowd wrote that 'literature is one thing and social protest and all forms of political propaganda are another' (1970:59). Marquard replied that the 'confusion in Mr O'Dowd's thinking' (1971:96) arose from 'the notion that politics involves action in the world and literature does not' and that 'Great Writers, unlike other men, can transcend their human condition and step outside society to do their writing'. Gardiner (1971:92-93) joined the argument against O'Dowd, claiming that his point of view lacked subtlety and complexity. In the mid-1970s, several important articles appeared in the radical journal, *Work in Progress*, in which the growing Marxian approach in South African literary studies confidently asserted that the conditions of literary production had everything to do with political and historical influence (Sole 1977, Couzens 1977). A very remarkable polemic then emerged in the wake of Black Consciousness and 'Soweto Poetry' (see Chapman 1982), between A.G. Ullyatt (1977) and various respondents about the 'dilemmas' in 'black poetry' (Ullyatt's phrases). Ullyatt's criticism of black poetry drew sharp rebuttals from Sole (1978), Jos Slabbert (1978), and David Maughan-Brown (1979). A later version of a similar argument occurred as a debate about the efficacy of liberalism in South African literary practice (Richard Rive 1983 and Stephen Watson 1983), also in *Contrast*. The debate about high literary standards ('Western', 'elitist') and politically engaged writing ('materialist') featured in the 1980s in ongoing exchanges in the *Weekly Mail* between critics and scholars such as Lionel Abrahams (1987), Andries W. Oliphant (1989a; 1989b), Stephen Watson (1989a; 1989b; 1989c), and Kelwyn Sole (1989), among others. For a penetrating scholarly exposition of the various implications of this debate and of the politicisation of writing in general, see Chapman (1988, 1991) and Watson 1986). Other interesting articles include Vaughan (1982), Cooper (1987), and Ryan (1988). See also the volume of twenty essays on teaching English in South

Africa edited by Wright (1990).

3. An important exception is Ndebele, who in his 1986 keynote address to the Jubilee Conference of the English Academy of Southern Africa declared that English as a language was 'tainted with imperial interests' (1987:220) and that English 'cannot be considered an innocent language' (p.229).

4. One of the major shifts in missionary thinking in the nineteenth century was from the humanitarianism in the early part of the century to racism in the latter part after the advent of Social Darwinism and 'scientific racism' (Bolt 1971; Biddiss 1975; Cornwell 1989). Early, millenarian missionaries wished to elevate their subjects to a position of equality, but later ones adopted the ideas of paternalism and trusteeship (Hunt Davis 1969:173; Brantlinger 1986:185; Cuthbertson 1986:213-14; Bosch 1991:309-10).

5. The 'episteme', a term derived from the work of Foucault, is explained by Macdonell (1986:87) as the 'ground of thought' on which 'at a particular time some statements – and not others – will count as knowledge'. It is a notion that tends to suggest that knowledge exists in 'great layers obedient to specific structural laws' (p.88). Spivak (1988a:280-81) writes that the 'clearest example of epistemic violence is the remotely orchestrated, far-flung, and heterogeneous project to constitute the colonial subject as Other'. She adds that Foucault 'locates epistemic violence, a complete overhaul of the episteme, in the redefinition of sanity at the end of the European eighteenth century'.

6. Legassick (1993:332), reviewing Crais (1992a) and Mostert (1992), writes that there is a 'fresh synthesis' in South African history in the approach, recently adopted by Crais and Mostert, in which 'the emphasis in the shaping of twentieth-century South Africa is decisively shifted from Afrikaners to British settlers, together with the British-ruled Cape state'. Legassick adds, with apparent approval, that both Mostert and Crais 'have integrated the decisive stages in the colonial subjugation of the Xhosa into an account of the shaping of the racial order'.

7. Foucault uses these terms as follows in his preface to *The Order of Things* (1970: xxiv): 'The history of madness would be the history of the Other – that which, for a given culture, is at once interior and foreign, therefore to be excluded (so as to exorcise the interior danger) but by being shut away (in order to reduce its otherness); whereas the history of the order imposed on things would be the history of the Same – of that which, for a given culture, is both dispersed and related, therefore to be distinguished by kinds and collected into identities.'

8. See, for example, Williams (1959:225); Hunt Davis (1969:200); Jordan (1973:37).

9. Richard Gray (1990b:143) writes that most British and North American missionaries, in contrast with continental Protestants (especially Germans), saw Christianity intimately linked with the 'introduction of African societies to

Western ways of life', incorporating aspects such as upright houses with chimneys and 'decent' clothing.

10. However, for a critique of Peires's arguments in this respect in *The Dead Will Arise*, see the *South African Historical Journal* 25 (1991:227-68).

## CHAPTER 3. A SAVAGE CIVILITY

1. Islam (1975:75) gives the date of publication as 1899. He writes that the poem is 'worth close examination for the way in which it explicitly sets forth Kipling's views on the role of the empire-builder in the world'. Islam argues further that for Kipling in the 1890s, the phrase 'white man' suggested not only 'a man with a white skin, it had a secondary symbolic meaning: "a man with the moral standards of the civilized world" ' (1975:75).

2. Drawing on Goody, Jean Comaroff (1985:143) suggests that literacy generated a greater awareness 'of the process of abstraction and a concern with knowledge and value as explicit systems beyond the immediate contexts that generate them'. Writing about cultural transformation among the southern Tswana, Comaroff argues that literacy 'transforms the consciousness of those who acquire it' (p.143). Among the Tshidi, she writes, literacy promoted an increasing elaboration of objective constructs (encoded in language) to describe coherent bodies of knowledge. In her view, the writings of S.M. Molema suggest that there developed among the literate a reflective concern with the process of cultural evolution itself (p.144; see 143-44). Goody (1980:131) argues that writing 'must take language out of the immediate referential context' and that this process makes it possible for concepts to be 'more easily manipulated, more easily turned upside down'. Comaroff (1985:144) adds that literacy appears to drive a wedge between the 'word' and the 'world': 'In the same way as money and time permit the detachment of value and productivity from their total context, so written words – impersonal, functionally specific, and seemingly transparent – permit the reification of speech and knowledge' (p.144). Scribner (1984:11) comments, 'Historically, literacy has been a potent tool in maintaining the hegemony of elites and dominant classes in certain societies, while laying the basis for increased social and political participation in others'. See also Fabian (1986) on linguistic colonialism in the former Belgian Congo.

3. On translation as a concept in historical, intercultural analysis, see Sanneh (1989).

4. Indeed, as Coetzee (1988b:12-35) suggests, surveillance was implicit in the seventeenth and eighteenth centuries, too, in what Coetzee calls the Discourse of the Cape: '... no less than in the science of Man that met and was frustrated by the real Hottentots, the modern science of Man has at its foundation a will to see a culture at work in a society. The science of Man is itself a discipline, one of what Foucault calls the disciplines of surveillance ...' (p.34). In *Discipline and Punish*,

the work to which Coetzee refers, Foucault deals with the timetable as a 'penal style' (1977:7) and as an example of what he calls the 'power of normalization' (p.308). As indicated below, there is rich evidence of a timetable-driven regimentation of human labour at Lovedale, and of the 'normalisation' of African subjects within what may arguably be described as a Western-humanistic 'Science of Man'.

5.　There is considerable scope for research into the manner in which conceptions of self were rigidly genderised in Lovedale's teaching and training. In his travelogue entitled *South Africa* (1878), the already famous writer Anthony Trollope concluded a chapter entitled 'Kafir Schools' with deep condescension in relation to educated young African women: 'If I had an Institution of my own to exhibit I feel sure that I should want to put my best foot forward, – and the best foot among Kafir female pupils is perhaps the singing of hymns and the hemming of linen' (p.223).

6.　Modern histories dealing directly with Lovedale include Shepherd (1940), Brock (1974), Burchell (1979) and White (1987), while more general historical works which devote some attention to Lovedale or to missionary activity in general include Hunt Davis (1969), Walshe (1970), Mills (1975), Peires (1981), George (1982), Odendaal (1983; 1984a), and Bundy (1988).

7.　The details cited here are from Odendaal (1983:23-106).

8.　See, for example, Hartman (1975); LaCapra (1983); Hutcheon (1988); Novick (1988); Lawrence & Taylor (1993).

9.　'Comedy' as employed here does not refer simply to the conventional sense of 'humorous' or farcical, but to the formal generic sense in terms of which a predominant aspect is the resolution of differences in society. In Shakespearean comedy misunderstanding, delusion, and the limitations of individual perception are 'comically' resolved in the denoument, where maturity and understanding lead to social well-being under a benevolent god.

10.　Examples of comedic, tragic and satirical emplotments in missionary discourse are offered in this chapter, while romantic narratives are discussed in Chapter 5 in relation to Robert Moffat and David Livingstone.

11.　I am indebted to Richard Elphick for suggesting that I bring into prominence the comedic emplotment of missionary narrative.

12.　A related idea was expressed in the 'sleep of ages' metaphor. See Pixley Seme's 1906 poem, 'The Regeneration of Africa' (in Mutloatse 1981).

13.　A heavy-handed, top-down approach to education was not unique to Lovedale or to colonial South Africa. Hartshorne (1992:220), reviewing the European derivation of missionary education in South Africa, observes that 'all these influences … were based on a perception of public education as the training of the "lower orders" in "the habits of good order, respect for property and authority"'. Hartshorne concludes 'This education bore all the marks of being designed to establish the "proper place" in society of those who received it'. Ivan Rabinowitz, discussing more recent trends, has suggested that 'current thinking in the debased phenomenology of "fundamental pedagogics" in South Africa is itself a product of Manichean antitheses and paternalistic disciplinary procedures, tricked out as "spiritual" development' (personal communication).

14. A conspicuous example is the influential work by C.T. Loram, *The Education of the South African Native* (1917:310), in which it is written, for example: 'The need [for universities for black South Africans] has not yet made itself felt in South Africa, and we should take cognisance of the danger (so apparent in India and Egypt) of educating any considerable number of individuals beyond the requirements of their race'.

15. Stewart's sense of 'character' can also be related to what Hobsbawm and Ranger (1983) would refer to as 'invention of tradition' – in this case, the tradition of gentility. See Ranger (1983:215-20).

16. A good general text in English on this theory is *Speech and Language in Psychoanalysis* (Lacan 1968).

17. Crais, however, takes pains to emphasise the less visible, 'hidden struggles' (1992a:221) of the working classes in the development of African nationalism.

## Chapter 4. Subversive Subservience

1. In references to *Imvo*, page numbers have been omitted because they were not always apparent on the original copies of the newspaper. The omission of page numbers is, however, not an impediment to quick reference since *Imvo* usually ran to four pages only and its English pieces (often editorial comment) were usually placed on the front page.

2. Jabavu was not completely independent in his control of the newspaper, since his venture was financially underwritten by R.W. Rose Innes and James W. Weir, but he asserted full editorial autonomy (see Odendaal 1983:105; Brock 1974:261). His newspaper was closed down in 1899 because his uncompromising line on the South African War became unpalatable to his sponsors. According to Switzer & Switzer (1979:4-5), other independent African newspapers did not begin to appear until the 1890s and early 1900s, in contrast to *Imvo*, which was established in 1884. Walter Rubusana founded *Izwi Labantu* in 1897, John Dube established *Ilanga lase Natal* in 1903, Silas Molema and Sol Plaatje set up *Koranta ea Becoana* in 1901, and others followed at slightly later dates.

3. Ngcongco (1974:43-44) writes that the circulation figures for *Imvo* are not available, but that a general impression existed that the newspaper was successful and widely read.

4. Lyotard (1984:19-20) writes that investigations into the nature of knowledge agree on the pre-eminence of the narrative form in the formulation of knowledge. Narratives 'allow the society in which they are told, on the one hand, to define its

criteria of competence and, on the other, to evaluate according to those criteria what is performed or can be performed within it'. Ashley (1982:50), relying on Peter L. Berger and Thomas Luckmann in *The Social Construction of Reality* (1967), writes, 'Legitimation is that machinery whereby explanations are provided for the nature of reality and occurs through the nature of language itself … and ultimately through the symbolic universe'.

5. Roux's chapter on 'Jabavu and the Cape Liberals' (1964:53-77) portrays Jabavu as an astute campaigner who gradually became the victim of 'special pleading' on behalf of his political backers and who eventually 'allowed himself to become ever more plainly the tool of a group of white politicians'. Roux's version of Jabavu shows no awareness of the ambivalence of Jabavu's position. Ncgongco (1974:90) follows Roux in the portrayal of Jabavu as a 'special pleader', while Odendaal (1983) does not argue for ambivalence in Makiwane's 'admission' that Europeans were superior to Africans. It must be emphasised to Odendaal's credit, however, that he argues elsewhere (1984b:17-18) for a more subtle understanding of the apparent conformity of leading African figures. Behind the 'mask of moderate passivity', Odendaal writes, 'there was a language of politics for speaking to the "nation"' (p.18). He adds, 'The ambiguity and subtlety of this has not been fully understood' (p.18). Work which takes issue with the view of African leadership figures as romantically deluded includes Hargreaves (1960), Ranger (1968), Isaacman and Isaacman (1977) and, more tangentially, Attwell (1994).

6. In the latter part of the nineteenth century, ideas based on Social Darwinism 'integrated the idea of the superiority of "advanced races" and that of human progress into a utopian blueprint' (Dietrich 1993:293). Takaki (1992:907) argues that a similar 'social construction of race' occurred in North America in the context of competition over land. On the discourse of race in South Africa, such as Makiwane appears to be participating in, see also Coetzee (1980) and Cornwell (1989). In general, see Bolt (1971), Biddiss (1975), Brantlinger (1988).

7. As Switzer & Switzer (1979:40) note, the ownership of *Imvo* remained in the Jabavu family until 1935, after which the newspaper was sold to Bantu Press. In a twist of irony, *Imvo* was bought by the National Party-supporting printing and newspaper company, Perskor, in the 1960s. But there is a further irony in the fact that *Imvo* under its Perskor-appointed editor, Blignaut de Villiers, in 1993-94 supported the African National Congress. De Villiers told me in a telephone conversation (26 May 1993) that 'politics make strange bedfellows' and it would be very impolitic for a newspaper with a black readership not to support African nationalism in the 1990s. My own observation of the newspaper confirmed that *Imvo* vigorously opposed the National Party and the former white government, which Blignaut described as 'illegitimate', in the run-up to the 1994 election.

8. For the account of Jabavu's fortunes in the 1990s, I am indebted to Ngcongco (1979:48 *et seq.*) and Odendaal (1983:171-90).

CHAPTER 5. MISSIONARY HEROES

1. The dissension between Moffat and Read was part of a larger context of missionary policy and London Missionary Society politics. Legassick (1969:436-46) describes how the 'crisis' of adulterous activities by LMS missionaries led to the appointment of Dr John Philip as LMS Superintendent at the Cape. Moffat was strongly opposed to the appointment. His antipathy towards Philip intensified when Philip warmed to the apparently likeable and more humane Read, whom the puritan Moffat regarded as 'beneath contempt' (Legassick 1969:440). Legassick sums Moffat up as 'cynical, dogmatic, and authoritarian' (p.449).

2. Moffat's forgiving attitude to Van der Kemp on the matter of his marriage to an ex-slave is in marked contrast to his upbraiding of James Read for committing adultery with a Khoikhoi woman. Apart from the broader dissension between Moffat and Read, Moffat seems to have objected to the 'moral collapse' he perceived in Read's adultery. Theological scruples dictated this kind of outrage in the ranks of the Reformed ministers of the Congregational persuasion. It is interesting that Moffat felt far less strongly about Van der Kemp's act of marrying across the colour line. Racism was presumably less important than morality at this early stage.

3. I am indebted to Tim Couzens for pointing out that for Moffat, 'panther' would have been used as a synonym for leopard.

4. According to Northcott (1961:21-23), Moffat's only formal theological training was based on a series of eighty lectures by London Missionary Society director William Roby. To study the lectures, Moffat as a youth copied each one down in his own longhand. Northcott writes that Moffat found in Roby's lectures three (deeply Calvinist) guiding principles for his theology of mission: acceptance, duty, and obedience. Accepting necessary sacrifice and suffering in the course of God's work would therefore have constituted an important part of Moffat's theology.

5. The application of cow dung on floors may have been more acceptable to Mary Moffat in view of the fact that it was widely practised by the trekboers. Nevertheless, her own barely suppressed ambivalence about confessing this habit to correspondents in Europe betrays a sense of shame about the possibility of Africanisation.

6. Brantlinger (pp.180-81), however, includes Livingstone in his description of great explorers whose writings are 'nonfictional quest romances in which the hero-authors struggle through enchanted, bedeviled lands towards an ostensible goal: the discovery of the Nile's sources, the conversion of the cannibals'.

7. See Saayman (1991:58-64) on the complexity of Soga's position in relation to the sharply opposed social and cultural contexts from which he emerged. See also Odendaal (1984b:17-18).

8. On Brownlee as a figure in his own right, see Bergh (1984).

9. On the War of the Axe as an historical phenomenon, see Le Cordeur & Saunders (1981) and Mostert (1992).

10. See Attwell (1994:14-16). In a personal communication (1994), Attwell notes that (i) Chalmers claims that the confessional passages come from the journal, which is demonstrably untrue; (ii) It seems reasonable to assume that Chalmers is referring to the private journal in existence (housed at Fort Hare) because he does say that the passages are written substantially in Xhosa, with Greek annotations. The journal at Fort Hare has passages in Xhosa with the odd Greek word, but nothing on the scale described by Williams. This leads Attwell to believe that Chalmers is referring at least in part to the Fort Hare journal, *and* that he is misrepresenting it; (iii) The confessional passages are rendered in entirely conventional English, in marked contrast to Soga's very peculiar style of writing. This means that anyone could have written them. 'The best we can do,' writes Attwell, 'is to recognise that there has been severe intervention by Chalmers (it is only the precise scale that is in doubt), and then to interpret that intervention on the basis of Chalmers's other statements.' Williams (1983:209) concurs. He comments that Chalmers took 'liberties' in his editing of Soga's written material, but nevertheless regards Chalmers's evidence on Soga as 'valuable'.

11. Soga was not alone in doing this. Celebrated examples include Bleek's *Zulu Legends* (1857), Callaway's *Nursery Tales, Traditions, and Histories of the Zulus* (1868), and Theal's *Kaffir Folk-Lore* (1882). The important difference is that Soga did this from within Xhosa culture. I am indebted to historian Patrick Harries for suggesting, in a reader's report, that such recordings of culture constituted a tradition, or convention, through which Europeans hoped to understand people to be converted and ruled, and in which a certain reverence for indigenous culture was expressed (in contrast to explicitly racist claims). According to Harries, folklore studies were a means of giving temporal and spatial coherence to the terms 'nation' and 'race', which may still have been regarded as innovative at the time of these studies. In this sense, Harries suggests, 'nation' was construed as a bulwark against the anarchy unleashed by capitalism and colonialism. Further, see Leroy Vail (ed.), *The Creation of Tribalism in Southern Africa* (1989), on ways in which tribal pasts were constructed for particular purposes in the colonial period. Ranger (1983) also deals with the ways in which various senses of tradition were invoked in colonial Africa.

12. Attwell (1994) takes a more affirmative line on what he describes as Soga's 'enunciative position'. For Attwell, Soga's 'adoption of missionary discourse in the English language would entail the transculturation and trans*valuation* of the very aims and instruments of the civilising mission' (p.4). Soga thus faced the challenge, in Attwell's reading, of reversing the tendency, in the colonies, in which the Enlightenment was historically realised as Eurocentrism (pp.4-5). Drawing on instances of polemical utterance by Soga, Attwell concludes

suggestively that Soga's position was 'paradoxical but also transformative, a curiously enlightened form of counter-enlightenment ... the consequence of Soga's in-betweenness' (p.13). Attwell describes Soga's 'currency' as '[i]ncorporation into a global and teleological history, the retention of racial distinctiveness, and adaptability to change' (p.13). Soga 'embraced the civilising mission and sought to establish a new enunciative position within it' (p.18). This is a telling account, although it tends to renarrativise Soga as a 'transformative' figure when such a recasting seems possible only from a present-day perspective. Attwell's position relies on a view of the continuity between Soga's 'currency' of African distinctiveness *vis-à-vis* Enlightenment universalism, and its present manifestations which the author finds in Nelson Mandela and the 1993 constitution. However, in contemporaneous context, Soga's transgressive enunciations appear to have been muted and rare. Attwell's account attributes more intentionality, within a postcolonial and strategic reading, than Soga seems to have mustered in his various, and contradictory, utterances.

Another way of seeing Soga's situation is to argue, as Odendaal (1984b:17-18) does, that Soga (and others in a similar position) 'spoke out of politeness', but that this did not detract from their 'basic black consciousness and aims'. Odendaal says over-reliance on English sources has led to a failure to recognise the 'essential African speaking behind the acquired, and of necessity, correct western constitutional voice'. Behind the 'formal mask of moderate passivity' was a 'language of politics' for speaking to 'the nation' as well as a 'language of politics for speaking to the white man'. Odendaal argues that the 'ambiguity and subtlety of this has not been fully understood'. While I agree that Soga's position was ambiguous and complex, I disagree that such a thing as an 'essential' African is at all recoverable to historians of the nineteenth century. As I have argued, in Soga's case, the subject-effects discernible are contradictory and indicate an ambivalently stranded subjectivity. In my view, Soga was neither a perfect convert nor an adherent of what today might be styled 'black consciousness'. His position seems more accurately described as one of irreducible ambivalence.

13. See also A.K. Soga's poem, 'Ntsikana's Vision', published in *Imvo Zabantsundu* in 1897 (in Mutloatse 1981), in which a similar blending of Xhosa and Christian elements is resolved by recasting Christianity as a universal truth.

# SELECT BIBLIOGRAPHY

## I  Archives and Manuscript Collections

James Stewart Papers: Manuscripts and Archives, Jagger Library, University of Cape Town.
Lovedale Collection, Cory Library for Historical Research, Rhodes University, Grahamstown.

## II  Newspapers and Periodicals

Free Church of Scotland. Home and Foreign Missionary Record, 1843-1850.
Glasgow Missionary Society Reports 1821-1843.
*Christian Express* 1876-1878.
*Lovedale News* 1876-1879
*Imvo Zabantsundu* 1884-1898
*Izwi Labantu* 1901-1902

## III  Books, Articles and Theses

Abrahams, Lionel. 1987. Poetry is difficult: That is the Price We Pay for Depth. *Weekly Mail* April 3.
Abrams, M.H. 1981. A *Glossary of Literary Terms*. 4 edn. New York: Holt, Rinehart & Winston.
_____ 1993. A *Glossary of Literary Terms*. 6 edn. New York: Holt, Rinehart & Winston.
Adam, Ian & Tiffin, Helen (eds). 1991. *Past the Last Post: Theorising Post-Colonialism and Post-Modernism*. New York: Harvester.
Adhikari, Mohamed. 1992. The sons of Ham: Slavery and the making of coloured identity. *South African Historical Journal* 27.
Ahmad, Aijaz. 1992. *In Theory: Classes, Nations, Literatures*. London: Verso.
Alcoff, Linda. 1991. The problem of speaking for others. *Cultural Critique* 20.

Alonso, Ana Maria. 1988. The effects of truth: Re-presentations of the past and the imagining of community. *Journal of Historical Sociology* 1 (1).

Anderson, Benedict. 1991. *Imagined Communities: Reflections on the Origin and Spread of Nationalism*. London: Verso.

Anderson, Mary R. 1992. Deconstruction and the teaching historian. *History of European Ideas* 14 (4).

Ankersmit, F.R. 1989. Historiography and postmodernism. *History and Theory* 28.

Anon. 1892. *Rivers of Water in a Dry Place*. London: Religious Tract Society.

Armstrong, James C. & Worden, Nigel A. 1989. The Slaves, 1652-1834. In Elphick, Richard & Giliomee, Herman (eds), *The Shaping of South African Society, 1652-1840*. Cape Town: Maskew Miller Longman.

Ashcroft, Bill, Griffiths, Gareth & Tiffin, Helen (eds). 1989. *The Empire Writes Back: Theory and Practice in Post-Colonial Literatures*. Routledge: London.

Ashforth, Adam. 1990. *The Politics of Official Discourse in Twentieth-Century South Africa*. Oxford: Clarendon Press.

Ashley, M.J. 1982. Features of modernity: Missionaries and education in South Africa, 1850-1900. *Journal of Theology for Southern Africa* 38.

Attwell, David. 1993a. *J.M. Coetzee: South Africa and the Politics of Writing*. Cape Town: David Philip.

_____ 1993b. Introduction. *Current Writing* 5 (2) (Special Issue on Post-coloniality).

_____ 1994. The Transculturation of English: The Exemplary Case of the Rev. Tiyo Soga, African Nationalist. Inaugural address, University of Natal, Pietermaritzburg.

Bergh, J.S. 1984. *Die Lewe van Charles Pacalt Brownlee tot 1857*. Archives Year Book for South African History 1981. Pretoria: Government Printer.

Bhabha, Homi K. 1983. The other question: The stereotype and colonial discourse. *Screen* 24 (6).

_____ (ed.). 1990. *Nation and Narration*. New York: Routledge.

_____ 1994. *The Location of Culture*. London: Routledge.

Biddiss, Michael D. 1975. Myths of the blood: European racist ideology 1850-1945. *Patterns of Prejudice* 9 (5).

Biersack, Aletta. 1989. Local Knowledge, Local History: Geertz and Beyond. In Hunt, Lynn (ed.), *The New Cultural History*. Berkeley: University of California Press.

Blaikie, W.G. No date. *David Livingstone: Missionary and Explorer*. London: Religious Tract Society.

Bleek, W.H.I. 1857. *Zulu Legends*. Ed. J. A. Engelbrecht. Pretoria: Van Schaik, 1952. (From Bleek's 1857 handwritten MS.)

Bloom, Harold. 1975. *A Map of Misreading*. New York: Oxford.

Bokwe, John Knox. 1914. *Ntsikana: The Story of an African Convert*. 2 edn. Lovedale: Lovedale Press.

Bolt, Christine. 1971. *Victorian Attitudes to Race*. London: Routledge.

Bosch, David J. 1991. *Transforming Mission: Paradigm Shifts in Theology of Mission*. New York: Orbis Books.

Boucher, Maurice (ed.). 1985. *Livingstone Letters 1843 to 1872: David Livingstone Correspondence in the Brenthurst Library Johannesburg*. Johannesburg: The Brenthurst Press.

Brantlinger, Patrick. 1986. Victorians and Africans: The Genealogy of the Myth of the Dark Continent. In Gates, Henry Louis Jr. (ed.), *'Race' Writing and Difference*. Chicago: University of Chicago Press.

_____ 1988. *Rule of Darkness: British Literature and Imperialism, 1830-1914*. Ithaca: Cornell University Press.

Brock, Sheila M. 1974. James Stewart and Lovedale: A Reappraisal of Missionary Attitudes and African Response in the Eastern Cape, South Africa, 1870-1905. Ph.D. thesis, University of Edinburgh.

Brown, Richard Harvey. 1987. *Society as Text: Essays on Rhetoric, Reason and Reality*. Chicago: University of Chicago Press.

Bruwer, E.C.D. 1988. From subsistence cultivator, to peasant, to farm worker. *Missionalia* 16 (2).

Bundy, Colin. 1988. *The Rise and Fall of the South African Peasantry*. 2 edn. Cape Town: David Philip.

Burchell, D.E. 1979. A History of the Lovedale Missionary Institution, 1890-1930. M.A. dissertation, University of Natal.

Callaway, Henry. 1868. *Nursery Tales, Traditions, and Histories of the Zulus*. Vol 1. London: Trubner.

Carlin, John. 1993. Love Affair with Britain (Interview with Nelson Mandela). *Saturday Star* 1 May.

Carroll, David. 1987. Narrative, Heterogeneity, and the Question of the Political: Bakhtin and Lyotard. In Krieger, Murray (ed.), *The Aims of Representation: Subject/Text/History*. New York: Columbia University Press.

Carusi, Annamaria. 1991a. The postcolonial Other as a problem for political action. *Journal of Literary Studies* 7 (3/4).

_____ 1991b. Post, Post and Post. Or, Where is South African Literature in All This? In Adam, Ian & Tiffin, Helen (eds), *Past the Last Post: Theorizing Post-Colonialism and Post-Modernism*. New York: Harvester.

Chalmers, John A. 1877. *Tiyo Soga: A Page of South African Mission Work*. Edinburgh: Andrew Elliot.

Chanaiwa, David. 1980. African Humanism in Southern Africa: The Utopian, Traditionalist, and Colonialist Worlds of Mission-Educated Elites. In Mugomba, Agrippah T. & Nyaggah, Mougo (eds), *Independence Without Freedom: The Political Economy of Colonial Education in Southern Africa*. Santa Barbara; Oxford: ABC-Clio.

Chapman, Michael (ed.). 1982. *Soweto Poetry*. Johannesburg: McGraw Hill.

_____ 1988. The liberated zone: The possibilities of imaginative expression in a state of emergency. *English Academy Review 5*.

_____ 1991. The Critic in a State of Emergency: Towards a Theory of Reconstruction (after February 2). In Petersen, Kirsten Holst & Rutherford, Anna (eds), *On Shifting Sands: New Art and Literature from South Africa*. Sydney: Dangaroo Press and Heinemann.

_____ 1993. Red People and School People from Ntsikana to Mandela: The significance of "Xhosa literature" in a general history of South African literature. *English Academy Review 10*.

Chrisman, Laura. 1993. The Imperial Unconscious? Representations of Imperial Discourse. In Williams, Patrick & Chrisman, Laura (eds), *Colonial Discourse and Post-Colonial Theory: A Reader*. New York: Harvester .

Christie, Pam. 1991. *The Right to Learn: The Struggle for Education in South Africa*. Johannesburg: Sached/Ravan.

Cobley, Alan Gregor. 1986. 'On the Shoulders of Giants': The Black Petty Bourgeoisie in Politics and Society in South Africa, 1924-1950. Ph.D. thesis, University of London. Published as *Class and Consciousness: The Black Petty Bourgeoisie in South Africa, 1924-1950*. New York: Greenwood Press, 1990.

Cochrane, James. 1987. *Servants of Power: The Role of English-speaking Churches 1903-1930*. Johannesburg: Ravan.

Coetzee, J.M. 1980. Blood, flaw, taint, degeneration: The case of S.G. Millin. *English Studies in Africa* 23 (1). (Also in 1988a.)

_____ 1988a. *White Writing: On the Culture of Letters in South Africa*. New Haven: Radix/Yale University Press.

_____ 1988b. Idleness in South Africa. In Coetzee, J.M., *White Writing: On the Culture of Letters in South Africa*. New Haven: Radix/Yale University Press.

_____ 1992. *Doubling the Point: Essays and Interviews*. Edited by David Attwell. Cambridge, Mass: Harvard University Press.

Comaroff, Jean. 1985. *Body of Power, Spirit of Resistance: The Culture and History of a South African People*. Chicago: University of Chicago Press.

Comaroff, Jean & Comaroff John. 1988. Through the looking glass: Colonial encounters of the first kind. *Journal of Historical Sociology* 1 (1).

_____ 1991. *Of Revelation and Revolution: Christianity, Colonialism and Consciousness in South Africa*. Chicago: University of Chicago Press.

_____ 1992. *Ethnography and the Historical Imagination*. Boulder, San Francisco and Oxford: Westview Press.

Comaroff, John L. 1989. Images of empire, contests of conscience: Models of colonial domination in South Africa. *American Ethnologist* 16 (4).

Cooper, Brenda. 1987. The value of the pearl: For now or forever? The question of the universal in a materialist aesthetic. *English Academy Review* 4.

Cooper, Frederick. 1994. Conflict and connection: Rethinking colonial African history. *American Historical Review* 99 (5).

Cornwell, Gareth. 1989. Race as science, race as language. *Pretexts* 1 (1).

Cousins, H.T. 1899. *From Kafir Kraal to Pulpit: The Story of Tiyo Soga*. London: Partridge.

Couzens, Tim. 1977. Criticism of South African literature. *Work in Progress* 2.

_____ 1980. 'The New African': Herbert Dhlomo and Black South African Literature in English 1857-1956. Ph.D. thesis, University of the Witwatersrand.

_____ 1985. *The New African: A Study of the Life and Work of H.I.E. Dhlomo*. Johannesburg: Ravan.

Crais, Clifton C. 1992a. *The Making of the Colonial Order: White Supremacy and Black Resistance in the Eastern Cape, 1770-1865*. Johannesburg: Witwatersrand University Press.

_____ 1992b. Representation and the politics of identity in South Africa: An eastern Cape example. *International Journal of African Historical Studies* 25 (1).

Curtin, Philip D. 1964. *The Image of Africa*. Madison: University of Wisconsin Press.

Cuthbertson, G.C. 1986. The Nonconformist Conscience and the South African War 1899-1902. Ph.D. thesis, University of South Africa.

_____ 1987. The English-Speaking Churches and Colonialism. In Villa-Vicencio, Charles (ed.), *Theology and Violence: The South African Debate*. Braamfontein: Skotaville.

_____ 1991. 'Cave of Adullam': Missionary reaction to Ethiopianism at Lovedale, 1898-1902. *Missionalia* 19 (1).

Davenport, T.R.H. 1978. *South Africa: A Modern History*. 2 edn. London: Macmillan.

_____ 1987. The Cape Liberal Tradition to 1910. In Butler, Jeffrey, *et al.* (eds), *Democratic Liberalism in South Africa*. Cape Town: David Philip.

Deane, David J. No date. *Robert Moffat the Missionary Hero of Kuruman*. London: S.W. Partridge.

De Kock, Leon. 1992a. Interview with Gayatri Chakravorty Spivak: New Nation Writers Conference in South Africa. *Ariel* 23 (3).

_____ 1992b. English and the colonisation of form. *Journal of Literary Studies* 8 (1/2).

_____ 1993a. The central South African story, or many stories? A response to 'Red People and School People from Ntsikana to Mandela'. *English Academy Review* 10.

_____ 1993b. Postcolonial analysis and the question of critical disablement. *Current Writing* 5 (2).

_____ 1995. Reading history as cultural text. *Alternation* 2 (1).

Dening, Greg. 1980. *Islands and Beaches: Discourse on a Silent Land. Marquesas 1774-1880*. Honolulu: University of Hawaii Press.

Dickason, Olive Patricia. 1984. *The Myth of the Savage: And the Beginnings of French Colonialism in the Americas*. Edmonton: University of Alberta Press.

Dietrich, Keith Hamilton. 1993. Of Salvation and Civilisation: The Image of Indigenous Southern Africans in European Travel Illustration from the Sixteenth to the Nineteenth Centuries. Ph.D. thesis, University of South Africa.

Doherty, C.M.W. 1990. A Genealogical History of English Studies in South Africa. M.A. dissertation, University of Natal.

Du Bruyn, Johannes Tobias. 1980. Die Aanvangsjare van die Christelike Sending onder die Tlhaping. M.A. dissertation, University of South Africa.

Dunton, Chris. 1993. Africa's language problem. *West Africa* (22-28 March).

Du Plessis, J. 1911. *A History of Christian Missions in South Africa*. London: Longmans, Green.

Du Preez, Max. 1993. En as F.W. die Horlosie Kon Terugdraai? *Vrye Weekblad* 7-13 May.

Du Toit, A.E. 1963. *The Earliest South African Documents on the Education and Civilization of the Bantu*. Pretoria: University of South Africa.

Eagleton, Terry. 1990. Nationalism: Irony and Commitment. In Eagleton, Terry *et al.*, *Nationalism, Colonialism, and Literature*. Minneapolis: University of Minnesota Press.

Elbourne, Elizabeth. 1991. Concerning missionaries: The case of Van der Kemp. *Journal of Southern African Studies* 17 (1).

_____ 1992. Early Khoisan Uses of Mission Christianity. Paper, conference on People, Power & Culture: The History of Christianity in South Africa, 1792-1992. University of the Western Cape.

Ellis, J.J. No date. *Life Story of David Livingstone*. London: 14 Paternoster Row.

Elphick, Richard. 1977. *Kraal and Castle: Khoikhoi and the Founding of White South Africa*. New Haven: Yale University Press.

_____ 1992. Writing about Christianity in History: Some Issues of Theory and Method. Keynote address, conference on People, Power & Culture: The History of Christianity in South Africa, 1792-1992. University of the Western Cape.

Elphick, Richard & Giliomee, Herman. 1989. *The Shaping of South African Society, 1652-1840*. Cape Town: Maskew Miller Longman.

Enklaar, Ido H. 1988. *Life and Work of Dr J. Th. Van Der Kemp 1747-1811*. Cape Town: A.A. Balkema.

Etherington, Norman. 1976. Mission station melting pots as a factor in the rise of South African black nationalism. *International Journal of African Historical Studies* 9 (4).

_____ 1994. Recent Trends in the Historiography of Christianity in Southern Africa. Paper delivered at the *Journal of Southern African Studies* 20th Anniversary Conference, York.

Fabian, Johannes. 1986. *Language and Colonial Power: The Appropriation of Swahili in the Former Belgian Congo 1880-1938*. Cambridge: Cambridge University Press.

Fanon, Frantz. 1961. *The Wretched of the Earth*. London: Penguin.

Fast, Hildegarde Helene. 1991. African Perceptions of the Missionaries and their Message: Wesleyans at Mount Coke and Butterworth, 1825-35. M.A. dissertation, University of Cape Town.

Foucault, Michel. 1970. *The Order of Things: An Archaeology of the Human Sciences*. London: Tavistock.

———— 1977. *Discipline and Punish: The Birth of the Prison*. Transl. Alan Sheridan. London: Ellen Lane.

———— 1982. The subject and power. *Critical Inquiry* 8.

Frame, Hugh F. 1944. *Roll On, Wagon Wheels*. Johannesburg: ELD Trust (repr. 1983).

Frye, Northrop. 1976. *The Secular Scripture: A Study of the Structure of Romance*. Cambridge, Mass.: Harvard University Press.

Gardiner, M.B. 1971. Writing and injustice. *Contrast* 7 (1).

Gates, Henry Louis Jr. 1987. Authority, (white) power and the (black) critic; it's all Greek to me. *Cultural Critique* 76.

Geertz, Clifford. 1983. *Local Knowledge: Further Essays in Interpretive Anthropology*. New York: Basic Books.

George, Ambrose Cato. 1982. The London Missionary Society and Education: A Study of the Eastern Frontier to 1852. M.A. dissertation, Rhodes University.

Gérard, Albert S. 1971. *Four African Literatures: Xhosa, Sotho, Zulu, Amharic*. Berkeley: University of California Press.

Godlonton, Robert. 1836. *A Narrative of the Irruption of the Kafir Hordes into the Eastern Province of the Cape of Good Hope, 1834-35*. Grahamstown: Meurant & Godlonton.

Goody, Jack. 1977. *The Domestication of the Savage Mind*. Cambridge: Cambridge University Press.

———— 1980. Thought and Writing. In Gellner, Ernest (ed.), *Soviet and Western Anthropology*. London: Duckworth.

Gray, Richard. 1990a. *Black Christians and White Missionaries*. London: Yale University Press.

———— 1990b. Christianity. In Roberts, A.D. (ed.), *The Colonial Moment in Africa: Essays on the Movement of Minds and Materials 1900-1940*. Cambridge: Cambridge University Press.

Gray, Stephen. 1979. *Southern African Literature: An Introduction*. Cape Town: David Philip.

———— (ed.). 1989. *The Penguin Book of Southern African Verse*. London: Penguin.

Greenstein, Ran. 1994. South African Studies and the Politics of Theory: Old Challenges and New Paradigms. Paper delivered at the *Journal of Southern African Studies* 20th Anniversary Conference, York.

Grove, Richard. 1989. Scottish missionaries, evangelical discourses and the origin of conservation thinking in southern Africa 1820-1900. *Journal of Southern African Studies* 15.

Gunner, E. 1986. The Word, the Book and the Zulu Church of Nazareth. In Whitaker,

Richard & Sienaert, Edgard (eds), *Oral Tradition and Literacy*. Durban: University of Natal Oral Documentation and Research Centre.

Guy, Jeff. 1983. *The Heretic*. Johannesburg: Ravan.

Hargreaves, J.D. 1960. Towards a history of the partition of Africa. *Journal of African History* 1.

Harington, A.L. 1980. *Sir Harry Smith – Bungling Hero*. Cape Town: Tafelberg.

Harris, Cornwallis. 1841. *The Wild Sports of Southern Africa*. 3 edn. London: Pickering.

Hartman, Geoffrey H. 1975. *The Fate of Reading and Other Essays*. Chicago: University of Chicago Press.

Hartshorne, Ken. 1992. *Crisis and Challenge: Black Education 1910-1990*. Cape Town: Oxford University Press.

Hobsbawm, Eric and Ranger, Terence (eds). 1983. *The Invention of Tradition*. Cambridge: Cambridge University Press.

Hodgson, Janet. 1985. Ntsikana: History and Symbol. Studies in a Process of Religious Change Among Xhosa-Speaking People. Ph.D. thesis, University of Cape Town.

Hofmeyr, Isabel. 1990. History Workshop positions: Introduction. *Pretexts* 2 (2).

_____ 1991. Jonah and the swallowing monster: Orality and literacy on a Berlin Mission Station in the Transvaal. *Journal of Southern African Studies* 17 (4).

_____ 1993. *"We Spend our Years as a Tale that is Told": Oral Historical Narrative in a South African Chiefdom*. Johannesburg: Witwatersrand University Press.

Horne, C. Silvester. 1929. *David Livingstone*. London: Macmillan.

Hunt Davis, Richard. 1969. Nineteenth Century African Education in the Cape Colony: A Historical Analysis. Ph.D. thesis, University of Wisconsin.

Hutcheon, Linda. 1988. *A Poetics of Postmodernism: History, Theory, Fiction*. New York: Routledge.

Hyam, Ronald. 1976. *Britain's Imperial Century 1815-1914*. London: Batsford.

Isaacman, Allen and Isaacman, Barbara. 1977. Resistance and collaboration in southern and central Africa, c. 1850-1920. *International Journal of African Historical Studies* 10.

Islam, Shamsul. 1975. *Kipling's 'Law': A Study of his Philosophy of Life*. London: Macmillan.

Jabavu, D.D.T. 1920. *The Black Problem*. New York: Negro University Press (repr. 1969).

_____ 1922. *The Life of John Tengo Jabavu: Editor of Imvo Zabantsundu, 1884-1921*. Lovedale: Lovedale Press.

Jabavu, Noni. 1960. *Drawn in Colour: African Contrasts*. London: John Murray.

_____ 1963. *The Ochre People*. Johannesburg: Ravan (repr. 1982).

JanMohamed, Abdul R. 1985. The economy of Manichean allegory: The function of racial difference in colonialist literature. *Critical Inquiry* 12.

Jay, Paul. 1992. Bridging the gap: The position of politics in deconstruction. *Cultural Critique* 22.

Jeal, Tim. 1973. *Livingstone.* London: Heinemann.

Jefferson, Ann. 1986. Structuralism and Poststructuralsim. In Jefferson, Ann & Robey, David (eds), *Modern Literary Theory.* 2 edn. London: Batsford.

Jenkins, Keith. 1992. The discursive turn: Tony Bennett and the textuality of history. *Teaching History* 66.

Jordan, A.C. 1973. *Towards an African Literature.* Berkeley: University of California Press.

Kallaway, Peter (ed.). 1984. *Apartheid and Education.* Johannesburg: Ravan.

Kantey, Mike. 1990. Foreword: Publishing in South Africa. In *Africa Bibliography 1989.* Comp. Hector Blackhurst. Manchester: Manchester University Press.

Kay, Stephen. 1833. *Travels and Research in Caffraria.* London: Harper.

Keegan, Tim. 1982. The Sharecropping Economy, African Class Formation and the 1913 Natives' Land Act in the Highveld Maize Belt. In Marks, Shula & Rathbone, Richard (eds), *Industrialisation and Social Change in South Africa: African Class Formation, Culture and Consciousness 1870-1930.* London: Longman.
_____ 1991. The overthrow of slavery. *Southern African Review of Books* 20/21.

Kistner, Ulrike. 1989. Literature and the national question. *South African Society for General Literary Studies Papers* 9.

Kramer, Lloyd S. 1989. Literature, Criticism and Historical Imagination: The Literary Challenge of Hayden White and Dominick LaCapra. In Hunt, Lynn (ed.), *The New Cultural History.* Berkeley: University of California Press.

Kros, C.J. 1992. They Wanted Dancing and not Merely the Lambeth Walk: A Reassessment of the 1940s School Disturbances with Particular Reference to Lovedale. African Studies Institute paper, University of the Witwatersrand, 27 July.

Kunene, Daniel P. & Kirsch, Randal A. 1967. *The Beginning of South African Vernacular Literature: A Historical Study* (Kunene) & *A Series of Biographies* (Kirsch). Los Angeles: University of California.

Kuzwayo, Ellen. 1985. *Call Me Woman.* London: The Women's Press.

Lacan, Jacques. 1968. *Speech and Language in Psychoanalysis.* Transl. Anthony Wilden. Baltimore: Johns Hopkins University Press.

LaCapra, Dominick. 1983. *Rethinking Intellectual History: Texts, Contexts, Language.* Ithaca: Cornell University Press.

Lambourne, Brigid. 1992. Methods of Mission: The Ordering of Space and Time, Land and Labour on Methodist Mission Stations in Caffraria, 1823-1835. African Studies Institute paper, University of the Witwatersrand, 24 August.

Landau, Paul Stuart. 1992. The Making of Christianity in a Southern African Kingdom: Gammangwato, *ca.* 1870-1940. Ph.D. thesis, University of Wisconsin, Madison.

Lawrence, Jon & Taylor, Miles. 1993. The poverty of protest: Gareth Stedman Jones and the politics of language – A reply. *Social History* 18 (1).

Le Cordeur, Basil A. (ed). 1988. *The Journal of Charles Lennox Stretch.* The Graham's

Town Series. Cape Town: Masker Miller Longman.

Le Cordeur, Basil & Saunders, Christopher (eds). 1981. *The War of the Axe: Correspondence Between the Governor of the Cape Colony, Sir Henry Pottinger, and the Commander of the British Forces at the Cape, Sir George Berkeley, and Others.* Johannesburg: Brenthurst Press.

Legassick, M.C. 1969. The Griqua, the Sotho-Tswana, and the Missionaries, 1780-1840: The Politics of a Frontier Zone. Ph.D. thesis, University of California, Los Angeles.

_____ 1980. The Frontier Tradition in South African Historiography. In Marks, Shula & Atmore, Anthony (eds), *Economy and Society in Pre-Industrial South Africa.* London: Longman.

_____ 1993. The state, racism and the rise of capitalism in the nineteenth-century Cape Colony. *South African Historical Journal* 28.

Livingstone, David. 1857. *Missionary Travels and Researches in South Africa.* London: Murray.

Lloyd, B.W. & Lashbrook, J. with T.A. Simons. 1978. *A Bibliography of Published Works By and About David Livingstone 1843-1975.* University of Cape Town Libraries.

Loram, C.T. 1917. *The Education of the South African Native.* London: Longmans.

Lovedale. 1887. *Lovedale: Past and Present: A Register of Two Thousand Names. A Record Written in Black and White, But More in White than Black.* Lovedale: Lovedale Press.

_____ 1892. *Outlines of the Literary Course at Lovedale: A Syllabus Prepared for the Use of Native Students.* Lovedale: Lovedale Press (James Stewart Papers (SP), BC 106 D16 University of Cape Town).

Lovejoy, Paul E. 1983. *Transformations in Slavery: A History of Slavery in Africa.* Cambridge: Cambridge University Press.

Lyotard, Jean-François. 1984. *The Postmodern Condition: A Report on Knowledge.* Transl. Geoff Bennington & Brian Massumi. Manchester: Manchester University Press.

Macdonell, Diane. 1986. *Theories of Discourse: An Introduction.* London: Blackwell.

Majeke, Nosipho (pseud. of Dora Taylor). 1952. *Role of Missionaries in Conquest.* Johannesburg: Society of Young Africa.

Manning, Patrick. 1990. *Slavery and African Life: Occidental, Oriental, and African Slave Trades.* Cambridge: Cambridge University Press.

Marks, Shula. 1975. The ambiguities of dependence: John L. Dube of Natal. *Journal of Southern African Studies* 1 (2).

_____ 1986. *The Ambiguities of Dependence in South Africa: Class, Nationalism, and the State in Twentieth-Century Natal.* Johannesburg: Ravan.

_____ 1993. Racial capitalism: A cultural or economic system? *South African Historical Journal* 28.

Marquard, Jean. 1971. Writing and injustice. *Contrast* 7 (1).

Marshall, Brenda K. 1992. *Teaching the Postmodern: Fiction and Theory*. New York: Routledge.

Mason, Peter. 1990. *Deconstructing America: Representations of the Other*. London: Routledge.

Maughan-Brown, D.A. 1979. Black literature debate: Human beings behind the work. *Contrast* 12 (4).

Miers, Suzanne & Roberts, Richard (eds). 1988. *The End of Slavery in Africa*. Madison: University of Wisconsin Press.

Mills, Wallace George. 1975. The Role of the African Clergy in the Reorientation of Xhosa Society to the Plural Society in the Cape Colony, 1850-1915. Ph.D. thesis, University of California, Los Angeles.

Moffat, Robert. 1842. *Missionary Labours and Scenes in Southern Africa*. London: John Snow.

Molema, S.M. 1920. *The Bantu Past and Present*. Edinburgh: W. Green & Son.

Molteno, F. 1984. The Evolution of Educational Policy. In Kallaway, Peter (ed.), *Apartheid and Education*. Johannesburg: Ravan.

Montrose, Louis A. 1989. Professing the Renaissance: The Poetics and Politics of Culture. In Veeser, H. Aram (ed.), *The New Historicism*. New York: Routledge.

Morphet, Tony. 1994. Promoting the English. (Review of *Essays and Lectures 1949-1991* by Guy Butler, ed. Stephen Watson) *Southern African Review of Books* 34.

Mostert, Noël. 1992. *Frontiers: The Epic of South Africa's Creation and the Tragedy of the Xhosa People*. London: Cape.

Mphahlele, Es'kia 1980. Landmarks of literary history in Southern Africa. *English Academy Review* 1980.

Mudimbe, V.Y. 1988. *The Invention of Africa: Gnosis, Philosophy, and the Order of Knowledge*. Bloomington and Indianapolis: Indiana University Press.

Mukherjee, Arun P. 1991. The exclusions of postcolonial theory and Mulk Raj Anand's 'Untouchable': A case study. *Ariel* 22 (3).

Mutloatse, Mothobe (ed.). 1981. *Reconstruction: 90 Years of Black Historical Literature*. Johannesburg: Ravan.

Nasson, Bill. 1991. *Abraham Esau's War: A Black South African War in the Cape: 1899-1902*. Cambridge: Cambridge University Press.

Ndebele, Njabulo S. 1987. The English language and social change in South Africa. *Triquarterly* 69. Also in *Rediscovery of the Ordinary: Essays on South African Literature and Culture*. Fordsburg: Congress of South African Writers (1991).

Ngconcgo, L.D. 1970. Jabavu and the Anglo-Boer War. *Kleio* 2 (2).

_____ 1974. *Imvo Zabantsundu* and Cape 'Native' Policy 1884-1902. M.A. dissertation, University of South Africa.

_____ 1979. John Tengo Jabavu 1859-1921. In Saunders, Christopher (ed.), *Black Leaders in Southern African History*. London: Heinemann.

Ngubane, Jordan K. 1971. South Africa's Race Crisis: A Conflict of Minds. In Adam,

Heribert (ed.), *South Africa: Sociological Perspectives*. London: Oxford University Press.

Norris, Christopher. 1982. *Deconstruction: Theory and Practice*. London: Methuen.

Northcott, Cecil. 1961. *Robert Moffat: Pioneer in Africa 1817-1870*. London: Lutterworth.

_____ 1973. *David Livingstone: His Triumph, Decline and Fall*. London: Lutterworth.

Novick, Peter. 1988. *That Noble Dream: The 'Objectivity Question' and the American Historical Profession*. Cambridge: Cambridge University Press.

Ntantala, Phyllis. 1992. *A Life's Mosaic*. Cape Town: David Philip.

Odendaal, André. 1983. African Political Mobilisation in the Eastern Cape, 1880-1910. Ph.D. thesis, Cambridge University.

_____ 1984a. *Vukani Bantu! The Beginnings of Black Protest Politics in South Africa to 1912*. Cape Town: David Philip.

_____ 1984b. Mayibuye I Afrika Nakwimbali Yelizwe: Towards Decolonising the History of Early African Politics in South Africa. Departmental Seminar, Department of History, University of South Africa.

O'Dowd, M.C. 1970. Writing and injustice. *Contrast* 6 (3).

Oliphant, Andries Walter. 1989a. Untitled letter. *Weekly Mail* April 21.

_____ 1989b. The New Illiteracy vs the Old Colonialism. *Weekly Mail* May 5.

Oliver, Roland & Atmore, Anthony. 1972. *Africa since 1800*. 2 edn. Cambridge: Cambridge University Press.

Orr, J. Edwin. 1975. *The Eager Feet: Evangelical Awakenings, 1790-1830*. Chicago: Moody Press.

Parry, Benita. 1987. Problems in current theories of colonial discourse. *Oxford Literary Review* 9 (1-2).

Paterson, William. 1790. *A Narrative of Four Journeys in the Country of the Hottentots and Caffraria in the Years 1777, 1778, 1779*. 2 edn. London: J. Johnson.

Peires, J.B. 1979a. Nxele, Ntsikana and the origins of the Xhosa religious reaction. *Journal of African History* 20 (1).

_____ 1979b. The Lovedale Press: Literature for the Bantu revisited. *History in Africa* 6.

_____ 1981. *The House of Phalo: A History of the Xhosa People in the Days of their Independence*. Johannesburg: Ravan.

_____ 1989. *The Dead Will Arise*. Johannesburg: Ravan.

Philip, John. 1828. *Researches in South Africa*. London: Duncan.

Plaatje, Sol T. 1917. *Native Life in South Africa*. London: P.S. King.

_____ 1978. *Mhudi*. London: Heinemann.

Pool, Robert. 1991. Postmodern ethnography? *Critique of Anthropology* 11 (4).

Potgieter, D.J. (ed.). 1975. *Standard Encyclopaedia of Southern Africa*. Vol. 2. Cape Town: Nasou.

Prakash, Gyan. 1992. Can the 'subaltern' ride? A reply to O'Hanlon and Washbrook. *Comparative Studies in Society and History* 34 (1).

Pratt, Mary Louise. 1992. *Imperial Eyes: Travel Writing and Trans-culturation*. London: Routledge.

Pringle, Thomas. 1834. *African Sketches*. London: Edward Moxon.

Ranger, Terence O. 1968. Primary resistance movements and modern mass nationalism in East and Central Africa. *Journal of African History* 9.

_____ 1983. The Invention of Tradition in Colonial Africa. In Hobsbawm, Eric & Ranger, Terence (eds), *The Invention of Tradition*. Cambridge: Cambridge University Press.

_____ 1986. Religious movements and politics in sub-Saharan Africa. *African Studies Review* 29 (2).

_____ 1987. Taking hold of the land: Holy places and pilgrimages in twentieth-century Zimbabwe. *Past and Present* 117.

_____ 1994. Protestant Missions in Africa: The Dialectic of Conversion in the American Methodist Episcopal Church in Eastern Zimbabwe, 1900-1950. In Blakely, Thomas D., Van Beek, Walter E.A. & Thomson, Dennis L. (eds), *Religion in Africa: Experience & Expression*. London: James Currey.

Ricoeur, Paul. 1971. The model of the text: Meaningful action considered as a text. *Social Research* 38 (3).

Rive, Richard. 1983. The liberal tradition in South African literature. *Contrast* 14 (3).

Robinson, R. & Gallagher, J.A. with Denny, A. 1961. *Africa and the Victorians: The Official Mind of Imperialism*. London: Macmillan.

Rorty, Richard. 1986a. The contingency of language. *London Review of Books* 8 (7).

_____ 1986b. The contingency of selfhood. *London Review of Books* 8 (8).

Ross, Andrew. 1986. *John Philip (1775-1851): Missions, Race and Politics in South Africa*. Aberdeen: Aberdeen University Press.

Ross, R. (ed.). 1982. *Racism and Colonialism: Essays on Ideology and Social Structure*. The Hague: Nijhoff.

Roux, Edward. 1964. *Time Longer than Rope*. Madison: University of Wisconsin Press.

Ryan, Rory. 1988. Literary-intellectual behaviour in South Africa. *boundary2* 15 (3).

Saayman, W.A. 1991. *Christian Mission in South Africa*. Pretoria: University of South Africa.

Said, Edward W. 1978. *Orientalism*. London: Routledge & Kegan Paul.

_____ 1993. *Culture & Imperialism*. London: Chatto & Windus.

Sangari, Kumkum. 1987. The politics of the possible. *Cultural Critique* 7.

Sanneh, Lamin. 1989. *Translating the Message: The Missionary Impact on Culture*. New York: Orbis.

_____ 1993. *Encountering the West. Christianity and the Global Cultural Process: The African Dimension*. New York: Orbis.

Saunders, C.C. 1970. The New African Elite in the Eastern Cape and Some Late

Nineteenth Century Origins of African Nationalism. In *The Societies of Southern Africa in the 19th and 20th Centuries* (Collected seminar papers, Vol. 1, University of London, Institute of Commonwealth Studies).

———— 1977. James Read: Towards a Reassessment. In *Societies of Southern Africa in the Nineteenth and Twentieth Centuries* (Collected seminar papers, Vol. 7, University of London, Institute of Commonwealth Studies).

Schapera, I. (ed.). 1974. *David Livingstone: South African Papers 1849-1853*. Cape Town: Van Riebeeck Society.

Schöttler, Peter. 1989. Historians and discourse analysis. *History Workshop* 27.

Schreuder, D.M. 1976. The cultural factor in Victorian imperialism: A case study of the British "Civilising Mission". *Journal of Imperial and Commonwealth History* 4 (3).

Scribner, Sylvia. 1984. Literacy in three metaphors. *American Journal of Education* 93.

Sheehan, Bernard W. 1980. *Savagism and Civility: Indians and Englishmen in Colonial Virginia*. New York: Cambridge University Press.

Shepherd, R.H.W. 1936. *Literature for the South African Bantu: A Comparative Study of Negro Achievement*. Pretoria: Carnegie.

———— 1940. *Lovedale, South Africa: The Story of a Century 1841-1941*. Lovedale: Lovedale Press.

———— 1945. *Lovedale and Literature for the Bantu*. Lovedale: Lovedale Press.

———— 1955. *Bantu Literature and Life*. Lovedale: Lovedale Press.

Siddle, D.J. 1973. David Livingstone: Mid-Victorian Field Scientist. In *David Livingstone and Africa*. Centre of African Studies, University of Edinburgh.

Slabbert, Jos. 1978. Black poetry debate: Dilemmas of bourgeois criticism. Open letter. *Contrast* 12 (2).

Slemon, Stephen. 1987. Monuments of Empire: Allegory/counter-discourse/post-colonial writing. *Kunapipi* 9 (3).

———— 1989. Modernism's last post. *Ariel* 20 (4).

Slemon, Stephen & Tiffin, Helen (eds). 1990. *After Europe: Critical Theory and Post-Colonial Writing*. Sydney: Dangeroo Press.

Sole, Kelwyn. 1977. Problems of creative writers in South Africa: A response. *Work in Progress* 1.

———— 1978. Black poetry debate: Prejudiced approach. *Contrast* 12 (2).

———— 1989. Untitled letter. *Weekly Mail* April 28.

———— 1994. Democratising culture and literature in a 'New South Africa': Organisation and theory. *Current Writing* 6 (2).

Spivak, Gayatri Chakravorty. 1976. Translator's Preface. In Derrida, Jacques. *Of Grammatology*. Baltimore: Johns Hopkins University Press.

———— 1985. The Rani of Sirmur. In Barker, Francis *et al.* (eds), *Europe and its Others*. Vol. 1. Colchester: University of Essex.

———— 1988a. Can the Subaltern Seak? In Nelson, Gary & Grossberg, Lawrence (eds), *Marxism and the Interpretation of Culture*. London: Macmillan.

_____ 1988b. Subaltern Studies: Deconstructing Historiography. In Guha, Ranajit & Spivak, Gayatri Chakravorty (eds), *Selected Subaltern Studies*. Oxford: Oxford University Press.

_____ 1990. Poststructuralism, Marginality, Post-coloniality and Value. In Collier, Peter & Geyer-Ryan, Helga (eds), *Literary Theory Today*. New York: Cornell University Press.

Stanley, Henry M. 1872. *How I Found Livingstone*. London: Sampson Low.

Stewart, James. 1880. *The Educated Kaffir, An Apology & Industrial Education, A Sequel.* Two Valedictory Addresses Delivered to the Lovedale Literary Society. Lovedale: Lovedale Press.

_____ 1884. *The Experiment of Native Education*. An Address Delivered to the Lovedale Literary Society. Lovedale: Lovedale Press.

_____ 1894. *Lovedale South Africa: Illustrated by Fifty Views from Photographs*. Edinburgh: Andrew Elliot.

_____ 1903. *Dawn in the Dark Continent*. London: Oliphant Anderson & Ferrier.

St Leger, F.Y. 1974. The African Press in South Africa. Ph.D. thesis, Rhodes University.

Switzer, Les. 1983. Reflections on the mission press in South Africa in the 19th and early 20th centuries. *Journal of Theology for Southern Africa* 43.

Switzer, Les and Switzer, Donna. 1979. *The Black Press in South Africa and Lesotho*. Boston: G.K. Hall.

Takaki, Ronald. 1992. The tempest in the wilderness: The racialization of savagery. *Journal of American History* 79 (3).

Theal, George McCall. 1882. *Kaffir Folk-Lore: A Selection from the Traditional Tales*. 2 edn. London: Sonnenschein, Le Bas & Lowry.

Thomas, Nicholas. 1994. *Colonialism's Culture: Anthropology, Travel and Government*. Cambridge: Polity Press.

Todorov, Tzvetan. 1984. *The Conquest of America: The Question of the Other*. Transl. Richard Howard. New York: Harper and Row.

Trollope, Anthony. 1878. *South Africa*. Vol. 1. London: Chapman and Hall.

Trump, Martin (ed.). 1990. *Rendering Things Visible: Essays on South African Literary Culture*. Johannesburg: Ravan.

Ullyatt, A.G. 1977. Dilemmas in black poetry. *Contrast* 11 (4).

Vail, Leroy (ed.). 1989. *The Creation of Tribalism in South Africa*. London: James Currey.

Van Wyk Smith, Malvern. 1991. The Metadiscourses of Postcolonialism: Some Reflections on 'Strong Othering' in the European Image of Africa. Keynote Address, Association of University English Teachers of South Africa conference, University of Fort Hare.

Vaughan, Michael. 1982. Literature and populism in South Africa: Some reflections on the ideology of *Staffrider*. *English Academy Review*.

Vesey, Godfrey. 1990. *Collins Dictionary of Philosophy*. London: Collins.

Walshe, A.P. 1969. The origins of African political consciousness in South Africa. *Journal of Modern African Studies* 7 (4).

_____ 1970. *The Rise of African Nationalism in South Africa*. Craighall: Donker.

Warwick, Peter. 1983. *Black People and the South African War 1899-1902*. Johannesburg: Ravan.

Watson, Stephen. 1983. Liberalism debate: Talk on Alan Paton criticized. Letter. *Contrast* 14 (4).

_____ 1986. Poetry and politicization. *Contrast* 16 (1).

_____ 1989a. On the Unforgiving Page, the Clichés Fall With a Heavy Thud. *Weekly Mail* April 14.

_____ 1989b. Untitled letter. *Weekly Mail* April 28.

_____ 1989c. As Baneful as Any Other Type of Ignorance. *Weekly Mail* May 5.

_____ 1990. Colonialism and the Novels of J.M. Coetzee. In *Selected Essays: 1980-1990*. Cape Town: Carrefour.

Wauchope, I. 1908. *The Natives and their Missionaries*. Lovedale: Lovedale Press.

White, Hayden. 1973. *Metahistory: The Historical Imagination in Nineteenth-Century Europe*. Baltimore: Johns Hopkins University Press.

_____ 1978. *Tropics of Discourse: Essays in Cultural Criticism*. Baltimore: Johns Hopkins University Press.

White, Timothy Raymond Howard. 1987. Lovedale 1930-1955: The Study of a Missionary Institution in its Social, Educational and Political Context. M.A. dissertation, Rhodes University.

Willan, Brian. 1984. *Sol Plaatje: A Biography*. Johannesburg: Ravan.

Williams, D. 1959. The Missionaries on the Eastern Frontier of the Cape Colony, 1799-1853. Ph.D. thesis, University of the Witwatersrand.

_____ 1970. African nationalism in South Africa: Origins and problems. *Journal of African History* 11 (3).

_____ 1978. *Umfundisi: A Biography of Tiyo Soga 1829-1871*. Lovedale: Lovedale Press.

Williams, Donovan (ed.). 1983. *The Journal and Selected Writings of The Reverend Tiyo Soga*. Cape Town: A.A. Balkema.

Wilson, Monica. 1983. *Freedom for My People: The Autobiography of Z.K. Matthews. Southern Africa 1901 to 1968*. Cape Town: David Philip.

Wright, Laurence (ed.). 1990. *Teaching English Literature in South Africa: Twenty Essays*. Grahamstown: Institute for the Study of English in Africa.

Young, Robert. 1990. *White Mythologies: Writing History and the West*. London: Routledge.

Zagorin, Perez. 1990. Historiography and postmodernism: Reconsiderations. *History and Theory* 29.

# INDEX